THE ROTTEN FRUITS OF ECONOMIC CONTROLS AND THE RISE FROM THE ASHES, 1965-1989

Thomas E. Hall

University Press of America,® Inc.
Lanham · Boulder · New York · Toronto · Oxford

4501 Forbes Boulevard
Suite 200
Lanham, Maryland 20706
UPA Acquisitions Department (301) 459-3366

PO Box 317
Oxford
OX2 9RU, UK

Printed in the United States of America
British Library Cataloging in Publication Information Available

Library of Congress Control Number: 2003110057
ISBN 0-7618-2680-7 (clothbound : alk. ppr.)
ISBN 0-7618-2681-5 (paperback : alk. ppr.)

™The paper used in this publication meets the minimum requirements of American National Standard for Information Sciences—Permanence of Paper for Printed Library Materials, ANSI Z39.48—1984

To Chris, Alex,
and Professor Bernard Udis

Table of Contents

List of Tables & Figures

Preface

I became interested in economics during my freshman year at the University of Colorado. I was enrolled in a principles of macroeconomics course taught by an absolutely outstanding teacher named Bernard Udis. This was the spring semester of 1973, so Professor Udis had plenty to talk about: the economy was booming, unemployment was low, and the Nixon price controls were in effect. Then, during my sophomore year, the oil embargo and first energy crisis took place, the economy slid into a serious recession, and inflation accelerated when the price controls expired. To a college student who did not have to worry about serious things in life such as holding a job or feeding a family, it was all very interesting. And thanks to that class I took from Professor Udis, I had some idea about why these things were happening.

The economy impacted me in more serious ways when I was a graduate student in California in the late 1970s. I was impoverished (as graduate students have been since time began), living on my wages as a teaching assistant, and savings from summer jobs. Prices of books and food were rising rapidly, which was problematic because expenditures on those two items are a significant portion of a graduate student's budget.

I was paid once a month for my work as a teaching assistant. On payday, I picked up my check and took it to the bank to deposit in my checking account. Then I headed to the savings and loan where I wrote a check (on my bank checking account) to deposit some of my salary into my savings account. A couple of weeks later, I moved funds from my savings account back to the checking account to cover expenditures during the rest of the month. I took these actions because: (1) my bank checking account did not earn interest (because a federal law prohibited it), and (2) a savings account at an S&L earned 0.25 percent higher interest than a savings account at a bank (due to a federal regulation). I was very poor at the time, so that 0.25 percent difference mattered to me. Things would have been simpler if I could have had my checking account at the S&L because then my financial transactions could have been done in one place (ATM machines were not available at the time). However, that was impossible because a federal rule prohibited S&Ls from offering checking accounts. Since the bank and S&L were just a block apart, I went to the trouble of dealing with two institutions. If the distance had been greater, I would have held my savings account at the bank and earned the lower interest rate.

Unfortunately for me (and other Americans in the same straights), putting funds in my savings account was an exercise in loss minimization. The problem was that it earned 5.5 percent interest, which was far below the market interest rate at the time (a federal regulation prohibited my S&L from paying more than 5.5 percent on the savings account). This was 1979, so the inflation rate was around 10 percent. Thus, the inflation-adjusted return on that savings account was negative 4.5 percent (= 5.5 % interest - 10.0 % inflation). And to add insult to injury, the 5.5 percent interest return was taxable income! But that was better than the alternative, which was keeping all of my balances in the checking account or in cash. If I had done that, my real financial wealth would have been shrinking at the inflation rate of 10 percent.

The problem of my pathetically low interest return would have been alleviated greatly if I had been wealthier. An initial purchase of $2,000 would have allowed me to open a money market mutual fund, and earn market interest rates which were around 11.0 percent at the time. But I did not have $2,000.

I made those trips to the bank and S&L on my bicycle. I owned an old car, but rarely used it. One reason was that gasoline was fairly expensive (due, in part, to federal government policy bungling in the energy sector). But a much more important consideration was that if I used my car, something truly awful would happen: I would have to buy gasoline at a gas station. That would involve sitting in my car for an hour or two, under that relentless Southern California sun, waiting in a line that was a few hundred yards long to buy gasoline. Please, God, anything but that!

I vividly remember riding my bicycle past a particularly long gasoline line one afternoon in late 1979, shaking my head in amazement at the foolishness that had caused that line to form. The fools were not the unfortunate people sitting in their cars wasting time and gasoline, the fools were the Washington politicians who first erected, and then maintained, a system of economic controls that kept the price of a gallon of gasoline about forty cents below the equilibrium price. Imagine if I had been able to offer the last driver in that line a choice: he or she could (1) wait in that line for three hours and pay $1 per gallon when they reached the pump, or (2) drive right up to the pump and pay $1.40

per gallon. Even though my financial situation was tight, I know how I would have answered.

These experiences (and several others from that era that I could relate) led to my interest in the consequences of government-imposed economic controls. The free market system is not perfect because it does not bring about the best economic outcome in every single case. But more often than not the free market generates results that are vastly superior to those caused by some of the destructive government policies that have occasionally been put in place. The people advancing these perverse policies of economic control almost always have good intentions, but they either know virtually nothing about economics and markets, or do not consider unintended results that their actions might cause. Left to run amuck, policymakers have the potential to cause real damage, which they did during the 1960s and 1970s. Fortunately, much was learned from experience, and this knowledge helped bring about the much-improved economic conditions the United States has enjoyed since the early 1980s.

This book is a description of the economic problems that began in the mid 1960s, what caused them, their consequences, and how the situation was eventually turned around for the greater good. The discussion is designed for someone who has a basic understanding of economics, and it is my sincere hope that readers find the subject matter as interesting as I did while working on it.

Several people assisted me with this project. First and foremost, my wife Chris helped by maintaining an environment conducive to my work. She is supportive, loving, and talented; I honestly do not know what I would do without her.

Special thanks go to Professor Dave Ferguson, who is the best international economist I know. He read every chapter, provided extensive comments, and wrote the first draft of the Bretton Woods chapter. He should be a coauthor of this book, but declined to have his name on the cover. Professor Gerald Granderson was a huge help on the energy economics sections, and Professor Jim Brock provided his (always) outstanding advice in the area of industry regulation. Several graduate students gathered data, proofread, and checked references: Cory Picklo, Moira McCaffrey, Margaret Dunleavy, Christopher Schilling, Christopher Ferguson, Stephanie Spear, and Sarah Buckley.

Chris Ferguson gets extra thanks for making some of the figures in the book, as does Jim Pater for making the manuscript camera ready. I acknowledge Blackwell Publishing for granting permission to reproduce the diagrams in figures 2.1 and 2.2, and the American Economic Association for permission to reprint the diagram in figure 2.3. Any errors are my responsibility.

Finally, I thank Professor Bernard Udis of the University of Colorado for getting an eighteen-year-old college freshman — who was clueless about what to major in–genuinely excited about studying economics three decades ago. I dedicate this book to my family, and to him.

Chapter 1

■ ■ ■

Perverse Economic Policies Can Destroy an Economy

During the Twentieth Century, the United States experienced incredible gains in economic well-being. To cite just a few statistics, inflation-adjusted per-capita income increased roughly sixfold, the standard workweek fell from sixty hours to forty, and average life expectancy at birth rose by over twenty years. Virtually no one living in the early 1900s could have envisioned the enormous wealth and prosperity this country would enjoy by the end of the century.

However, the road to prosperity was not smooth. While there were sustained intervals of relative macroeconomic stability that featured significant gains in income and wealth (e.g., the 1920s and 1990s), two intervals stand out in terms of macroeconomic instability: the Great Depression which occurred from 1929–1941, and the boom-bust years of 1965–1982. What distinguishes these periods is that an unprecedented number of policy errors were committed which created economic volatility with bouts of very high unemployment.

The Depression featured the worst economic performance of the entire century, perhaps in all of U.S. history.[1] From 1929–1941, the United States experienced two severe recessions, widespread bank failures, massive long-term unemployment, and such widespread poverty during the first recession (1929–1933) that the welfare system in place could not begin to handle all the cases. The Depression was such an unpleasant and profound experience for those who lived through it that years later many of them continued to pinch pennies and distrust banks to such an extent that they would hide cash in their homes rather than hold bank deposits.

While the economic problems from 1965–1982 were nowhere near as severe as those experienced during the Depression, the period stands out as the most unstable of the post World War II era. Major problems included macroeconomic instability in the form of boom-bust cycles of economic output, high and rising inflation, and serious economic distortions caused by government-imposed controls. The year 1965 marks the start of an inflation build-up that lasted over fifteen years and included two bouts of double-digit inflation. Meanwhile, the economy expanded and contracted with surprising regularity; during a span of just fourteen years the United States experienced four recessions, two of which were the most severe since the Depression. Additional problems included two energy crises, severe shortages of various products, a major foreign currency crisis involving the U.S. dollar, and huge declines in real values of financial assets. The American public was most unhappy with the course of economic events and vented their frustrations on their political leaders: over a period of just seven years, three presidents (Nixon, Ford, and Carter) failed to retain office.[2]

1.1 The Depression Expanded the Role of Government

The economic problems experienced during 1929–1941 and 1965–1982 had one important feature in common: they were man-made. In both cases well-intentioned officials in government and at the Federal Reserve carried out economic policies they thought were proper, but which created economic disasters. The Great Depression was started by officials at the Federal Reserve who were concerned that member banks were helping fuel the late 1920s stock market advance by issuing loans to brokerage firms. So the Federal Reserve engineered a monetary contraction to end the stock market boom, and thereby started a recession. The recession spread around the world because the U.S. monetary contraction raised interest rates which attracted foreign capital. The world was on the gold standard at the time, so this capital inflow took the form of gold. Other countries tried to stop their gold outflows by raising interest rates which caused their economies to slide into recession as well.

Perverse economic policies pursued in the United States and elsewhere transformed the recession into the Great Depression. The United States set off an international trade war by enacting the Smoot-Hawley tariff in 1930; over sixty countries retaliated by raising their tariff rates. U.S. federal income taxes were raised in 1932 in an effort to balance the federal budget. Most important of all, the Federal Reserve failed to come to the aid of banks experiencing runs on their deposits, so there was a nationwide collapse of the banking system. Meanwhile, restrictive policies were being pursued in other countries as well. For example, in 1931 Germany's central bank (the Reichsbank) tried to stop a gold outflow by raising the discount rate from 5.0 to 10.0 percent which caused economic conditions there to worsen considerably. Policies such as these turned what started out as fairly standard recessions in several countries into the greatest economic disaster of all time.[3] The Depression led to social upheavals in a few particularly hard-hit countries, with the worst case occurring in Germany where poor economic conditions allowed Adolph Hitler to rise to power and eventually start World War II in Europe. Tens of millions of people lost their lives because of bad economic policies pursued in the United States, Germany, and elsewhere.

Social upheaval in the United States took the form of President Franklin Roosevelt's New Deal. A commonly-held view during the 1930s was that the Great Depression represented a failure of capitalism, so in the minds of many the way to end the economic misery was to have the government become more involved in regulating the economy. In this way, the New Deal was a major step forward on the road to economic controls because prior to the Depression the federal government's role in the economy was (by today's standards) very limited: it maintained the military, regulated interstate commerce, enforced antitrust law, supplied currency and coins, financed public projects, and collected taxes (which were small in relation to income). In addition, the Federal Reserve had been established in 1913 to regulate member banks and provide credit for the needs of trade. Beyond that, there wasn't much else the federal government did in terms of economic control. The New Deal brought enormous changes because the government began regulating banking, agriculture, and manufacturing to a much greater extent than had been the case before. In addition, the public sector's share of aggregate spending rose dramatically as the federal government tried to stimulate economic activity by hiring millions of people for work relief programs, distributing direct relief welfare payments, and becoming a producer of goods and services such as electricity, old-age insurance, and mortgage insurance.

Some of the changes made during the Depression had a great deal to do with creating the economic instability from 1965–1982. One reason this occurred is because some of the laws enacted during the New Deal caused severe economic disruptions years later. Perhaps the best example is the Banking Act of 1933 which was designed to prevent a repeat of the terrible bank failures that had devastated the U.S. economy during the early 1930s. Among other things, the law authorized the Federal Reserve to set maximum interest rates banks could pay on time and savings deposits. The idea underlying this rule was that banks would be less likely to fail if they could not compete by offering high interest rates on deposits, and taking on risky high-yield assets in order to be able to pay those rates. These deposit rate ceilings did not cause serious disruptions until the 1960s when inflation drove market interest rates well above the ceiling rates depositors could earn at banks and thrifts. Many Americans responded by withdrawing their deposits from banks and thrifts, and instead purchasing other financial instruments such as bonds that earned market rates. This deposit outflow caused a serious profit squeeze at depository institutions. In addition, it caused severe cutbacks in the amount of financial capital available to the homebuilding industry which was instrumental in generating the turbulent boom-bust cycles in new house construction that occurred from 1965–1982.[4]

The second way that events during the 1930s led to the economic instability of 1965–1982 was through the manner in which the Depression changed economic thought. The horrendous 1929–1933 recession was the impetus for John Maynard Keynes to write his magnum opus *The General Theory of Employment, Interest, and Money* (Keynes 1936). In this book, he forcefully and convincingly argues that the recession was caused by a major decline in aggregate demand.[5] Keynes's proposed solution to the massive unemployment that resulted was to stimulate aggregate demand using expansionary monetary and/or fiscal policies. These ideas overlapped nicely with New Deal programs like work relief which were designed to accomplish precisely what Keynes prescribed: the federal government hired millions of people to do various tasks such as building roads, dams, and buildings, and when these workers spent their earnings it generated income for others which enhanced the expansionary effects of the program. However, despite these policies high unemployment was still a problem in the late 1930s, partly because the demand stimulus generated by the New Deal was too small to lift the U.S. economy out of the Depression (Brown 1956).

A demand stimulus powerful enough to end the Depression finally occurred in 1940–1941. It resulted from a combination of the lagged effects of the late 1930s monetary expansion, huge increases in U.S. military spending following France's surrender to Germany in June 1940, and rising sales of military hardware to Great Britain. This demand stimulus was a major cause of the final push toward full employment, and defense spending played a huge role: 46 percent of the increase in U.S. aggregate demand between 1940 and 1941 resulted from rising U.S. government defense purchases.

The fact that huge increases in government purchases were instrumental in driving output back to full employment led many economists to believe that Keynes had been right: a policy-induced demand expansion could end the Depression. As a result, economists paid increasing attention to his work, and by the 1950s reached a general consensus that the federal government *can and should* use aggregate demand policies to reduce fluctuations in economic output, in particular to prevent another Great Depression. In fact, Keynes's work had such an enormous impact on the economics profession that the major debate in macroeconomics during the 1950s and 1960s was not whether aggregate demand management policies could stabilize economic activity, but whether monetary or fiscal policy was the best way to do it![6]

1.2 Controlling Foreign Exchange Rates

The Great Depression also led to major changes in the international monetary system. During the 1930s countries became less economically dependent on each other because world trade declined dramatically. There were a number of reasons why this happened: the worldwide recession of the early 1930s, the tariff war set off by the passage of Smoot-Hawley, and an economic autarky (independence) program carried out by Germany. Many considered this trend toward economic independence to be one of the reasons why World War II occurred, arguing that countries would be much less likely to go to war if they were heavily dependent on each other for trade. Therefore, logic dictated that if policies were taken to enhance world trade, future wars would be less likely.

This was the background to the Bretton Woods conference which took place in New Hampshire in 1944. Delegates from several countries met and agreed on a system that served as the framework for the international monetary system for nearly thirty years. The International Monetary Fund (IMF) was created to administer a fixed exchange rate system for member countries' currencies, and the World Bank was established to lend funds to countries needing financial aid to rebuild. The basic idea underlying the Bretton Woods agreement was to rebuild countries devastated by the war so they could become integral parts of the world order, and fix exchange rates as a way to enhance trade since stable exchange rates reduce the uncertainty associated with exchange rate risk.

The exchange rate system was the component of the Bretton Woods

Agreement that caused problems years later. The IMF fixed exchange rates, but over time the supply and demand for foreign currency schedules shifted around because economic conditions in the member countries changed. Thus, disequilibrium positions occurred, but this contingency was supposedly taken care of because countries could borrow funds from the IMF to cover disequilibrium positions that were thought to be temporary. In the event that a disequilibrium persisted, a country could change its exchange rate after consultation with the IMF.

However, when the need arose, there was considerable reluctance on the part of countries to change their exchange rates. If a country's currency was undervalued, it meant that their products were priced in foreign markets below what they would have been if their currency rose toward its equilibrium value. Countries in this position wanted to avoid exchange rate changes because they enjoyed the benefits of a high level of exports. For countries with overvalued currencies, exchange rate adjustment meant that their currency would fall in value which many interpreted as a sign of economic weakness. In addition, a currency devaluation would raise import prices which puts upward pressure on measured inflation. So countries with overvalued currencies as well as countries with undervalued currencies were reluctant to allow their exchange rates to change. As a result, exchange rate adjustments were far and few between, and almost always when a country was experiencing a major crisis in their balance of payments. Meanwhile, when a crisis was brewing, currency speculators would get involved and intensify the problem by betting that the exchange rates would, in fact, change. For example, in the case of a country with an overvalued currency, speculators would bet that the currency would be devalued. It was a bet the speculators would either win or not lose on, because the only possible outcomes were that the exchange rate would either be devalued or remain unchanged; there was no chance the exchange rate would rise in value. Meanwhile, speculators betting that the exchange rate would be devalued only worsened the balance of payments crisis which made devaluation even more likely. In this roundabout way, the system of fixing exchange rates, originally designed to enhance trade by reducing uncertainty about exchange rate changes, actually ended up increasing uncertainty.[7]

1.3 Bill Phillips's Discovery

During the 1950s, while macroeconomists were busy debating the merits of monetary versus fiscal policy as stabilization tools, a graduate student at the London School of Economics named Bill Phillips published a research paper that went on to have an enormous impact on the conduct of U.S. economic policy. His article appeared in the November 1958 issue of *Economica*, and using several decades of U.K. data reports an inverse relationship between the unemployment rate and the rate of change in nominal wages (Phillips 1958). Phillips's work gained wide exposure two years later when American economists Paul Samuelson and Robert Solow (1960) replicated Phillips's results using U.S. data, reporting a negative correlation between unemployment and the inflation rate (instead of the change in nominal wages). Samuelson and Solow found the relationship to be quite strong in the sense that almost all of the data points were close to the fitted line. This relationship became known as the Phillips curve.

At first glance this statistical result may seem innocuous, but in fact it has enormous policy implications. It suggests that a trade-off exists between inflation and unemployment. In other words, economic policymakers can pick and choose where they wanted to be on the fitted line. Want less inflation? Go ahead and reduce it, but you have to be willing to accept higher unemployment. What about lowering the unemployment rate? You can, if you're willing to accept more inflation. This apparent trade-off was made-to-order for economists advocating activist demand management policies because they could choose whatever unemployment rate they wanted by simply setting the inflation rate at the level necessary according to the estimated Phillips curve.

Policymakers' attempts to exploit the Phillips curve relationship helped create a great deal of the economic instability that occurred from 1965–1982. The 1960 presidential election took place during a recession, and this followed a decade when many economists felt that the U.S. economy was underperforming. In fact Paul Samuelson–who was one of Kennedy's economic advisors–dubbed the decade the "stagnant '50s" (Samuelson 1968, 9). When Kennedy assumed the presidency in 1961, he staffed the Council of Economic Advisors with economists eager to improve the economy's performance, and who believed in both the Phillips curve and activist demand management policies. Kennedy backed their efforts because he had campaigned on a platform to promote economic expansion. So when Kennedy arrived at the White House in 1961, the stage was set: economic advisors who wanted to expand the economy, believed in the Phillips curve, and had the support of the president of the United States.

President Kennedy proposed tax cuts, and a few years later government spending rose dramatically when the Johnson administration expanded U.S. involvement in the Vietnam War and created several new social programs. Meanwhile, the Federal Reserve did their part by generating rapid monetary growth. An economic boom was underway by 1962, and in 1965 the U.S. economy reached full employment. During those years the unemployment rate fell from 6.7 percent to 4.5 percent, while the CPI inflation rate rose from 1.0 percent to 1.6 percent. These numbers were very much in line with the magnitudes predicted by Samuelson and Solow's estimated Phillips curve, lending credence to the view that the economy could be manipulated for the greater good.

1.4 Problems Develop

The year 1965 is a critical one because it marks the start of an inflationary build-up which lasted over fifteen years. Figure 1.1 shows the CPI inflation rate from 1959–1999. Inflation accelerated in late 1965 because that year the U.S. economy reached and then exceeded full employment. President Johnson's economic advisors realized what was happening during 1965:IV when "GNP rose by the largest amount in history...[which] exceeded anyone's expectations or desires" (Okun 1970, 66). They urged Johnson to push for a tax increase to slow down the economy, but he was reluctant to do so because there was little Congressional support. Instead, the Federal Reserve stepped in and started raising short term interest rates in an effort to reduce aggregate demand growth. The policy took hold during 1966; economic growth slowed, unemployment rose, and inflation fell slightly. The growth slowdown continued during 1967, and the CPI inflation rate stabilized at around 3.0 percent. The Federal Reserve had managed to cool off the economy and stabilize inflation without throwing the economy into a recession.

This policy success, along with the fact that the expansion had begun in 1961 (making it the longest since World War II), led economists to sing the praises of the "new economics," the idea that activist aggregate demand policies could stabilize economic activity. For a few

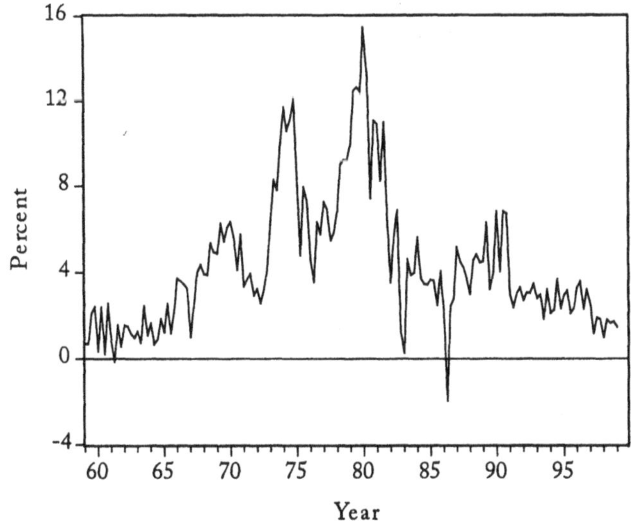

Fig. 1.1 CPI Inflation Rate, 1959–1999

years the economics profession was held in high esteem-- the popular press was actually praising economists and putting their photographs on magazine covers. The new economists were euphoric: consider the comments of Walter Heller, Chairman of the Council of Economic Advisors during the Kennedy and Johnson administrations (1967, 3 & 9):

> Interwoven with the growing Presidential reliance on economists has been a growing political and popular belief hat modern economics can, after all, deliver the goods... economists who can meet a crisis and help carry an expansion into its sixth year may still be worth their salt. As Business Week put it, the record of five years of "remarkable growth– and remarkable stability–in the U.S. economy...has raised the prestige of economists–especially those who espouse the so-called new economics–to an all-time high"...
>
> We now take it for granted that the government must step in to provide the essential stability at high levels of employment and growth that the market mechanism, left alone, cannot deliver.

Paul Samuelson waxed enthusiastic a year later (1968, 8):

> *The New Economics really does work.* Wall Street knows it. Main Street, which has been enjoying 92 months of advancing sales, knows it. The accountants who chalk up record corporate profits know it. The children of the workingmen do not know it: but their mothers do, and so do the school nurses who measure the heights and weights of this generation and remember the bony structure of the last. You can bet that the statisticians in the Kremlin know it–down to the last hundred million of GNP.

A growing number of economists were reaching the conclusion that judicious use of aggregate demand policies could keep the economy growing while avoiding the serious recessions which had plagued the United States in the past. In fact, enthusiasm for the new economics was so high that in 1967 economists actually held a conference titled "Is the Business Cycle Obsolete?"[8] Little did they know the situation was about to unravel.

1.5 Sayonara to the Phillips Curve

The Phillips curve relationship began to disappear in 1968 when the inflation rate accelerated by more than a percentage point while the unemployment rate barely fell. By the early 1970s, the inflation-unemployment trade-off was completely gone because both inflation and unemployment rose:

Year	Unemployment	CPI Inflation
1969	3.5 %	5.5 %
1970	4.9 %	5.7 %

Precisely this outcome had been predicted a few years earlier by economists Milton Friedman and Edmund Phelps who argue that the inflation-unemployment trade-off is just a short-run relationship.[9] They claim that when inflation occurs, unemployed workers eventually start to expect it, so they adjust their wage demands upward which causes them to take longer to find jobs. Thus, for a given level of inflation, the unemployment rate rises. As a result, over time there is no inflation-unemployment trade-off, in fact in the long-run any inflation rate is consistent with a fully employed economy.

Despite the fact that Friedman and Phelps had demonstrated that the inflation-unemployment tradeoff was not a stable relationship, this point was ignored by most policymakers. During the 1970s, officials in government and at the Federal Reserve repeatedly poured demand stimulus onto the economy, which led to overheated business conditions and rising inflation. When the public complained about inflation, the policies would be reversed and the economy thrown into a recession with rising unemployment. This cycle occurred repeatedly: from 1965-1982 the United States experienced one growth recession (1966–1967), and four recessions with falling output (1969–1970, 1973–1975, 1980, and 1981–1982).[10]

The economic instability during this period was associated with distortions caused by government-imposed controls. In the summer of 1971, President Nixon imposed wage and price controls in an effort to tame inflation. This absurd policy of treating the symptom of inflation instead of the cause accomplished little beyond generating shortages of several products, and helping to create the conditions that resulted in two energy crises. Thanks to Nixon's price controls, the American public was treated to distortions and inconveniences in the form of (to name just a few) long lines to purchase gasoline, school and plant shut-downs due to shortages of heating oil and natural gas, shortages of various meat products, and unfinished houses due a lack of new toilets.

1.6 Some Indicators of Instability

The unstable economic conditions that occurred from 1965–1982 can be seen in the behavior of several economic indicators. Referring back to figure 1.1, note that from the late 1960s to early 1980s each peak of the inflation rate was higher than the previous peak. This illustrates the upward trend of inflation; it was such a serious problem by the late 1970s and early 1980s that it was a key reason why Jimmy Carter lost the 1980 presidential election. Unemployment followed a similar pattern: figure 1.2 shows the unemployment rate ratcheting up as well. At each trough in economic activity the unemployment rate was higher than it had been at the previous trough. This fact caused considerable consternation among Americans; to many it was indicative of an economy with fewer and fewer opportunities for advancement.

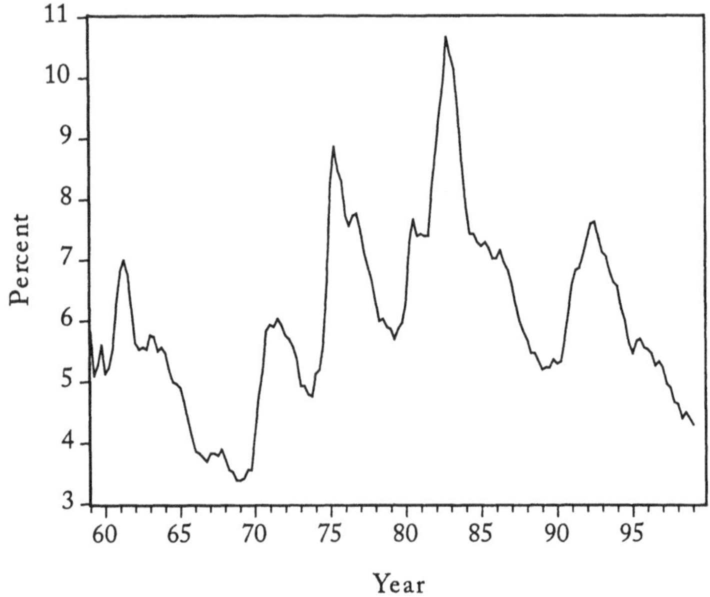

Fig 1.2 Civilian Labor Force Unemployment Rate, 1959–1999

Inflation causes lenders to demand compensation for expected future price increases, which is why interest rates often follow the same general pattern as inflation. Figure 1.3 shows the yield on 90-day Treasury bills. During the 1970s, interest rates cycled up, rising to levels unprecedented in modern times. When yields peaked in the early 1980s, they did so at values not seen in the United States since the Civil War when Confederate Army troops were encamped outside Washington D.C.

The 1970s inflation was a global problem, in large part because the 1972–1973 economic boom was experienced worldwide. One effect of this worldwide expansion shows up in the prices of commodities, which are raw materials such as oil, foodstuffs, and various metals that are traded on world markets. Figure 1.4 shows the index of commodity prices, and the pattern is remarkable: after being relatively stable during the 1960s, the index shot up dramatically in the 1970s. In fact, between 1972 and 1979, commodity prices tripled.

The high inflation experienced in the United States and elsewhere had many pernicious effects, and one of the more serious was the dam-

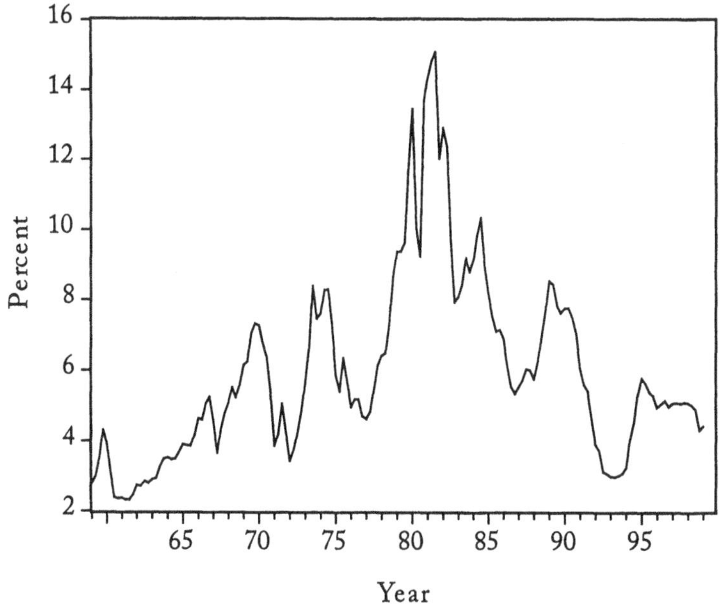

Fig 1.3 Yield on 90 Day Treasury Bills, 1959–1999

age done to equity values. Figure 1.5 plots the Dow Jones Industrial Average from 1946 to 1999. Stock prices rose substantially from 1950–1967, but then stagnated for the next several years until the next bull market began in 1982. A major reason why stock prices had a flat trend during the 1970s was because of the inflation taking place which damaged equity values in two ways. First, it drove up interest rates which reduced the present value of expected dividends. Second, it caused corporate profits to be overstated, because while revenues rose with inflation, historical accounting costs did not. Thus, corporate incomes were overstated which meant that income tax liabilities were too. As a result of these factors, the nominal values of corporate equities were essentially flat for about fifteen years (1967–1982). During that same period, the U.S. price level increased roughly threefold, meaning that in inflation-adjusted terms a figurative bloodbath took place on Wall Street. Real estate, which tends to be a good hedge against inflation, was a vastly superior investment during the inflationary 1970s than were stocks or bonds.

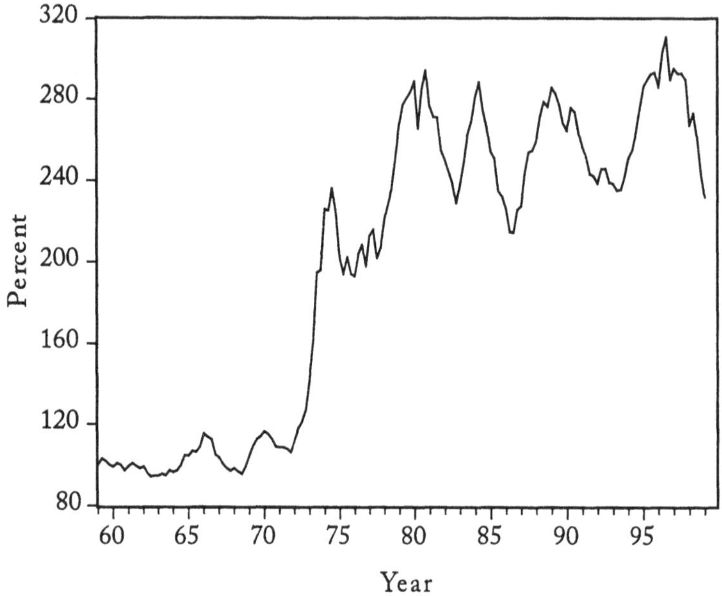

Fig 1.4 Index of Commodity Prices, 1959–1999

1.7 The Wrong Conclusion

Karl Marx once said that history repeats itself–the first time as tragedy, the second time as farce. The tragedy was the Great Depression: a man-made economic policy disaster that caused massive uemployment, widespread poverty, and ultimately led to a world war that resulted in the deaths of millions of people. In the midst of this catastrophe, people naturally wanted to take steps to prevent a reoccurrence, and this is why governmental control over the economy was dramatically increased. This change took place because the prevailing attitude at the time was that the Depression was caused by a *failure of capitalism*. Therefore, the way to prevent a repeat performance was to control the market system more rigorously.

This view was well-meaning, but mistaken. The Great Depression did not result from a failure of capitalism. Instead, above all else, the Depression proves that *perverse economic policies can destroy an economy.* Capitalism did not fail during the 1930s, policymakers in government and at the Federal Reserve did! They pursued badly-designed policies because they had poor knowledge of the

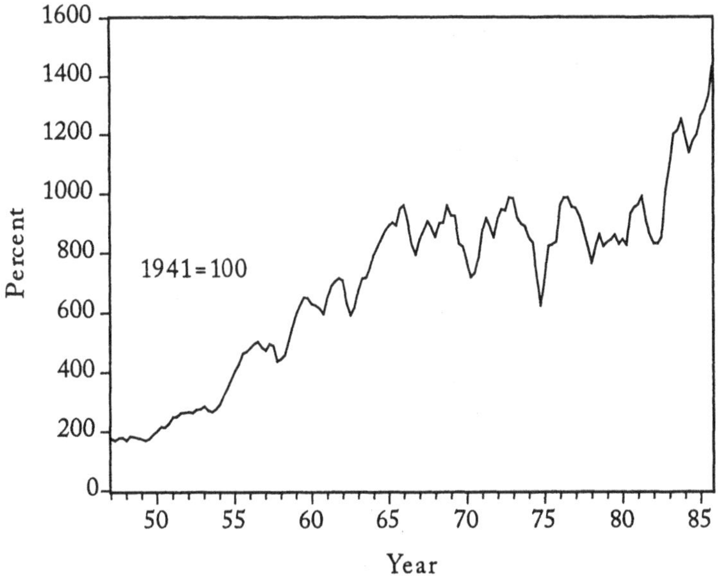

Fig 1.5 Index of Stock Prices, 1947–1986

economy, were confused, and in some cases incompetent. The result was the mother of all macroeconomic disasters.

The farce was the sequence of events that led to the U.S. economic instability 1965–1982. During and after the Depression, much was learned about how the economy operates, in particular how changes in aggregate demand influence economic activity. After World War II, policymakers took this newfound knowledge and used it over a period of years to repeat the same mistake again and again– overstimulating the economy, then creating a recession to reduce inflation, followed by another inflationary boom, then a recession....And these weren't mild booms and busts, these were major inflation accelerations followed by severe recessions associated with significant increases in unemployment. The mistakes policymakers made during the 1930s are understandable because knowledge about aggregate economic relationships was not well-developed, and many key participants simply did not know better. Such an explanation carries far less weight when applied to the 1970s because many people *did* know better. And for those who were ignorant, the knowledge existed and was fairly easy to obtain.

The purpose of this book is to explain how the economic mess the United States experienced from 1965–1982 came to pass, and how the problems were eventually solved. It is an interesting story about the evolution of macroeconomic thinking, and how people learn (albeit slowly) from past mistakes. To accomplish this task, we draw on the abundance of previous work that exists on these topics. It turns out that the economic prosperity which occurred from 1982–2000 can be traced to sound policies that were learned from mistakes made during the 1960s and 1970s.

CHAPTER 2

■■■

The Phillips Curve

> *His wartime experiences, combined with a natural aversion to controversy in general, and political controversy in particular, may...partially explain one of the mysteries of contemporary macroeconomics: why Phillips remained silent, in print at least, while the curve, with which he was eponymously associated, was used, by others, to justify the policy of tolerating inflation in order to achieve permanently low levels of unemployment, which he had specifically cautioned against.*
> *—Robert Leeson (1994, 616).*

On several occasions people have advocated policies without carefully considering all of the ultimate consequences. One famous example was the 1919-1933 prohibition of alcoholic beverages in the United States. The underlying idea was simple: alcohol consumption causes social problems, therefore if alcohol is prohibited people will not drink (or at least drink considerably less), and society will be better off.

While there is evidence that prohibition reduced alcohol consumption, it hardly fell to zero. Liquor was illegally imported from Canada and Mexico which did not prohibit alcohol production, and Americans manufactured alcoholic beverages in their homes. So while alcohol consumption did decline, it did not stop, nor did the social problems associated with it. Meanwhile, a whole new set of problems arose. With prohibition there was an incentive to manufacture more potent forms of alcohol because it was easier to conceal smaller quantities. This desire to increase potency resulted in unscrupulous bootleggers using dangerous additives such as denatured alcohol which directly resulted in some deaths (Thornton 1991, 100-105). There was also a tremendous increase in organized crime: Chicago's Al Capone is just the most famous example of the innumerable criminals who committed murder and mayhem in an effort to control alcoholic beverage distribution. While this was going on, public officials such as police officers, prosecutors, judges, and mayors were corrupted by payoffs from liquor distributors in exchange for keeping the criminal justice system off their backs. In effect, the criminal element ended up controlling many local governments. The results of alcohol prohibition were not quite what the proponents had in mind.

The Phillips curve is another example of an idea that was adopted without enough thought given to the ultimate consequences. The curve itself was developed in 1958 by an economist named Bill Phillips who was working on his Ph.D. at the London School of Economics. He was trying to provide statistical evidence for a proposition he thought obvious, that during periods of high labor demand, wages rise rapidly and unemployment is low. During periods of low labor demand, wages fall slowly and unemployment is high. He never advocated using his results as the basis for policies designed to reduce unemployment. Yet his results were latched onto by economic policymakers in the United States who tried to reduce unemployment by raising the inflation rate. This misuse of Bill Phillips's results goes a long way toward explaining how the United States developed a serious inflation problem by the late 1960s. The results were disastrous: the United States ended up with more inflation and more unemployment.

2.1 Bill Phillips

> *Bill Phillips was a great and modest man. Not only did he give a tremendous stimulus to applied economic research on wage determination and inflation, but his pupils and colleagues in London, Canberra and Auckland respected him for his integrity and competence, and loved him for his humanity and enthusiasm.*
> *—C.A. Blythe (1978, xvii).*

Alban William Housego (Bill) Phillips (1914-1975) lived an interesting, although sadly abbreviated, life.[1] He was born in New Zealand and grew up on his family's dairy farm. In 1929, at the age of fifteen, he left home to become an apprentice electrician which he did until 1935. He then moved to Australia where he kicked around for the next two years working at a variety of jobs, including a brief stint as a crocodile hunter. In 1937 Phillips decided to travel to Britain by way of China and Russia, a journey which took him almost a year, in part because he was traveling through Manchuria during the war between China and Japan. During the journey he took a correspondence course in electrical engineering from the British Institute of Technology.

Shortly after he arrived in London (with ten shillings in his pocket) he took the electrical engineering exam and passed it. For the next several months he worked in the electrical industry.

In 1939 he decided to study economics, so he enrolled at the London School of Economics. His initial tour there was brief, however, because shortly after he enrolled World War II erupted. Phillips joined the armed forces and was sent to the South Pacific as an armament officer. In 1942 he committed an act of great bravery that earned him a military citation. He was on board a ship that was attacked by Japanese aircraft. Phillips grabbed a machine gun and quickly set up a mounting so the weapon could serve as an anti-aircraft gun. For the next three and a half hours Phillips manned the gun even though at one point a bomb hit the deck he was standing on. His military citation mentioned his "outstanding courage" and that he "set a most valuable example of coolness, steadiness and fearlessness to all in his vicinity" (Blythe 1978, xv).

Unfortunately, Phillips was taken prisoner a short time later and spent the rest of the war in a Japanese prison camp. The conditions were appalling: the prisoners were beaten, tortured, starved, and many were literally worked to death. An estimated 27 percent of all Anglo-Americans interned in Japanese prison camps died (Leeson 1994, 611). Phillips was among the fortunate who lived, but like so many others who survived the ordeal his health was ruined. He weighed ninety-eight pounds when he returned from the war, and while he regained his weight, he never regained vigorous health. He was hindered by poor health for the rest of his life. A massive stroke in 1969 when he was just fifty-four years old effectively ended his professional life. He died in 1975 at the age of sixty.

Although Phillips's career was relatively short, he had a huge impact on the economics profession. After the war he reentered the London School of Economics and published several papers while working on his Ph.D. degree. His areas of expertise were control theory and macroeconomics. He was most proud of his work in control theory, but ironically it was one of his papers in macroeconomics that made him famous throughout the world. The article was published in 1958 and is titled "The Relation Between Unemployment and the Rate of Change of Money Wage Rates in the United Kingdom, 1861-1957." Phillips himself didn't consider it his best work. In fact, he claimed to have written the paper over the course of a weekend (Leeson 1994, 613).

The paper itself is hardly pretentious. Phillips simply provides statistical evidence about the relationship between unemployment and wage changes. He argues that during periods of high labor demand there is high wage growth and low unemployment, and during periods of low labor demand wages are falling and unemployment is high. Furthermore, he posits a nonlinear relationship because when unemployment is low wages rise rapidly, but when unemployment is high wages fall slowly because "workers are reluctant to offer their services at less than the prevailing [wages]" (Phillips 1958, 283).

To investigate this proposition, Phillips plots rates of unemployment against rates of change in nominal wages using annual British data from 1861-1913. This is Phillips's figure 1, which is reproduced here as figure 2.1. Clearly, an inverse relationship exists between nominal wage growth and the unemployment rate, and for the most part the data points are reasonably close to the fitted line.

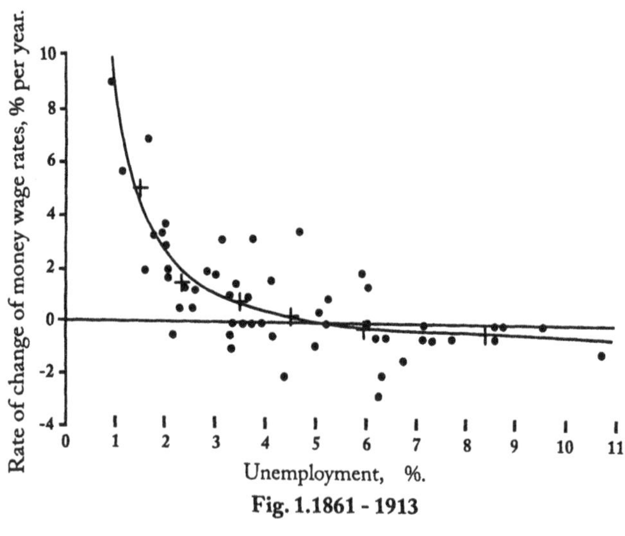

Fig 2.1 *Source: Phillips (1958, 285), reprinted with permission.*

There are, however, points that lie some distance from the estimated line, and Phillips provides explanations for why this might happen. One factor he considers is import prices. He contends that if import prices rise significantly during a particular year, workers might demand a cost of living adjustment in the form of higher nominal wages. When this happens, for a given rate of unemployment the change in wages may then be higher than during a 'normal' year, in other words, the data point would lie to the right of the fitted line. During a year when import prices fell significantly, workers might not demand a cost of living adjustment, so wages may change more slowly and the data point would lie to the left of the fitted line.

The economy's stage in the business cycle could also result in points away from the fitted line. For a given unemployment rate, Phillips argues that during periods of falling unemployment (during economic expansions) wages would be rising faster than they would be when unemployment is rising during an economic recession. In other words, when the unemployment rate is falling and hits, say, 4.0 percent during an economic expansion wages would be rising more rapidly than when the unemployment rate reaches the same 4.0 percent value while it is rising during a recession. Therefore, data points would tend to lie to the right of the fitted line during economic expansions, and to the left during economic recessions.

The final reason Phillips cites for why data points may be off the fitted line is industrial strife. For example, widespread strikes would raise the unemployment rate for a given rate of wage changes, and result in data points to be right of the fitted line. The opposite would be true during times when organized labor was relatively calm.

Phillips draws the curve fitted with data from 1861-1913, and on the same diagram plots data covering 1948-1957. This is Phillips's figure 11 and is reproduced here as figure 2.2. Note how close the data points are to the fitted line. The implication of this exercise (although Phillips never says this) is that the relationship is stable over time.

One of the great ironies of modern macroeconomics is how Phillips' results, which he himself considered obvious and relatively minor work, went on to become the centerpiece of very important economic policy decisions. Phillips's biographers (e.g., Leeson 1994) make it clear that Phillips himself never advocated using his findings as a tool for economic policy other than indicating what unemployment rate might result if a policy of price stability were pursued. Yet when his findings were used as an economic policy tool, Phillips was silent on the matter. No one knows exactly why, although Leeson (1994) thinks it might have been because Phillips was a man who was always looking forward; by the time his results were being used for economic policy decisions he had moved on to other interests. In addition, he detested conflict and rather than becoming involved in a major debate he was probably more comfortable just ignoring the entire issue.

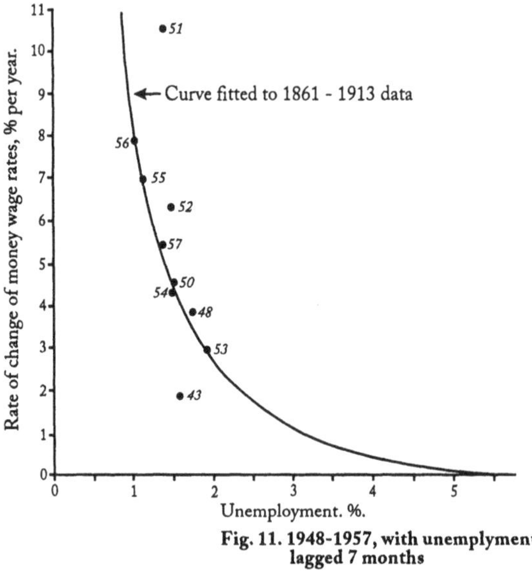

Fig 2.2 *Source: Phillips (1958,297), reprinted with permission.*

2.2 Paul Samuelson and Robert Solow

> *In order to achieve the nonperfectionist's goal of high enough output to give us no more than 3 per cent unemployment, the price index might have to rise by as much as 4 to 5 per cent per year. That much price rise would seem to be the necessary cost of high employment and production in the years immediately ahead.*
> *—Paul Samuelson and Robert Solow (1960, 192).*

Paul Samuelson (b. 1915) and Robert Solow (b. 1924) are very accomplished men with much in common. Both received their Ph.D.s from Harvard, spent their careers at the Massachusetts Institute of Technology, and received Nobel Prizes in Economic Science. Samuelson earned his award for incorporating mathematics into economic theory, Solow for developing the standard neoclassical model of economic growth which is commonly referred to as the Solow Growth Model. Economists owe a huge debt to both Samuelson and Solow for their major strides in the development of economic theory.

Samuelson and Solow are also major figures in our story of the Phillips curve. They collaborated on a paper published in 1960 titled "Analytical Aspects of Anti-Inflation Policy" which investigates the source of U.S. inflation during the 1950s. While this inflation was low compared to what Americans would experience during the 1970s, at the time the prevailing rates of around 3.0 percent in 1956 and 1957 were considered high, especially in light of "little evidence of over-all high employment and excess demand" (Samuelson and Solow 1960, 181). Their investigation focuses on whether the inflation emanated from the demand side ("demand pull") or the supply side ("cost push").

In the course of their study they estimate Phillips's relationship with U.S. data, making one minor change: instead of using nominal wage growth on the vertical axis as Phillips does, they use the inflation rate. This is not a substantive alteration because nominal wages rise

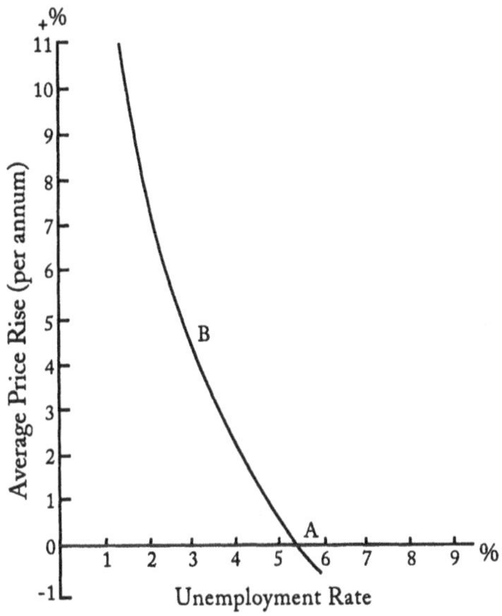

FIGURE 2

MODIFIED PHILLIPS CURVE FOR U.S.

This shows the menu of choice between different degrees of unemployment and price stability, as roughly estimated from last twenty-five years of American data.

Fig 2.3 *Source: Samuelson and Solow (1960, 192), reprinted with permission.*

at roughly the same rate as prices. The fitted line looks much like the one Phillips reports, downward sloping and nonlinear. Samuelson and Solow refer to the line as the Phillips curve, and it is reproduced here as figure 2.3.[2] They view the downward sloping line as illustrating a tradeoff between inflation and unemployment. Low unemployment can be achieved, but at the cost of high inflation. Conversely, low inflation can be attained, but in this case society must be willing to tolerate high unemployment.

Samuelson and Solow contend that the relationship may not be stable over time. In particular, they argue that economic policies could shift the curve. On the structural side, weaker labor unions, better information flow about existing job vacancies, and improved labor mobility would cause the curve to shift left, meaning that a given inflation rate would be consistent with a lower unemployment rate. Factors causing higher structural unemployment would shift the curve to the right.

A particularly intriguing section of the paper considers the affect of aggregate demand changes on the location of the Phillips curve. They offer two possibilities. The first is that a reduction in aggregate demand growth causes unemployment to rise, but in the short-run inflation does not fall. However, over time "the low-pressure demand would so act upon wage and other expectations as to shift the curve downward in the longer run-- so that over a decade, the economy might enjoy higher employment with price stability than our present-day estimates would indicate" (1960, 193).[3]

The second possibility is that aggregate demand changes may have the opposite effect. Low aggregate demand growth might cause "larger and larger amounts of structural unemployment...[causing] an upward shift of our menu of choice, with more and more unemployment being needed just to keep prices stable" (1960, 193).[4] According to Samuelson and Solow, they have no idea which of the two possible outcomes is more likely.

In sum, Samuelson and Solow's contribution to the Phillips curve is twofold. First, they present the statistical relationship as being between the unemployment and inflation. Second, and more importantly, they view the results being suggestive of a tradeoff between the two. In other words, ignoring structural factors such as the power of labor unions, if society wants less unemployment it must be willing to accept more inflation. Conversely, if society desires less inflation, it must be willing to endure more unemployment. Yet at the same time, by acknowledging the fact that demand policy could alter wage and price expectations and cause the curve to shift, Samuelson and Solow anticipated the potential danger of a policy of raising inflation in an effort to reduce unemployment. Unfortunately, they (along with many others) ignored this possibility.

2.3 The Critical Misinterpretation

> *I remember that Paul Samuelson asked me when we were looking at these diagrams [of inflation and unemployment] for the first time, 'Does that look like a reversible relation to you?' What he meant was 'Do you really think the economy can move back and forth along a curve like that?' And I answered 'Yeah I'm inclined to believe it,' and Paul said 'Me too.'*
> *—Robert Solow (taken from Leeson [1997, 145]).*

The critical misinterpretation that Samuelson, Solow, and many others made about the Phillips curve was that it presented a stable, exploitable tradeoff between inflation and unemployment. The idea was that society could simply choose where it wanted to be on the Phillips curve and, very importantly, remain there for a prolonged period of time. Economists and policymakers in positions of power ignored the possibility, which Samuelson himself considered but dismissed because empirical evidence was lacking, that creeping inflation could eventually become galloping inflation (Samuelson 1964, 791). In other words, a higher and higher inflation rate might be necessary to maintain the same unemployment rate.

Keynesian economists whole-heartedly embraced the notion of an exploitable Phillips curve. They believed that monetary and (especially) fiscal policies could be used to maintain high employment and help avoid recessions, or at least make them milder than they otherwise would be. To economists who thought in these terms, the Phillips curve was a very attractive concept: low unemployment is attainable if society is simply willing to tolerate some inflation! Keynesian economists (including Samuelson and Solow) discounted the suggestion that aggregate demand changes might eventually shift the Phillips curve.

Keynesian economists received their big opportunity to apply their ideas to actual policy decisions when John F. Kennedy became president. Kennedy was a Democrat (as were most Keynesians), and had studied economics at Harvard under the tutelage of John Kenneth Galbraith, a well-known Keynesian. So it was natural for Kennedy to staff his economic advisory positions with Keynesian economists. His first Council of Economic Advisors consisted of three well-known members of that group: Walter Heller, Kermit Gordon, and James Tobin. From then on, through to the end of the Johnson administration, all of the senior members of the Council were well-known Keynesians.

Table 2.1 - Growth Rates of M2 and Nominal GDP, 1960-1970

Year	M2 growth	Nominal GDP Growth
1960	4.9%	3.8%
1961	7.4%	3.5%
1962	8.1%	7.4%
1963	8.4%	5.5%
1964	8.0%	7.4%
1965	8.1%	8.5%
1966	4.6%	9.5%
1967	9.3%	5.8%
1968	8.0%	9.2%
1969	3.7%	7.9%
1970	6.6%	5.4%

Source: Council of Economic Advisors (1998, 361).

The 1960 presidential election took place in the midst of a mild recession, and during the campaign Kennedy pledged to promote economic recovery. At the time of his inauguration (January, 1961) the unemployment rate stood at 6.7 percent which suggests that the U.S. economy was operating below capacity. So the pieces were in place: an economy with excess capacity, economic advisors who wanted to stimulate aggregate demand to promote recovery, and a president sympathetic to their view.

The demand stimulus during the 1960s was brought about by a combination of expansionary monetary and fiscal policies. On the monetary front, the Federal Reserve began aggressively purchasing government securities starting in February 1961. From February to August of that year they added about $700 million worth of securities to their portfolio, and then raised it by another $1.6 billion from September to December (Eastburn 1965, 92). Table 2.1 shows the results of these actions. By 1962, M2 was rising at a rate of over 8.0 percent, and the growth rate remained in that neighborhood for the next three years. This monetary stimulus helped cause nominal GDP growth to more than double during 1961-1962, and it stayed high for the next several years.

Fiscal policy also contributed to the expansion of demand. The Cold War was at its height in the early 1960s over the Soviet Union's attempts to place nuclear missiles on the island of Cuba, which is located just ninety miles off the Florida coast. At the time, there was considerable talk about the "missile gap," the alleged fact that the United States had a much smaller arsenal of nuclear missiles than the Soviets did.[5] In an effort to close this gap, U.S. defense spending rose with much of the increased outlays going for missile purchases. From 1960-1962, current dollar defense spending rose $7.4 billion, which accounts for almost 9.0 percent of the rise in GDP during that period. After 1962 defense spending stabilized until 1965 when the Vietnam War build-up began. From 1965-1968 current dollar defense spending rose $30 billion, accounting for 6.4 percent of the rise in GDP over that same period (Council of Economic Advisors 1996, 281).

Tax policy was expansionary as well. An investment tax credit was instituted in 1962, providing a 7.0 percent credit for the purchase of new capital goods. That same year President Kennedy proposed reductions in income tax rates, but Congress was slow to act. The House of Representatives passed the bill in 1963, but the Senate did not approve it until February 1964, three months after President Kennedy was assassinated. The Revenue Act of 1964 reduced personal income tax rates by about 20 percent, lowered the top rate from 91 to 70 percent, cut withholding rates from 18 to 14 percent, and reduced the corporate income tax rate from 52 to 48 percent. At the time, it was the biggest tax cut in U.S. history (Campagna 1987, 307).

These expansionary monetary and fiscal policies helped cause a decade-long economic boom. Table 2.2 shows the annual unemployment and inflation rates from 1960-1970. Issues of the Economic Report of the President during the 1960s repeatedly cite 4.0 percent unemployment as being consistent with a fully employed economy. For this reason, the unemployment rates of over 5.0 percent recorded during the first half of the decade were considered high because they indicated excess capacity in the economy. The unemployment rate finally broke through the 4.0 percent barrier in 1966, but (as the Phillips curve predicted) at the expense of accelerating inflation.

The situation started to unravel in the late 1960s when inflation started to gallop. The unemployment rate fell to the 3.0 percent range in 1968, but inflation was accelerating dramatically. Then, during 1969 the unemployment rate fell just 0.1 percent while inflation rose 1.3 percentage points. The possibility that Samuelson and Solow had considered in 1960, but ignored afterwards–that a demand stimulus might cause the Phillips curve to shift–was apparently happening. Interestingly, a formal explanation for why this might occur had already been provided by Milton Friedman and Edmund Phelps.

Table 2.2 - Labor Force Unemployment Rate and CPI Inflation Rate, 1960-1970

Year	Unemployment Rate	CPI Inflation Rate
1960	5.5%	1.7%
1961	6.7%	1.0%
1962	5.5%	1.0%
1963	5.7%	1.3%
1964	5.2%	1.3%
1965	4.5%	1.6%
1966	3.8%	2.9%
1967	3.8%	3.1%
1968	3.6%	4.2%
1969	3.5%	5.5%
1970	4.9%	5.7%

Source: Council of Economic Advisors (1999, 377 & 399).

2.4 Milton Friedman and Edmund Phelps

Phillips' analysis of the relation between unemployment and inflation is deservedly celebrated as an important and original contribution. But, unfortunately, it contains a basic

> *defect— the failure to distinguish between nominal and real wages...Implicitly, Phillips wrote his article for a world in which everyone anticipated that nominal prices would be stable and in which that anticipation remained unshaken and immutable whatever happened to actual prices and wages.*
> *—Milton Friedman (1968, 102).*

Milton Friedman and Edmund Phelps are both famous economists. Friedman (b. 1912), taught at the University of Chicago for many years, and is now associated with the Hoover Institution. In 1976 he received a Nobel Prize in Economic Science for his work in monetary analysis and consumption theory. Phelps (b. 1933) has long been associated with Columbia University and arguably deserves a Nobel Prize of his own. Working independently of each other, these two men developed a concept that went on to become a bedrock of macroeconomic thinking, and revolutionized the way economists think about economic policy. The idea is called the natural rate hypothesis.

They developed their theory in the context of the Phillips curve. The natural rate hypothesis argues that the measured unemployment rate tends toward a natural rate in the long-run, and that this natural rate of unemployment is independent of the inflation rate. In other words, in the long-run there is no downward sloping Phillips curve, instead the long-run Phillips curve is vertical.

At the same time, they argue that the relationship plotted by Phillips, and later Samuelson and Solow, is an unstable short-run relationship. There is a tradeoff between inflation and unemployment in the short-run, but only for a given rate of expected inflation. If aggregate demand growth changes, it causes the inflation rate to change, and people will eventually expect this new inflation rate and adjust their behavior accordingly. When this occurs, the short-run Phillips curve shifts.

In essence, Friedman and Phelps were formalizing a point made earlier by Samuelson and Solow. Recall that in Samuelson and Solow's article, they explain that restrictive aggregate demand policies could potentially shift the Phillips curve to the left over time by lowering "wage and other expectations" (Samuelson and Solow 1960, 193). However, while raising this possibility they never emphasize it because they also consider an alternative scenario: that a restrictive demand policy could shift the curve to the right if economic slack created long-term structural unemployment. Friedman and Phelps focus on the former possibility: that aggregate demand changes, by changing the actual inflation rate, eventually change the expected inflation rate. This expected inflation rate is important because it influences wage rates sought by unemployed workers.

Friedman and Phelps develop their framework by considering frictionally unemployed workers. These are people 'between jobs,' they possess skills that match up with existing vacancies, but a time-consuming job search is necessary to find employment. A representative unemployed worker is assumed to have a reservation wage, which is the lowest nominal wage offer at which he or she will accept employment. These reservation wages are assumed to be based on the expected future inflation rate. If expected inflation rises, workers raise their reservation wages in order to maintain the same real (inflation-adjusted) reservation wage.

The Friedman-Phelps version of the Phillips curve is shown in Figure 2.4. They define the long run as the time when expectations of inflation are correct. When this is true, unemployment is at the natural rate, U_n. In this case, frictionally unemployed workers take a certain number of weeks on average to find jobs which results in U_n. Assume initially that the inflation rate (p) is 2.0 percent, and the expected inflation rate (p^e) is 2.0 percent, so the economy is operating at full employment (point 1 on the diagram).

Now suppose the actual inflation rate rises to 4.0 percent, but the expected inflation rate remains at 2.0 percent. With the higher inflation rate, nominal wages rise more rapidly, but since the expected inflation rate is still 2.0 percent unemployed workers don't realize that the faster wage growth is due to rising inflation. Since the expected inflation rate has not changed, neither have reservation wages. As a result, the unemployed workers mistakenly view the rising wage offers as being higher real wages, which they are not. In fact, real wages have fallen because prices are rising faster than nominal wages. Thus, the frictionally unemployed are fooled into accepting job offers sooner than they would have if their expected inflation rate was 4.0 percent instead of 2.0 percent. The average number of weeks people are unemployed declines, as does the measured unemployment rate. The economy is now operating at point 2 on the diagram. Therefore, a tradeoff exists between inflation and unemployment, but only for a given expected inflation rate. This tradeoff is represented by the line $SRPC_1$ (= Short Run Phillips Curve.).

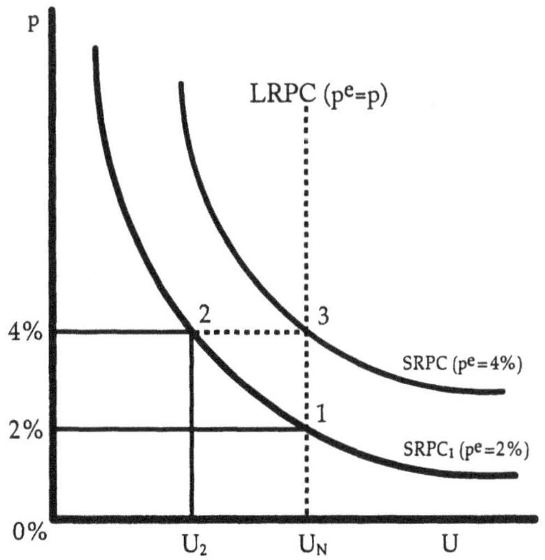

Fig. 2.4 The Friedman - Phelps Natural Rate Phillips Curve

The economy will not stay at point 2, however, because expectations of inflation are incorrect. Eventually people figure out that the inflation rate is 4.0 percent, and raise their reservation wages accordingly. When this happens, the frictionally unemployed take longer to find jobs, the same average number of weeks as when actual and expected inflation were both 2.0 percent. The economy is now operating at point 3 in the diagram-- back at full employment with a 4.0 percent actual and expected inflation rate. Thus, there is no permanent trade off between inflation and unemployment. In the long-run, the Phillips curve is a vertical line passing through points 1 and 3.

Economic policymakers during the 1960s behaved as if they could simply pick a point on the downward sloping Phillips curve and stay there. The Friedman-Phelps view demonstrates that the trade-off between inflation and unemployment is only a short-run relationship. In the long-run, the economy can be fully employed with any inflation rate, including zero. Furthermore, attempts to stimulate the economy by raising aggregate demand growth are doomed to fail because the economy will just return to full employment with a higher inflation rate. In the end, all policymakers succeed in doing is generating inflation that will require a painful recession to eradicate.

2.5 America Discovers Inflationary Expectations

> *The Democratic advisers in the Kennedy-Johnson administrations had argued that a substantial reduction in the unemployment rate could be achieved at the cost of only a moderate acceleration of inflation, and with an inflation rate of only 3.0 percent in the four quarters ending in 1967:4 their gamble appeared to have paid off.*
>
> *This policy framework collapsed with amazing speed after 1967 as the result of the interaction of events and economic writings. My graduate school classmates and I were acutely aware of the timing of this turn in the intellectual tide, as we began our first teaching jobs in the fall of 1967 and almost immediately found our graduate school education incapable of explaining the evolution of the economy. The most important ingredient in this intellectual revolution was the influence of the Friedman-Phelps "natural rate hypothesis."*
>
> *—Robert J. Gordon (1980, 134).*

The development of macroeconomic thought is replete with cases of economic theories being developed to explain events that already took place. For example, Keynes developed his aggregate demand-based theory in response to the Great Depression, and the real business cycle model was developed to explain the role of supply-side factors that were important during the 1970s. In contrast, the Friedman-Phelps version of the Phillips curve is an unusual case in macroeconomics: a theory that predicted a major macroeconomic event before it actually took place. It is easy to imagine both Milton Friedman and Edmund Phelps looking over the economic data during the late 1960s and early 1970s, nodding their heads in confirmation, and telling anyone who would listen "I told you this would happen!" The two men had come up with the intellectual equivalent of a basketball slam dunk.

Annual inflation and unemployment rates for the United States from 1961-1973 are plotted in figure 2.5, and three interesting patterns appear in this diagram. First, during the 1960s the behavior of inflation and unemployment did follow a downward sloping relationship. Second, the behavior of inflation referred to by Robert J. Gordon is clear in the figure. The inflation rate was stable in the 3.0 percent range during 1966-1967, and then increased dramatically during 1968 and 1969. Third, the points for 1970, 1971, and 1972 are well away from any line fitted with the data from the 1960s. In other words, any semblance of a stable Phillips curve completely disappeared after 1969.

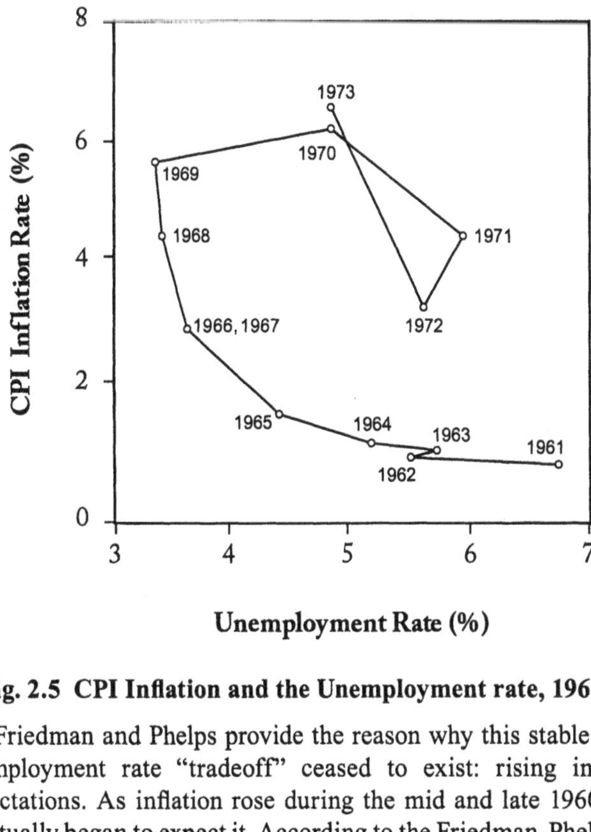

Fig. 2.5 CPI Inflation and the Unemployment rate, 1961–1973

Friedman and Phelps provide the reason why this stable inflation-unemployment rate "tradeoff" ceased to exist: rising inflationary expectations. As inflation rose during the mid and late 1960s, people eventually began to expect it. According to the Friedman-Phelps theory, workers raised their reservation wages, and by doing so took longer to find new jobs. As a result, the measured unemployment rate rose.

Evidence that expected inflation rose during the 1960s is available thanks to a man named Joseph Livingston. In 1946, Livingston began surveying economists on their expected future values of several economic variables, one of which was the consumer price index. Although he asked about the expected price level, from this data we can calculate an expected inflation rate by simply taking the difference between the survey-average expected price level one year ahead and calculating the percent change between that number and the actual price level when the survey was taken. Table 2.3 shows the expected one-year ahead inflation rates using the December observations from the Livingston survey. It is clear what happened: in the late 1960s inflation expectations rose. Thus, we see in figure 2.5 that inflation rates of over 4.0 percent were no longer high enough to keep the unemployment rate below 4.0 percent because higher expected inflation had shifted the

Table 2.3 - Expected CPI Inflation From the Livingston Survey

Year	Expected CPI Inflation
1961	1.4 %
1962	1.3 %
1963	1.2 %
1964	1.4 %
1965	1.9 %
1966	2.5 %
1967	3.2 %
1968	3.3 %
1969	4.1 %
1970	4.3 %

Source: Federal Reserve Bank of Philadelphia, http://www.phil.frb.org.

Phillips curve to the right.

Thus, in the span of just a few short years the great experiment in aggregate demand management unraveled. The Keynesian economic policymakers thought they could raise the inflation rate and permanently reduce unemployment. But, as Friedman and Phelps predicted, driving up the inflation rate would not keep unemployment down because eventually people would expect higher inflation. This process is precisely what happened, and by the early 1970s the United States ended up with the double whammy of higher inflation and higher unemployment.

The sad part of this story is that this was just the beginning: policymakers in Washington apparently didn't learn anything from this episode because during the 1970s they repeated the same mistake two more times. They overstimulated the U.S. economy in an effort to reduce unemployment, and both times the United States ended up with more unemployment and more inflation.

CHAPTER 3

■■■

The Bretton Woods System

There are only two mechanisms that are consistent with a free market and free trade. One is the fully automatic international gold standard...[which] is neither feasible nor desirable...The other is a system of freely floating exchange rates determined in the market by private transactions without governmental intervention.
—Milton Friedman (1962, 67).

On July 1, 1944, less than a month after the Allied invasion of Normandy, while World War II was still undecided in both Europe and the Pacific, 730 delegates from forty-four countries had enough confidence in the outcome of the war to meet in Bretton Woods, New Hampshire and plan the Post-War monetary world. They did not want to resurrect the gold standard because there was widespread agreement that it had been a major reason why the Depression had spread around the world. Yet at the same time, there was a general desire to bring back the stability of foreign exchange rates that existed while the gold standard was in place.

The Bretton Woods Agreement that resulted from this conference was nothing more than a price-fixing regime, where foreign exchange rates were the prices being fixed. The belief was that setting exchange rates would bring about the desired stability. But as anyone who has ever studied supply and demand analysis knows, fixing prices leads to market disequilibrium because in the dynamic world we live in supply and demand schedules shift around. This is exactly what happened: during the time Bretton Woods was in force (1947-1971), enormous changes took place in the world economy, yet rates of exchange among several currencies were held constant, in some cases for intervals lasting more than twenty years. Huge disequilibrium positions arose, and the adjustment that finally took place when the system imploded in 1971 was considered a "world financial crisis." It was a crisis that need never have occurred because it was created by yet another well-intentioned governmental program of economic control.

3.1 The World Before Bretton Woods

To understand why the Bretton Woods system was implemented in the first place, readers should be familiar with the world's monetary systems prior to World War II. In those times, there were only two alternative exchange rate systems for organizing international trade and finance, and correcting payments imbalances between nations: a commodity (gold) standard, and floating exchange rates. Both systems provided free market solutions to the problem with only a limited role required of governments. The preferred system was the commodity standard, usually gold (or silver), in which each government fixed their national currency in value to gold, and this price was maintained through government purchases of the commodity. In the pure form of this system, the governments' role was limited to setting the price of gold in terms of units of domestic currency, and buying and selling gold in quantities necessary to maintain this price.

The gold standard was expensive to operate because it required governments to maintain large stocks of the metal to ensure that these sales and purchases were effective. However, the system worked. In the United States, the price of gold was kept at $20.67/ounce (with only one small change and a Civil War suspension) for a period that stretched from the ratification of the U.S. Constitution in 1791 until 1933.

Internationally, since each country on the gold standard fixed the price of gold in terms of their own currency, foreign exchange rates were objectively measured as the ratio of gold content in the respective currencies. For example, in the United States one dollar was valued at 23.22 grains of gold, and in Britain one pound (the British unit of account) was worth 113 grains of gold.[1] Thus, the objective price of a British pound in terms of dollars (the $/pound exchange rate) was (113 grains of gold / 23.22 grains of gold), or $4.87/pound.

Although a free market for pounds and dollars existed (for example, in New York and London), the equilibrium exchange rate stayed within a narrow range around $4.87/pound. To see why, suppose that the United States experienced a severe winter that caused an increase in demand for British woolens. In this case, Americans would demand more pounds to buy British clothing, and the value of the pound would rise toward $5/pound. But the exchange rate would be brought back down as profit-seeking individuals sent gold to London, where gold purchased for $4.87 in the United States could be sold for 1 British pound. The

British pounds could then be sold on the foreign currency market for more than $4.87. The act of selling pounds and buying dollars in New York would cause the pound to lose value (and the dollar to gain value), and the exchange rate would fall back toward $4.87/pound.

Thus, during the years the gold standard was in force, exchange rates tended to stay within narrow ranges around the gold ratios of any two countries' currencies. These stable rates made the public confident in the value of currency, and increased their willingness to hold money. Steady currency values also tended to provide stable prices for goods traded internationally, which reduced the risks associated with using the two different currencies required to buy foreign goods. Confidence in money and reduced risk promoted the growth of trade between nations, and thus, growth of the world economy. These were the chief benefits of the system, and the reasons governments promoted the system.

However, while exchange rates were stable, the quantity of money in the economy was not. As trade balances expanded and contracted, gold payments (and thus, money) flowed from country to country. As the quantity of money increased and decreased, economic activity and the domestic price level rose and fell outside governments' ability to control it. For example, suppose a drought in the United States reduced U.S. wheat exports. This would result in a U.S. balance of payments deficit, and a gold outflow. As a result, the U.S. money supply would fall which would lower prices, and possibly cause a recession. This example illustrates the major problem with the gold standard: a country's economic health could depend heavily on its international payments position.

When countries engaged in war, they temporarily abandoned the gold standard. A major reason why is that a country would experience high government expenses during hostilities. After using a significant portion of their gold stock to pay for armaments, a nation was usually unable to maintain the gold backing necessary for the monetary gold standard. The default system in this situation was the free, or floating, exchange rate system. With payment in gold suspended by the government, and their money no longer set at a fixed price with gold, the foreign exchange rate of their currency was determined by supply and demand in foreign exchange markets. The usual result was a dramatic fall in the price for the currency of a country at war. For example, during and after World War I, the British pound fell in value from $4.87/pound in 1914 to a low of $3.40/pound during 1920 (Kindleberger 1973, 28).[2]

The floating exchange rate system in place during wars was typically associated with volatile movements in exchange rates because governments printed large quantities of money to pay for wartime expenses. These volatile exchange rates caused prices for internationally traded goods to be unstable, which increased the risks associated with international transactions. Variable rates also led the public to lose confidence in the domestic currency. For these reasons, floating exchange rates were viewed negatively as a temporary expedient until governments could return to the stability of gold.

During the 1930s the gold standard also took on negative image because it was blamed for spreading the Great Depression around the world. This occurred because when one country experienced a recession, it purchased fewer imports, which produced a trade surplus and caused a net gold inflow. One country's inflow was another country's outflow, and the nations losing gold experienced falling money stocks, which in turn caused recession in those countries.[3] Thus, the recessions that began in 1929 spread around the world so that by 1931 virtually every industrialized country in the world was in serious economic trouble. By 1936, most major nations had left the gold standard, no longer willing to pay such a high price for the system.

When countries abandoned the gold standard during the Depression, they floated their exchange rates and expanded their money supplies to help restore prosperity. While this was happening, the flexible rate system fell into even further disrepute because conventional wisdom at the time maintained that governments were manipulating their exchange rates at the expense of their neighbors. By selling quantities of their own currency in foreign exchange markets, nations were allegedly forcing their currency to fall in value relative to other currencies. Thus, by lowering the price of their exports and raising the price of imports, they were supposedly attempting to restore domestic prosperity at the expense of their trading partners.

So when the conferees met at Bretton Woods in 1944, neither the gold standard nor the floating rate system were viewed as desirable solutions to the international monetary situation of the post-war world. It was felt that countries could no longer be expected to sacrifice their domestic economy to their foreign payments position through the gold standard, or to have the self-discipline to resist the temptation of manipulating floating rates to their advantage. The Bretton Woods Conference faced the huge task of finding a new, generally-accepted solution to the problems of international finance.

3.2 Competing Plans

The underlying premise of the Bretton Woods negotiations was: never again would nations be expected to sacrifice domestic prosperity to the needs of international finance. To help bring about this goal, two main proposals were put forth, one British and one from the United States.[4] The British proposal was designed by John Maynard Keynes, the most prominent economist of his day. His system was a compromise solution in the sense that it attempted to capture both the stable exchange rates of the gold standard, and the monetary flexibility of the freely floating exchange rate system. The long-run correction of payments imbalances was to be achieved through government adjustment of exchange rates.

Keynes proposed a system with the following characteristics:

[1] Par values of currencies would be set and maintained by governments, pegged within a ±5 percent band by the purchase and sale of currencies in the market. When necessary, exchange rates would be re-pegged in an orderly and non-competitive manner.
An international clearing union, similar to a world central bank, would be established to provide international liquidity or credits to help governments cover payments imbalances between exchange rate re-pegging. The clearing union would have the power to create a new world money, to be called "bancor," which would provide the necessary liquidity.

[2] Currencies would not be backed by gold.

[3] Countries that maintained excessive payments surpluses would pay an interest penalty. This was designed to equalize the incentives to correct imbalances for both deficit and surplus nations.

The U.S. Department of the Treasury's proposal took a somewhat different view:

[1] Exchange rates would be fixed. Rates could change only if there was an 80 percent approval vote of the membership to do so. (Votes were in proportion to national reserves, and at the time, the United States held well over 20 percent of the world's total. Thus, the United States proposed veto power for itself.)

[2] The United States opposed Keynes's proposed clearing union because of concerns that since it could create money, it might be an engine for inflation. Instead, the U.S. plan included a limited $5 billion stabilization fund designed to provide loans to member states which would be used to help support the price of their currencies.

[3] The United States proposed using gold for national reserves, and to provide backing for currencies (in 1949, the U.S. stock of gold reserves was valued at $24.6 billion, constituting approximately two-thirds of the world's total).[5]

[4] The United States opposed applying penalties on surplus nations (the United States expected to have a surplus in its balance of payments).

The actual agreement reached produced the expected compromises:

[1] Par values would be pegged and maintained within a ±2 percent band. Re-pegging would take place in response to "fundamental disequalia," and with the mutual agreement of the nations involved.

[2] The International Monetary Fund (IMF) was established to supervise adjustment of exchange rates. The IMF would lend to provide liquidity to governments with international payments imbalances that were thus having problems maintaining the par values of their exchange rates. The source of this liquidity was to be a pool of deposits of national reserves from each member nation. Credit would be provided under tight restrictions.

[3] Gold backing for currencies was optional. The United States chose to set the price of gold at $35/ounce, and to support this price by paying gold in exchange for dollars presented to it by governments (as opposed to private individuals or other organizations).

[4] A penalty clause for surplus countries was established (but never used).

Depending upon your point of view, this was either a creative new system, or merely an exercise in government price fixing.

3.3 Foreign Exchange Markets

To understand why the Bretton Woods system, which helped restore growth and prosperity to the industrialized world after WWII, came to a sudden and dramatic end in 1971, we must look at how free markets operate. In particular, we need to examine the workings of the markets

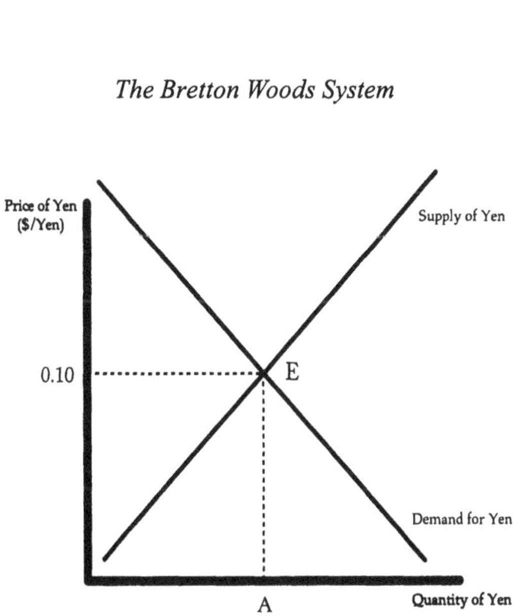

Fig. 3.1 The Foreign Exchange Market

for currencies used in international trade and investment transactions. In free markets, quantities of goods and services are traded by many buyers and sellers, and the prices of these goods are determined by the relative strength and interplay of the supply and demand.

The demand and supply for foreign currencies establishes such a market, which is shown in figure 3.1. Looking at it in terms of trade and investment between the United States and Japan, the demand for Japanese yen is derived from U.S. demand for Japanese goods (U.S. imports) and investment opportunities in Japan (capital flows from the United States to Japan). The greater is the dollar price of yen (i.e., the larger the $/yen exchange rate), the higher will be the price of Japanese imports. In this case, Americans will purchase fewer imports from Japan which results in the downward sloping demand schedule for yen shown in figure 3.1.

The supply of yen is derived from the Japanese desire to invest in the United States and/or buy U.S. exports. Yen must be sold (supplied to the foreign exchange market) in order to buy dollars, which will then be used to buy U.S. goods. The higher the dollar price of yen, the cheaper U.S. dollars will be in terms of yen, and thus, the lower will be prices paid by Japanese for U.S. goods. Thus, the supply of yen schedule in figure 3.1 slopes up.

The point at which the demand and supply of yen are equal (point E in figure 3.1) implies both an equilibrium exchange rate, and that the balance of payments (trade and investment flows) between the United States and Japan is balanced. The latter result occurs because at the equilibrium point U.S. flows to Japan (represented by the demand for yen) equal Japanese flows to the United States (represented by the supply of yen). However, note that as soon as an equilibrium exchange rate is determined in the market, the situation will be altered. For example, when Japanese producers put new goods on the market, the demand for Japanese goods will increase, and prices of these goods will fall when technological improvements occur. These developments would cause the demand for yen to increase. Similarly, if U.S. farmers face drought or floods, the price of U.S. crops would rise which would reduce U.S. exports of these products. This would cause a decline in the supply of yen.

To appreciate the problem with the Bretton Woods system of pegged exchange rates, one need only envision the supply and demand for yen schedules shifting while exchange rates are held constant. In fact, the very instant the governments involved set par values for currencies, they became obsolete as measures of market reality.

As an illustration of this point, figure 3.2 shows what would happen if there were a crop failure that reduced U.S. production of oranges.

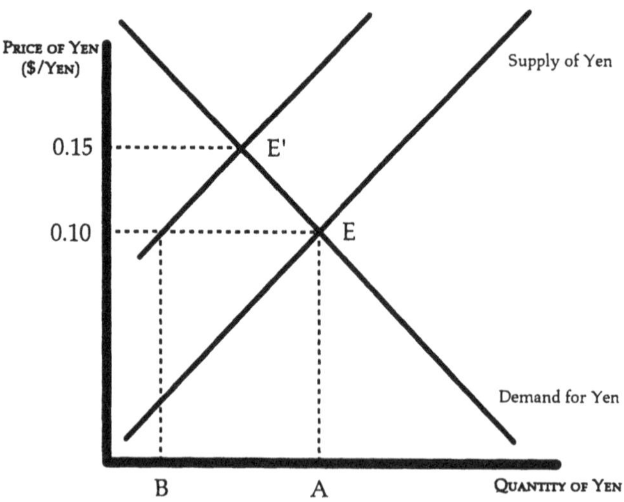

Fig. 3.2 Failure of the U.S. Orange Crop

There would be fewer purchases of U.S. oranges by the Japanese, so they would require fewer dollars. In figure 3.2, the supply of yen would shift to the left, and if the exchange rate is fixed (at $0.1/yen in figure 3.2), there is an excess demand for yen. This implies a balance of payments deficit for the United States, and surplus for Japan, both equal to the distance BA.

If exchange rates were freely flexible in the market, this payments imbalance would be corrected automatically. The excess demand for yen would cause the exchange rate to rise toward $0.15/yen. This, in turn, would make U.S. goods cheaper to the Japanese, and Japanese goods more expensive to Americans. The result would be an increase in U.S. exports and a reduction in U.S. imports, to the point at which the payments imbalance has been eliminated (at E'). However, under the Bretton Woods agreements, this new equilibrium position did not automatically occur because exchange rates were allowed to change only in a narrow range around the par value ($0.10/yen in our example).

Therefore, a policy of fixing exchange rates creates an ongoing problem with payments imbalances because the demand and supply for foreign exchange schedules are constantly shifting. These long-term payments imbalances were the Achilles Heel of the Bretton Woods system, because there are only four ways to correct a balance of payments deficit:

[1] floating, or re-pegging the exchange rate.

[2] government purchases of excess currency in the foreign exchange market using monetary reserves (national stocks of gold, foreign currency, or borrowed reserves, such as IMF "liquidity").

[3] Domestic macroeconomic policy changes designed to reduce demand for imports or attract foreign capital. Examples include reducing the growth of aggregate demand, or raising domestic interest rates to generate large inflows of foreign investment, both of which might create a recession.

[4] Exchange controls, which are limitations on the ability of citizens to purchase foreign exchange.

Since exchange rate stability was one of Bretton Woods' major goals (and for reasons discussed below), the system consistently ignored solution (1), re-pegging exchange rates, except for long-term "fundamental disequilibria." This solution was chosen only as a last resort, and usually in the face of a financial crisis. Another goal of the system, free and efficient trade, conflicts with exchange controls (solution (4)).

This leaves solutions (2) and (3). Having the government buy up excess currency on the foreign exchange market (solution (2)) is a short-term answer that papers over the imbalance with scarce international reserves and limited credit, but does not correct the cause of the problem. The use of macroeconomic policy to correct the imbalance (solution (3)) would work, but at the expense of the national economy which is what the conferees at Bretton Woods did not want to happen.

Thus, there exists only one long-run solution to a payments deficit that does not conflict with the goals of free trade and pursuing domestic macroeconomic policies independent of the external balance position: devaluation of the currency. However, under the Bretton Woods system, this was not automatic. Joint decisions by a national government and the IMF were required to correct payments imbalances using this method. In the meantime, the imbalances would be covered using scarce national monetary reserves, the claim upon these resources depending upon the frequency that exchange rates were re-pegged to approach market equilibrium values.

3.4 In the Beginning

As WWII ended, the world was faced with almost intractable problems of rebuilding. Years of war had destroyed industrial capacity in Europe and Asia, and the factories and machines left standing were worn out from years of producing war materials at full tilt. There was a huge need to restore manufacturing capacity, and the people of Europe and Asia badly needed consumer goods. In addition, while reconstruction was being accomplished, nations needed the international liquidity (or credit) required to re-establish trade, to feed their citizens, and to import the needed capital goods.

Thus, during the late 1940s world trade moved largely in one direction: from the United States to the rest of the world. From 1946–1949, the United States ran a trade surplus of $32 billion by selling enormous amounts of investment and consumption goods to Europe and Asia. This trade surplus was partially offset by a U.S. capital outflow of $26 billion as America handed out foreign aid and loans to the countries that were rebuilding (Rolfe and Burtle 1973, 59). Thus, the United States ran a balance of payments surplus during those years of $6 billion.

This U.S. payments surplus meant that the rebuilding countries were running payments deficits. These deficits abroad led the U.S. policymakers to form the opinion that some of the foreign aid being distributed was being wasted by the rebuilding countries because they were using a portion of it to buy up their excess currencies on foreign exchange markets. For this reason, and to help those countries rebuild and restore prosperity, in 1949 the United States urged them to accept large currency devaluations. These countries were left with little choice but to agree because the United States told them that if they did not devalue, the U.S. would cut their foreign aid (Rolfe and Burtle 1973, 67).

So in 1949, the currencies of several countries were devalued against the U.S. dollar, most by double digit amounts. Some of the largest devaluations were of the former Axis countries' currencies. For example, the Japanese yen was re-pegged at a par value of $.00278/yen (360 yen per dollar) which represented a dramatic reduction in its value relative to what had been the case before the war. Prior to the Great Depression, the dollar/yen exchange rate had been $0.5/yen, and in the 1930s the yen was devalued 50 percent to $0.25/ yen. Thus, in 1949 the yen was devalued to almost 100th of its pre-war Depression value. This may have been justified by the state of destruction of the Japanese economy, but it had the effect of making Japanese goods extremely cheap, and provided the framework for the Japanese post-war "miracle" based upon export-led growth. When one considers that the $/yen exchange rate was unchanged for the next twenty-two years in the face of Japan's re-emergence as an industrial power, the first clues can be seen of future problems that would develop with Bretton Woods "price fixing."

The 1949 currency devaluations were successful in the sense that the deficit countries experienced higher import prices and lower export prices, so their payments deficits rapidly diminished. This prevented wasting resources defending exchange rates, and as recovery progressed, their industries could also anticipate a strong demand for their exports because of the competitive prices that were derived from the low prices of these currencies.

3.5 Long-Term Surpluses and Deficits

During the early post WWII years, the United States was in the unique position of being the largest economy in the world not destroyed by the war. U.S. exports soared as the country supplied the food, consumer goods, and capital equipment for the industrialized world to survive and rebuild. The Marshal Plan, which distributed billions of dollars of foreign aid, along with private corporate investment, provided scarce liquidity and investment funds abroad through grants and loans in order to restore production. As a result, the U.S. economy not only supplied goods and services to the destroyed industrial nations, it also became banker to the world. Confidence in the new Bretton Woods system, the strength of the U.S. economy, and the decision to back the dollar with gold combined to make the dollar the trusted world money, much in demand for international trade and finance. U.S. international long-term capital loans were made in dollars, and U.S. dollars were accepted around the world as a means of payment.

Since the United States would redeem dollars for gold at $35/ounce, a dollar was a promise to pay on demand. The more the United States acted as a world bank by lending to other countries and providing liquidity by issuing dollars, the more vulnerable America became to large demands for its gold. The seeds were being sown for future trouble because as dollar balances built up in Europe and Japan, potential claims against the U.S. gold stock gradually began to exceed the supply available. Other countries used dollars not just for international transactions, but also as international reserves which was a substitute for maintaining gold stocks. This placed the dollar in an important role, but also meant that a change in value of dollar would alter the worth of national reserve holdings of those countries, and thus their national wealth.

The Bretton Woods system specified revaluation of currencies in the face of "fundamental," or long-run, payments imbalances. However, following the initial devaluations in 1949 almost every member country resisted changes in their exchange rates. Countries running deficits did not devalue their currencies, even though continued deficits implied that an increasing amount of reserves were needed to purchase their currency in order to support its price at the par value. The longer these countries resisted devaluation, the more reserves they would have to borrow, possibly becoming deeply indebted to the IMF, other central banks, and even private commercial banks. Delaying devaluation and correction of payments deficits made financial crises inevitable.

Yet if devaluation was such an obvious solution, why were governments unwilling to do so in the face of long-standing deficits? The answer is that national economic and political well-being and success were tied to the price of currency. Devaluation was considered a sign of failure and weakness, rather than merely a means to balance the international payments accounts of the nation.

Meanwhile, countries with surpluses in their payment accounts were not interested in changing the value of their currencies either. In their minds, they were in an ideal situation—reserves flowed into their coffers, and they become rich and respected. Raising the value of their currency would cut off this process. Thus, they were unwilling to cooperate with deficit countries in currency devaluations, and often did not see the connection between their surpluses and the deficits of their trading partners. Their surpluses were credited to a strong, well-managed economy. Deficits were supposedly a result of poor policies and, perhaps, weak national self-control.

As time went by, these fixed exchange rates became less and less realistic which created rare opportunities for speculators to profit from this price fixing. Speculators had a one-way bet; there was absolutely no risk that countries with long standing deficits would raise the price of their currencies, so only two other outcomes were possible: the currency would either fall in value or remain the same. Speculators sold these currencies with delivery promised in the future at a lower expected price (called selling short). There would be large profits if the currency was devalued, while the worst-case scenario for the speculator was that governments would make accommodating purchases of their currencies and put off devaluation. In this case speculators would only lose the brokerage fee on their speculative sale. The result was a herd mentality.

While speculators were selling the currency of a particular country, that government had to purchase its own currency to support its price. Financial crisis was the inevitable result, and when devaluation finally occurred the speculators took their profits. The situation would quiet down until the next country with a persistent balance of payments deficit made another devaluation both necessary and obvious to speculators, and the process would repeat itself. The great irony was that instability and crises became the periodic and inevitable result of a system designed to produce stability in international financial markets.

An interesting example of this process in action took place during the 1960s with the British pound. When Harold Wilson took office as British Prime Minister in October 1964, his new Labor government faced a brewing crisis. The Bank of England was using 50 million pounds worth of gold and foreign exchange reserves each day to buy pounds in the face of a selling wave by speculators. Eventually, the value of the total stock of British reserves was down to one billion pounds. Mr. Wilson could have devalued the pound, but chose instead to impose a 15 percent tariff surcharge, cut government expenditures, and go hat-in-hand to borrow reserves from the United States and Japan, all in an effort to continue propping up the pound.

The Labor Party came into office promising a new program of expanded welfare state benefits, but chose to sacrifice these goals in order to maintain the price of the pound at above-realistic market values. Politically, this seems irrational; the Wilson government could have easily blamed the previous government for the mess, devalued, and gone on with their program. Instead they put off devaluation for three years and were forced to fight off periodic pound crises with accommodating sales of reserves and high interest rates designed to both attract foreign investments in pounds and slow the growth of the economy. Employment suffered as a result. Wage freezes, tariffs and government spending cuts were all used to put off devaluation.

The ultimate and inevitable financial crisis came to a head in the fall of 1967, triggered by the closing of the Suez Canal, and labor strikes in Britain. On November 18, 1967, after three years of pain and sacrifice, the pound was devalued 14.3 percent. Evidence of how a devaluation was seen as failure, rather than merely a change in a price designed to move the market toward a more realistic equilibrium exchange rate, is seen in the following section of a *New York Times* article titled "D-For Devaluation-Day" (taken from Meier 1982, 66):

> The BBC was showing a Doris Day movie. Shaw's "Heartbreak House" was playing at the Lyric, where the manager called out an American who had asked to be notified if the news came during the show. "That does it", said the manager, "I'm emigrating."
>
> As the sun set on the British Empire, the reverberations were already beginning to show.

3.6 Dollar Shortage Becomes Glut

The 1957 Treaty of Rome began the process that ultimately led to the formation of the European common market and the evolution toward today's European Union (EU). It also signaled a time when recovery from World War II was complete. Just ten years before, the EU countries and Japan had been prostrate from the war and desperate for U.S. dollars to finance recovery. By the late 1950s their economic infrastructure and trade had been rebuilt, and exports from these countries were increasing, aided by diminishing barriers to trade.

Although the dollar continued to serve as a reserve currency and source of liquidity, the rate of increase in the demand for dollars was falling. The United States was running balance of payments deficits which were causing the growth of the supply of dollars in world markets to exceed the growth of demand, and the dollar shortage of earlier years began to be transformed into a surplus and even glut. This created a dilemma for the United States because some of these dollars were being returned to the United States in exchange for gold. While the U.S. gold stock was large, it was also limited.

As gold was being withdrawn, the ratio of dollars outstanding to gold held in U.S. government vaults increased. Trust in the stability of the dollar began to erode, and periodic crises occurred as speculators bet that the overpriced dollar would be devalued. This left the U.S. government with the problem of managing the crises; meanwhile, foreign governments continued to return their dollars to the United States in exchange for gold. In the longer-run, the only way to restore stability was to either (1) keep the U.S. economy in a slow growth environment with tight money and high interest rates in order to reduce imports and attract foreign investments, or (2) devalue the dollar. Slowing the growth of the U.S. economy in order to balance the international portion of it (approximately 10 percent share of the total) was not considered either politically acceptable or economically wise in the long-run. Economists referred to this as "letting the tail wag the dog." Instead of having the dog (the U.S. economy) wag its tail (the exchange rate) to balance international payments, the whole U.S. economy would have to be lowered to keep the tail steady.

The alternative was devaluation of the dollar, which would reduce both the payments deficit and the quantity of dollars flowing into world markets. Unfortunately, U.S. trading partners did not consider this solution acceptable. Surplus countries, such as Japan, Germany, and France had created the foundations of their postwar prosperity upon the growth of cheap exports. A dollar devaluation, which would raise the prices of their exports, was unacceptable to the leaders of those countries. In addition, Japan, Germany and France's balance of payments surpluses had increased their reserves tremendously, primarily in the form of U.S. dollars. Dollar devaluation would also reduce the value of their national reserves. They argued that they held these dollars out of generosity and the kindness of their hearts, so it was unfair and unacceptable for the United States to punish them by making them poorer.

During the 1960s, the U.S. balance of payments deficits continued and expanded as the dollar became increasingly overvalued. It became more and more obvious to speculators that their bets on a dollar devaluation were "one way" and virtually risk-free. Long-term solutions were put off even as U.S. manufacturing industries lost confidence in their own efficiency, and began to look to the successful Japanese corporations (built on the foundation of the cheap yen) for advice and counsel in management techniques.

U.S. economic policies during the 1960s contributed to the worsening situation. The ongoing effort to exploit the Phillips curve relationship led the Federal Reserve to raise the rate of monetary growth. As more and more dollars were printed, many found their way onto the foreign currency market. This rapid monetary growth caused inflation to accelerate which made U.S. exports even more overpriced and further increased the U.S. balance of payments deficits. The trade surpluses of earlier years gradually eroded, and became deficits by 1971. The U.S. gold stock, which was worth $26 billion in 1950, was down to about $11 billion by 1970.

The United States was showered with gratuitous advice from its major trading partners, but none of it included dollar devaluation. One typical recommendation called for an increase in the gold price of the dollar, from $35/ounce to $70/ounce. This change would have increased the dollar value of the U.S. gold stock, but would not have corrected the real problem, which was an overvalued dollar. At $70/ounce the United States would have paid out less gold per dollar, but the balance of payments deficits would have continued. Only a change in the value of the U.S. dollar relative to several currencies including the Japanese yen, W. German deutschmark, French franc, would correct the U.S. payments imbalance.

These unhelpful solutions raised the level of U.S. frustration with its trading partners. President Richard Nixon became increasingly impatient hearing and worrying about the price of foreign currencies, and finding his domestic policy options limited by the demands of international finance. He expressed this frustration on the Watergate Tapes:

"I don't give a [expletive deleted] about the lira" (Volcker and Gyohten 1992, 90).

3.7 Crisis?

U.S. involvement in the Bretton Woods agreement ended on August 15, 1971 when President Nixon halted U.S. participation by suspending payments of gold for dollars. The United States stopped defending the price of the dollar, and no longer fought off the actions of speculators in foreign currency markets. By allowing the dollar to float, Nixon solved the U.S. payments imbalance problem with the stroke of a pen.[6] Many people considered this action as just further proof that the United States was a declining economic power, and widely predicted that the dollar would soon be displaced from its role as the world's leading currency. However, this interpretation was incorrect: allowing the dollar to float was actually an exercise of U.S. power in international monetary affairs. After all, America's trading partners would not cooperate in devaluing the dollar, so the United States just went ahead and did it on its own. President Nixon's action was also recognition that pegging exchange rates had not brought stability to foreign exchange markets.

Following Nixon's announcement, the Japanese and German governments continued to support the dollar because they considered it to be in their national interest. During the next three months they bought billions of dollars trying to support its price, and thus maintain the value of their national reserves. For example, just during August, Japan bought $4.4 billion which was greater than "their $2.9 billion of total dollar holdings at the end of 1970" (Council of Economic Advisors 1972, 155). By the end of October, the Bank of Japan held $11.6 billion. In the end, the Europeans and Japanese had to accept the market reality and allow the dollar to fall to its equilibrium price.[7]

U.S. trading partners believed that this free market realignment in the value of the dollar was only temporary. They expected the United States to return to the fold by reestablishing a new par value for the dollar with respect to other major currencies, and then supporting this new rate. However, as time passed, the U.S. became more and more satisfied with freely floating exchange rates and automatically balanced payments accounts.

The official end of U.S. involvement in the Bretton Woods system exchange rate system occurred in 1973 when an international conference was held at the Smithsonian Institute in Washington, D.C. U.S. trading partners expected this conference to ratify the new lower-priced dollar, and then fix new par values. However, what actually happened was official acceptance of the floating dollar. The U.S. dollar would float as it had been since 1971, but now the other countries officially agreed that was free to do so.

The European Common Market (now the European Union, or EU) continued on with Bretton Woods in the form of what became the European Monetary System (EMS). Currency exchange rates were pegged within the EU, and all floated together against the dollar and yen. This arrangement was called the "snake" because the European currencies were fixed against each other, yet floated together against the dollar. When the currencies' values were plotted against each other, the diagram resembled the reptile.

However, as the snake slithered on, it had problems which are represented by three numbers: 2, 6, 15. Initially exchange rates in the EMS were set within a ±2 percent range to be maintained through government accommodating transactions. Over time, however, difficulty in maintaining these limits caused the EU to widen them to ±6 percent, and due to a major crisis in 1992, the band was expanded to ±15 percent. Clearly, the snake had to be allowed to wiggle more and more as successive financial crises occurred. In the end, ±15 percent was actually a 30 percent band, which effectively meant that rates were floating freely most of the time.

3.8 Floating Rates Save the Day

An event occurred in 1973 which might have turned into an absolute catastrophe if the United States had still been participating in the Bretton Woods system. As punishment for U.S. and Dutch support of Israel during the 1973 Yon Kippur War, the Islamic member states of the Organization of Petroleum Exporting Countries (OPEC) announced large increases in oil prices, plus an embargo against the United States and Holland. The price of a barrel of crude oil rose from \$3/barrel to \$12/barrel.[8] Since in the short-term the demand for oil is highly inelastic, a quadrupling of the price of oil caused an enormous increase in revenue to OPEC countries. Because oil is bought and sold on world markets with U.S. dollars, this price hike raised the demand for dollars which kept the U.S. dollar secure as the world currency.

If this event had occurred prior to Aug. 15, 1971, the probable result would have been a world financial crisis of gigantic proportions. The oil price hike caused annual OPEC dollar earnings to roughly triple to around $100 billion, and every one of those dollars would have represented a Bretton Woods obligation to exchange them for gold, and for the United States to support the dollar's value in foreign exchange markets (Council of Economic Advisors 1975, 190). The U.S. gold stock was nowhere near large enough to handle that many claims, so under these circumstances OPEC's oil policy and the resulting claims on the U.S. gold stock may have been viewed as an act of war. Indeed, the potential for the triggering of World War III presents a frightening picture.

However, as we know, such a disaster did not take place, in large part because the U.S. was no longer fixing the price of the dollar. In the new floating dollar regime, OPEC countries had only three choices of what to do with their "Petro dollars":

[1] Sell them. Sales of these vast quantities of dollars would most certainly have caused a large decline in the value of the U.S. dollar on world markets. The result would have been huge capital losses to OPEC holders of dollars.

[2] Spend them on U.S. goods and services. Buying U.S. exports would have maintained the dollar's value at high levels.

[3] Invest them in U.S. financial markets. This would maintain the price of the dollar, and also produce future income for OPEC countries in the form of interest and dividends to replace oil revenues when the wells eventually began to run dry.

That OPEC did not choose to dump their dollars on world markets is not surprising. To import enormous amounts of U.S. goods with these dollars was also an unlikely choice. OPEC nations typically have high personal incomes, but small populations. There is a limit on the number of American Cadillacs Saudi families could absorb.

Therefore, OPEC's obvious choice for these funds was to invest them. This was called "recycling the petrodollars," and it meant that the U.S. could continue to buy oil without fear that the dollar would collapse in international markets. A world financial crisis was averted, and perhaps even World War III. The world was lucky indeed that the dollar's value was no longer fixed by U.S. membership in the Bretton Woods system.

Thus, the Bretton Woods system, which was created amidst the crisis of World War II, fortunately was not fully in place to create further crisis during the 1970s. Years later, its end is not mourned in the United States, although the existence of the euro indicates the European desire to continue fixing exchange rates. Fortunately, as far as the United States is concerned, Bretton Woods was replaced by a system that embraced the reality of the marketplace. Because the original Bretton Woods system was designed to fight this reality, it was ultimately a costly experiment whose burial created the opportunity for a new era of free trade and growth.

Chapter 4

■■■

Inflation and the Federal Reserve

> *What explains the failure of the Fed to achieve its own objectives? In its public apologia for its distressing performance, the Fed has been pulling out every ancient and discredited cliche: "You can't push on a string," "You can lead a horse to water, but you can't make him drink," and so on ad nauseam. In short, "Don't blame us. We're innocent victims of forces beyond our control." As a longtime Fed watcher, I can assure you that this is par for the course. Whenever things go well the Fed is delighted to claim credit. Whenever they go badly, forces outside its control are responsible.*
>
> *—Milton Friedman (1975)*

Rapid monetary growth and the resulting high inflation were the root cause of many of the macroeconomic problems that plagued the United States during the 1970s. The dramatic rise in the U.S. money supply caused the demise of the Bretton Woods system and the dollar depreciation that followed. This fall in the value of the dollar was an important factor in causing the 1973-1974 energy crisis. High inflation also raised nominal interest rates which, in tandem with the deposit rate ceilings in place at the time, exacerbated the 1970s boom-bust cycle of new home construction and placed many thrift institutions in financial peril. Inflation was also a major factor in the U.S. stock market's abysmal performance during the decade.

Economists generally agree that inflation results from excessive money creation. Since the Federal Reserve controls the U.S. money supply, it follows that they were responsible for the high U.S. inflation during the 1970s. This chapter focuses on the Federal Reserve, and addresses the issue of why they pursued inflationary monetary policies.

4.1 Arthur F. Burns

> *Outside the Fed, Burns won an exalted reputation as the stern enemy of inflation. He delivered many eloquent lectures on the subject, scolding Congress and other audiences forteir lack of self discipline. Among his colleagues at the Fed, however, there was considerable cynicism about*

the chairman's pious rhetoric...His stewardship was recorded indelibly in America's prices: the Consumer Price Index was at 116 when Burns took charge of the central bank. When he retired the price index was at 195 and rising...In retirement, Arthur Burns began lecturing on the "anguish of central banking."
—William Greider (1987, 341-42).

The reputations of several politicians and economists were tarnished by the events of the 1970s. In politics, a clear loser was President Richard Nixon who resigned in 1974 as a result of the Watergate scandal. Among economists, perhaps none emerged from the decade more badly scarred than Arthur Frank Burns (1904-1987). He served as an economic advisor to President Nixon from 1968-1971, and then as chairman of the Federal Reserve Board of Governors from 1971-1978. As such, he was a major player in determining U.S. economic policies during those years.

Burns was a child when he emigrated from Austria to the United States.[1] In the early 1920s he enrolled at Columbia University, which awarded him his Ph.D. in 1934. He taught at both Rutgers and Columbia, and numbered among his students none other than Milton Friedman, who would later become the Federal Reserve's most vocal (and famous) critic. After receiving his Ph.D., Burns teamed up with his former teacher, the great business cycle economist Wesley C. Mitchell who was nearing the end of his brilliant career spent determining the causes of economic fluctuations and patterns of economic activity over business cycles.[2] Working together at the National Bureau of Economic Research they developed what many call the Burns and Mitchell business cycle dating technique which is described in *Measuring Business Cycles.*[3] This methodology was a major advance in economics because it provides the framework to classify economic variables as leading, coincident, or lagging indicators. For this reason, Arthur Burns (who did most of the work on the book) is credited with inventing of the index of leading economic indicators.

Burns became a major player in national economic policy in 1953 when President Eisenhower appointed him chairman of the Council of Economic Advisors. After completing his three-year term, Burns continued his life as a Washington insider, advising presidents and serving as a regular fixture on the public speaking circuit. Over the years he developed a friendship with Richard Nixon, and after Nixon was elected president in 1968 he appointed Burns to a newly-created cabinet level position called Counselor to the President. Nixon had a great deal of respect for Burns because of "his superior intellect and because he always followed the practice he once described to me of 'telling the President what he needs to hear, not just what he wants to hear'" (Nixon 1978, 519-20).[4]

In early 1971 the chairmanship of the Federal Reserve Board of Governors opened up when Nixon declined to reappoint William McChesney Martin who had held the position for nearly twenty years. Nixon wanted to replace Martin whom he blamed for his loss to Kennedy in the close 1960 presidential election. That election took place during a mild recession, and many observers–including Nixon–thought that Nixon would have won if the economy had not been contracting. Nixon blamed the Federal Reserve, and therefore Martin, for the recession (Greider 1987, 329). So Nixon replaced him with Arthur Burns, who assumed the position on January 31, 1971.

Burns held the chairmanship for the entire seven-year term until President Carter replaced him with G. William Miller. After leaving the Federal Reserve, Burns went back on the public speaking circuit until 1981 when President Ronald Reagan appointed him U.S. Ambassador to West Germany. He held that position until 1985, and then died two years later. Burns position as a major public figure of his era is attested to by the fact that "the speakers at his memorial service included a Nobel-laureate economist, a United States senator, the secretary of state, the chairman of the Federal Reserve Board, and two former presidents of the United States" (Wells 1994, 248).

During his tenure at the Federal Reserve, many economists criticized Burns for his role in creating the economic instability taking place at the time, as well as his unwillingness to accept responsibility for the high inflation that was occurring. Although the problems were not entirely his fault, he was clearly involved. It is true that the inflation buildup began in the 1960s, long before Burns ever served at the Federal Reserve. In addition, the big monetary expansion of the early 1970s that began immediately after the 1970 Penn-Central Railroad commercial paper default also occurred before Burns arrived on the scene. However, Burns's cardinal sin in the eyes of many economists was to engineer rapid monetary growth and accompanying high inflation during 1971, 1972, and the first half of 1973, and then repeat the performance a few years later, all the while claiming that *the Federal Reserve had nothing to do with it!*

An example of Burns's version of events can be found in his speech titled "The Menace of Inflation," which he delivered in May 1974.[5] He argues that the high U.S. inflation rates during 1973 and 1974 were the result of "special factors" including poor crop harvests, rising oil prices, and the worldwide economic boom of 1972-1973. Most importantly, according to Burns, the inflation problem "lies chiefly in the rising aspirations of people everywhere [because they] depend less and less on their own initiative, and more and more on government, to achieve their economic objectives." The result is the "awesome imbalance of the federal budget [which places] tremendous pressures...on our credit mechanisms and the supply of money has grown at a rate inconsistent with price stability" (Burns 1978, 162-3). So in Burns's mind the federal budget deficits, not the Federal Reserve, caused the inflationary monetary growth.[6] Burns contends that the Federal Reserve should not be blamed for the inflation because "one essential ingredient in this struggle [against inflation] is continued resistance to swift growth in money and credit. The Federal Reserve, I assure you, is firmly committed to this task...we are not going to be a willing party to the accommodation of rampant inflation" (1978, 165).

Another example of Burns' mind-set shows up in his speech titled "Our Inflation in Historical Perspective" (Burns 1980). In his discussion of the late 1970s inflation, he describes its pernicious effects, and then lists the various factors he considers responsible for it: trade unions, monopolies, stagnant productivity, government regulations, federal budget deficits, excessive monetary growth, the collapse of Bretton Woods and resulting dollar devaluation, poor harvests, and rising oil prices. While he lists monetary growth as a factor, nowhere in this speech is the Federal Reserve mentioned. Burns concludes with seven proposed solutions to help reduce inflation. When the issue of monetary growth is addressed, he proposes that Congress adopt "a concurrent resolution stressing the importance of restrictive monetary policies in ending inflation" (Burns 1980, 7). Apparently the Federal Reserve needed Congress to order them to control monetary growth in a prudent manner.

In Burns's defense, he had been educated in the 1920s and 1930s when the consensus view among economists was that nonmonetary factors were the cause of inflation (Hetzel 1998). Burns believed in the cost-push view which argues that rising prices are caused by firms with monopoly power pushing up prices, and increased business costs that get passed on to buyers in the form of higher prices. Cost increases result from factors such as labor unions demanding higher wages, or bad weather reducing crop yields. In addition, once inflation gets started it tends to self-perpetuate because when people experience inflation they begin to expect it, so workers keep demanding ever-higher wages to compensate. Burns was hardly alone in holding these views on inflation: at the time, virtually all politicians and a large number of economists adhered to them as well.

If money growth does not cause inflation, then what role does the Federal Reserve have in the economy? Those adhering to the nonmonetary theory of inflation believed in what is called the credit view of monetary policy which contends that monetary policy primarily impacts the economy through its affect on interest rates. According to this view, the Federal Reserve can control interest rates, which influences aggregate demand because household consumption spending and business investment spending both depend in part on interest rates. For example, an easy monetary policy causes low interest rates which raises spending, and a tight policy is consistent with high interest rates that reduces spending.

This credit view contains two serious flaws. The first is that it ignores the idea that money creation can raise spending independent of the interest rate effect. In other words, if new money is created, it raises spending for two reasons: the interest rate effect, and because some of the newly-created money is directly spent by households on consumption goods and services. The second problem is that the credit view ignores the longer-run affects of monetary growth on interest rates. An increase in the monetary growth rate causes interest rates initially to fall, as the credit view contends. But that is hardly the end of the story. Spending rises, due to both lower interest rates plus the fact that some of the new money is being directly spent. Higher spending means higher nominal income, which raises the demand for money because people are engaging in more transactions. This increase in the demand for money drives interest rates back up toward their levels that prevailed before the monetary growth rate rose. Meanwhile, prices start to rise; inflation is taking place and over time people expect it to continue. When this occurs, lenders demand compensation because they believe loans will be repaid in dollars that are worth less due to rising prices, so they charge higher interest rates. The end result is that while the increase in monetary growth initially lowered interest rates, over time interest rates rise back up, in fact they end up being higher then they were originally.

Two conclusions emerge from this analysis. First, an increase in the monetary growth rate can cause inflation. Second, an easy monetary policy is consistent with lower interest rates, but only in the short-run. In the longer-run, an easy monetary policy causes high interest rates, which is exactly opposite to the conclusion offered by the credit view.

This discussion of interest rate behavior is a critical point to understand. For example, adherence to the credit view is a major reason why the Federal Reserve conducted such destructive monetary policies during the early 1930s. Tight policies carried out during 1928 and 1929 led to high interest rates, as the credit view predicts. But then the recession began (in August 1929), and then seriously deepened so that by early 1931 short-term rates were well below where they had been when the recession started. The Federal Reserve, which adhered to the credit view, considered those low rates to be indicative of an easy monetary policy, which was precisely the opposite of what was true. So in January 1931, the Federal Reserve Board proceeded to sell of a large portion of their bond portfolio because credit was in such 'abundance.' This action contracted the economy even further, helping turn the recession into the Great Depression.

The Federal Reserve faced the opposite situation in the 1970s. As the easy monetary policies took hold, the economy boomed and inflation rose which drove up interest rates. Arthur Burns's credit view mind-set led him to believe (1) that the rapid monetary growth was not responsible for the inflation, and (2) that the high interest rates prevailing indicated that monetary policy was tight, not easy. In addition, Burns blamed the high interest rates on the fact that the federal government was running budget deficits. Throw into the equation Presidents Nixon and Carter, both of whom made it perfectly clear to Burns that they wanted interest rates to be lower, and the result was rapid monetary growth during both presidential administrations, carried out in a doomed effort to reduce interest rates.

At the time, there were a number of economists who understood what was happening, but their views were largely ignored by the Washington establishment. Led by Milton Friedman and Anna Schwartz, a group of economists called monetarists had been arguing since the 1950s that inflation is primarily caused by rapid monetary growth, and that easy monetary policies eventually result in high interest rates.[7] Burns was familiar with these arguments, in fact he claimed he was sympathetic to them, although his actions suggested otherwise. Even though events during the 1970s proved that the monetarists' arguments were correct, at the time monetarists were considered a fringe group, so a relatively small number of people listened to them.

4.2 Phantom Excess Capacity & the Perils of Interest Rate Targeting

During the early 1970s, there was widespread belief that the economy was operating below capacity. For example, in 1971 the unemployment rate hovered around 6.0 percent, and this number was widely viewed as being above the rate consistent with a fully employed economy. The 1972 *Economic Report of the President* states that "reduction of unemployment in 1972 is the primary objective of this year's economic policy" (1972, 108). The desired outcome was 5.0 percent unemployment by the end of the year. The Council of Economic Advisors acknowledged that 4.0 percent (the 1960s unemployment target) was unattainable without inflation accelerating because over time demographic changes had put upward pressure on the unemployment rate. Reduced U.S. involvement in the Vietnam War resulted in large numbers of men leaving military service and entering the labor force. Also, the baby boom cohorts were entering the labor force, along with increased proportions of women.[8] In addition, some economists claimed that increasingly generous unemployment compensation had reduced the incentive to find work.

In hindsight, the problem was that the natural rate of unemployment had been impacted by these factors to a much greater extent than policymakers realized. The 1972 *Economic Report of the President* uses the 1956 unemployment rate of 4.1 percent as a benchmark (because that year employment was high and inflation was low), and adjusts it for demographic changes that had taken place over time (Council of Economic Advisors 1972, 114-116). The result is an estimated benchmark unemployment rate for 1971 of 4.5 percent, which is considerably below the 6.0 percent rate the United States was experiencing at the time. Contemporary estimates (for example, Gordon 2000) place the natural rate of unemployment during 1971 at 6.4 percent which means that in reality the 6.0 percent unemployment during 1971 was very close to capacity. In other words, economic policymakers intended to pour stimulus onto a fully-employed economy because they mistakenly thought considerable excess capacity existed. The Federal Reserve would carry out their role in the stimulus plan by pushing down interest rates.

The Federal Reserve conducts their monetary policy through interest rate targeting. This is a process where the central bank chooses a target value for an interest rate, and then changes the supply of credit in order to keep the actual rate within a narrow band around the target value. The rate the Federal Reserve has targeted for the past several decades is the federal funds rate, which is the rate on overnight interbank loans. Executing this policy is actually quite simple: if the federal funds rate rises above the target value, the Federal Reserve conducts open market purchases which creates bank reserves and pushes the federal funds rate down. If the federal funds rate falls below the target, the Federal Reserve sells securities which reduces bank reserves and drives the federal funds rate up.

Why does the Federal Reserve target interest rates? One reason is because it's easy to monitor conditions. Interest rates are quoted constantly during trading hours, so the Federal Reserve can always stay appraised of how close rates are to their target. In contrast, if instead they targeted a measure such as the M2 money supply, that data is published just once a week and occasionally subject to large revisions.

Another reason they target interest rates is because the banking industry desires stable rates. Banks pay interest on deposits to attract funds, and then lend those funds out at higher interest rates. The difference between the average rate banks earn on their loans and securities (banks' assets) and the average rate they pay on their deposits (banks' liabilities) is called the interest margin, and it's an important indicator of bank profits. If interest rates are stable, then the interest margin will be too, which gives bankers more profit stability, certainty about the future, and also enhances their ability to plan ahead. Ironically, for reasons discussed below, this policy of targeting interest rates probably led to a greater degree of interest rate instability than would have been the case if the Fed had not been targeting interest rates.

A third reason why the Federal Reserve targets interest rates is because of their belief that the demand for money is unstable. The Federal Reserve has long maintained that the U.S. financial system regularly experiences innovations in payments and savings options. For example, the increased use of credit cards alters the way people pay for goods and services, which may influence how much money they wish to hold.

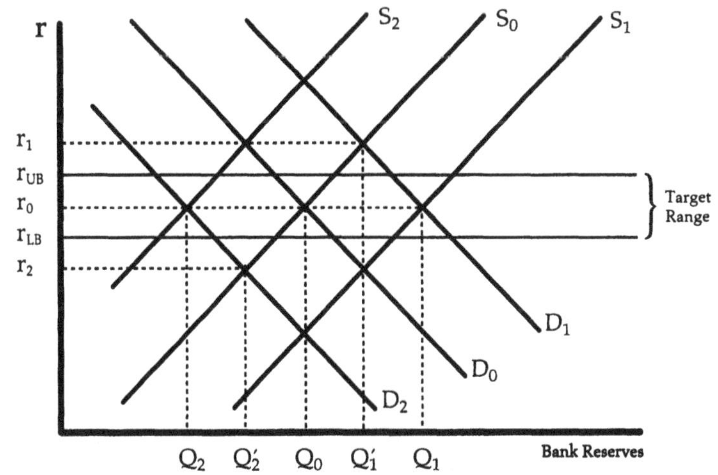

Fig. 4.1 Interest Rate Targeting

Similarly, when the financial industry develops and markets a new type of account (for example, the money market mutual fund), the public changes the manner in which they store their wealth, and how much of that wealth they wish to hold in various forms of money.

The Federal Reserve's view is illustrated in Figure 4.1 which shows the supply and demand for bank reserves (which reflects the supply and demand for credit). Assume initially that the supply schedule is S_0 and the demand schedule is D_0, which results in an equilibrium interest rate of r_0 and quantity of bank reserves Q_0. Also assume that the Federal Reserve decides they want to target the interest rate on bank reserves (the federal funds rate) between an upper bound, r_{ub}, and a lower bound, r_{lb}. Now suppose that the demand for bank reserves is subject to short run instability in the sense that it shifts between D_1 and D_2 because of various financial innovations taking place. When the demand rises to D_1 the Federal Reserve increases the supply to S_1 to keep the interest rate within the target range. As a result, the quantity of bank reserves rises to Q_1. If the demand falls to D_2, the Federal Reserve reduces the quantity to S_2 so the interest rate stays within the target range. In this case the quantity of bank reserves falls to Q_2.

Note what is happening here. If the demand for money and credit (and, therefore, bank reserves) is subject to short run instability, but this instability takes place within a finite range (between D_1 and D_2), then a policy of targeting interest rates makes sense. By shifting the supply schedule to maintain a stable interest rate, the quantity is unstable, but within a relatively narrow range (between Q_1 and Q_2). So the Federal Reserve manages to achieve interest rate stability (which the banking industry likes), and keep the quantity of money and credit reasonably stable.

It is worth considering what would happen in Figure 4.1 if the Federal Reserve kept the supply schedule at S_0. As the demand schedule shifted between D_1 and D_2, the interest rate would become unstable between r_1 to r_2, while the quantity varies between Q_1' and Q_2'. In other words, the quantity of money and credit would be less volatile than if the Federal Reserve targeted interest rates, but interest rates become unstable (which makes bankers' lives more difficult). The fact that the Federal Reserve places such a high value on stable interest rates, and believes that money demand instability takes place within a relatively narrow range, is why they target interest rates instead of the quantity of money.

Critics of interest rate targeting contend that this policy is not only unnecessary, but does more harm than good. Their basic argument is that the demand for money is actually stable in the sense that it behaves in a predictable manner with respect to income and interest rates. The fact that money demand is positively related to income means that it rises during economic expansions, and falls (or grows more slowly) during recessions. This procyclical behavior of money demand, in combination with interest rate targeting, creates a procyclical money supply. To see why, consider what happens during a typical economic expansion. As nominal GDP rises, so does the demand for money and credit. This increase in demand causes a rightward shift in the demand for bank reserves, which prompts the Federal Reserve to create additional bank reserves so as to maintain the stable interest rate. Creating bank reserves causes the supply of money and credit to rise, which raises aggregate demand and drives up nominal GDP even further. This increase in nominal income causes the demand for money and credit to continue rising, which leads the central bank to create even more bank reserves, and the process continues. The end result is that the Federal Reserve is raising the supply of money and credit during an economic expansion, which could eventually cause the economy to produce above capacity and raise the rate of inflation.

When inflation becomes a problem, the Federal Reserve tries to slow the economy down by raising the target interest rate. If a recession results, the growth of the demand for money and credit will fall. But in order to maintain the target interest rate the Fed must contract the growth of money and credit. In this way, they can end up pursuing a contractionary monetary policy during a recession, which can increase the severity and length of the economic downturn.

4.3 Boom and Recession

Table 4.1 shows the annualized rates of inflation, M1 growth, and real GDP growth from 1971:I to 1975:IV.[9] The combination of interest rate targeting and trying to hit an unemployment target below the natural rate resulted in high rates of monetary growth during 1971, 1972, and early 1973. Due in part to this rapid monetary growth, the economy boomed from mid 1971 until the first quarter of 1973, with output growth well above the long run annual average of around 3.0 percent. When inflation began to rise dramatically during the second quarter of 1973, the Federal Reserve reversed course. They reduced the rate of monetary growth by raising the target federal funds rate, and by late 1973 it had slowed considerably. As inflation rose, an increased proportion of aggregate demand growth was accounted for by rising prices, meaning that the proportion attributable to output growth declined.[10] By the second half of 1973 the economy's growth rate had slowed to about 2.0 percent.

The U.S. economy slid into a recession in November, 1973.[11] Meanwhile, the Federal Reserve kept the monetary growth rate low; M1 grew at an annualized rate of just 3.6 percent during 1974:II-1974:III. Critics of interest rate targeting contend that these slow rates of money growth are an example of procyclical monetary policy in action– the Federal Reserve did not lower the target interest rate fast enough, so as the economy slid into recession ever slower monetary growth rates were necessary to maintain the target federal funds rate. They contend that the 1973-1975 recession would have been milder if the Federal Reserve had maintained more stable monetary growth.

A number of economists, most notably Milton Friedman, complained bitterly about the Federal Reserve's monetary policies during this period. Largely in response to these complaints, Congress in 1975 passed a resolution stating that the Federal Reserve should set targets

Table 4.1 - Quarterly GDP Deflator Inflation Rate, M1 Growth, and Real GDP growth, 1971–1975

Period	inflation rate(%)	M1 growth (%)	real GDP growth(%)
1971:I	6.5	6.9	9.1
1971:II	7.3	8.5	2.9
1971:III	4.5	6.8	3.6
1971:IV	5.3	3.2	6.6
1972:I	4.4	7.7	4.9
1972:II	2.6	6.5	9.5
1972:III	5.2	8.3	5.8
1972:IV	5.1	9.7	8.1
1973:1	5.9	8.1	9.5
1973:II	8.2	4.6	2.2
1973:III	8.1	4.7	1.6
1973:IV	9.5	4.9	2.3
1974:I	5.4	6.7	-3.9
1974:II	8.4	3.6	-3.7
1974:III	13.4	3.6	-2.3
1974:IV	10.9	4.7	-7.5
1975:I	9.8	2.9	-9.9
1975:II	6.2	6.1	5.6
1975:III	8.8	7.3	11.4
1975:IV	7.3	3.3	3.3

Source: Council of Economic Advisors, various issues. Quarterly growth figures are at annualized rates.

for monetary aggregates and make them public. This effectively forced the Federal Reserve to report target ranges for the monetary aggregates, but this exercise turned out to be more show than substance. They reported target ranges for the monetary aggregates, but at a wide range of values; for example, a typical range for M1 growth might be 3.0 percent to 6.0 percent. This information was used to form a "target cone" for each monetary aggregate which is shown in figure 4.2. Using the actual value of M1 as the starting point, the Federal Reserve projected a cone where the top line corresponds to the high end of the target (6.0 percent in our example), and the bottom line represents the lower end (3.0 percent). Meanwhile, the Federal Reserve was still targeting the federal funds rate, in fact placing far more emphasis on that goal than on hitting the monetary target. Partly for this reason, they repeatedly missed their monetary growth targets, overshooting them during the mid-to-late 1970s.

Overshooting the monetary growth target during a particular year presented the Federal Reserve with a dilemma: should the new targets correct their past mistake, or should they ignore the fact that they missed the target and start fresh? In other words, should they draw the new target cone from the midpoint of the previous cone, or from the actual money supply which lies outside the previous cone?

They chose the latter tactic. Every time they announced new monetary targets, they started with the actual value of the money supply, which is represented by the second cone shown in figure 4.2. This process of compounding the errors over time is called "base drift" and is an important part of the story about how and why the Federal Reserve generated inflationary monetary growth during the 1970s. To many it was proof-positive that the Federal Reserve was doing nothing more than paying lip service to monetary targeting while what they were really doing was targeting interest rates. As Melton notes, "the targets ap-

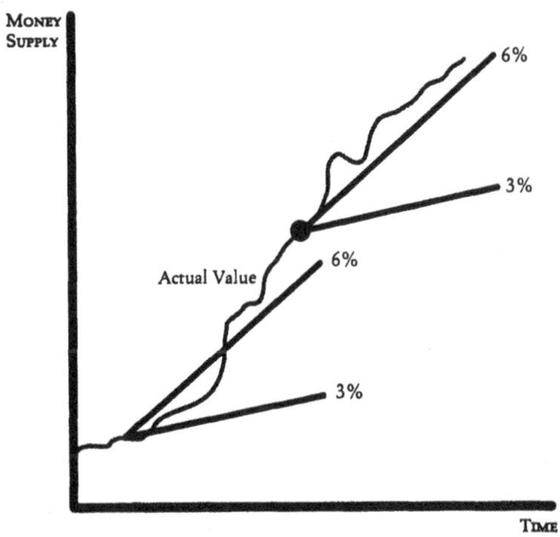

Fig. 4.2 Base Drift

peared to be chasing after the aggregates instead of serving as a serious guide to policy" (Melton 1985, 33).

4.4 No Learning Curve?

The Federal Reserve was a major player in helping overstimulate the U.S. economy during the 1960s, and then again during the early 1970s. One would think that after those two episodes, Federal Reserve officials would have started listening to their critics and realized there were problems with how they were conducting their policies. However, this was not the case. The Federal Reserve generated excessive rates of monetary growth one more time, and in doing so helped create inflation rates the American public considered completely unacceptable. This third bout of high inflation was instrumental in costing Jimmy Carter a second term as U.S. president.

Once again, policymakers were trying to hit an unemployment target below the natural rate. The 1978 *Economic Report of the President* estimates a "benchmark unemployment rate" of 4.9 percent, by which they mean the labor force unemployment rate in a fully-employed economy (Council of Economic Advisors 1978, 84). Contemporary estimates such as Gordon's (2000) place the natural rate of unemployment at just over 6.0 percent during the mid and late 1970s. Thus, the policy of trying to attain an unemployment rate below 5.0 percent was doomed to result in yet another round of accelerating inflation.

Table 4.2 shows the rates of unemployment, CPI inflation, real GNP growth, and M1 growth during the mid and late 1970s. Monetary growth became expansionary at the end of 1974 following the Federal Open Market Committee's meeting in December. The Committee noted the continuing drop in aggregate economic output, along with the fact that inflation was moderating somewhat. Based on this information, the FOMC "concluded that the economic situation and outlook called for somewhat more rapid growth in monetary aggregates over the months ahead than had occurred in recent months" (Board of Governors of the Federal Reserve System 1975, 86). Monetary growth increased in 1975, and then rose even faster during 1976 and 1977.

Despite the Federal Reserve's efforts to push down interest rates and stimulate economic activity, Federal Reserve chairman Arthur

Table 4.2 - Annual Rates of Unemployment, CPI Inflation, Real GDP Growth, and M1 Growth, 1975-1979

Year	Unemployment Rate (%)	CPI Inflation (%)	Real GNP Growth (%)	M1Growth(%)
1975	8.5	6.9	-0.6	4.8
1976	7.7	4.9	5.6	6.5
1977	7.1	6.7	4.9	8.2
1978	6.1	9.0	5.0	8.2
1979	5.8	13.3	2.9	6.8

Source: Council of Economic Advisors (1997)

Burns fell out of favor with President Carter, mostly because Burns repeatedly criticized Carter's economic policies in public. Largely for this reason, when his term as chairman ended, he was replaced.[12]

4.5 William Who?

> *[G. William Miller] was a...mildly conservative Democrat who supported Jimmy Carter for President in 1976, and was warmly regarded by the President and his economic advisers. They thought of him as a "team player," a Fed chairman who cooperated closely with the President's economic goals...Wall Street analysts complained that Miller was much too cooperative, too timid about raising interest rates high enough to suppress inflation.*
> —*William Greider (1987, 20).*

"William Who?" is a headline on the front page of the December 29, 1977 issue of *The Wall Street Journal*. This headline is printed atop an article announcing that President Carter had chosen G. William Miller to replace Arthur Burns as chairman of the Federal Reserve Board of Governors.

It was a strange choice. Miller was a lawyer by training with virtually no experience in the economics profession or in economic policy. His only prior association with the Federal Reserve was serving on the Board of Directors of the Federal Reserve Bank of Boston. Miller's major claim to fame was that he had been the CEO of Textron Corporation, which is an industrial conglomerate perhaps best known for producing Bell helicopters. The appointment surprised a great many people because Miller wasn't on anyone's short-list of likely candidates except the person whose list counted most: President Jimmy Carter.

Miller's tenure at the Federal Reserve was short and controversial. He served for just seventeen months before being appointed by President Carter to the position of U.S. Secretary of the Treasury as part of a cabinet shake-up in 1979. His term at the Federal Reserve was controversial because many view him as ranking along-side Arthur Burns as the two most politicized appointments ever to the chairmanship of the Federal Reserve Board of Governors.

Jimmy Carter wanted lower interest rates, in fact he campaigned on that theme. However, Carter had a very weak understanding of macroeconomic relationships. For example, during a 1976 presidential debate against President Gerald Ford, Carter made the absurd statement that "Congress can modify the supply of money by modifying the income tax laws" (from Melloan and Melloan 1978, 73). With respect to interest rates, Carter failed to realize (as did many others) that lower rates in the short run can mean higher rates in the long run.

Figure 4.3 shows the 90-day Treasury bill rate from January 1976 to December 1979. Miller took over the Federal Reserve chairmanship at the end of January 1978 which is indicated by the vertical line at the February observation. Short-term interest rates declined briefly after Miller took over, but then rose dramatically during late 1978 and 1979. It is difficult to ascertain precisely when the U.S. economy reached full

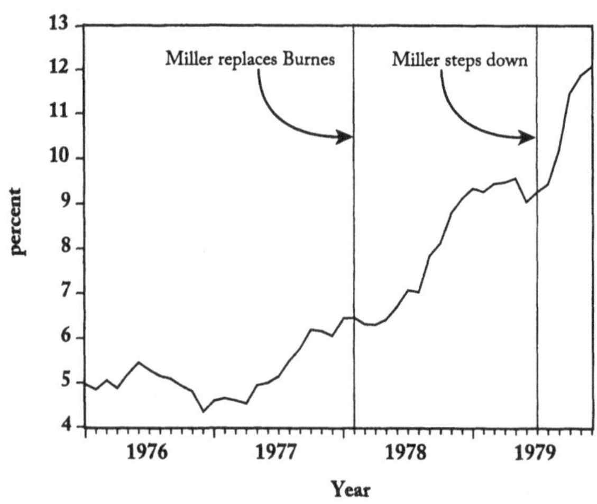

Fig. 4.3 90-Day Treasury Bill Rate, 1976–1979

employment, but it probably happened during the summer of 1978 when the labor force unemployment rate fell below 6.0 percent. Inflation was significantly higher during 1978 than it had been the previous year. However, despite obvious indications of an overheated economy, President Carter wanted the stimulus to continue, and the G. William Miller-led Federal Reserve provided it during 1978 and into 1979. But the 'low interest rate policy' of rapid monetary growth, along with a major hike in oil prices in 1979, helped raise inflation and inflationary expectations. The result was a T-bill rate of over 9.0 percent by the time Miller left the Federal Reserve. The low interest rate policy, originally started during Arthur Burns's tenure, had blown up in Carter's and Miller's faces.

In sum, the 1970s inflation was largely the result of poorly-designed policies carried out by the Federal Reserve. Politicized Fed leaders chasing unemployment targets below the natural rate, in combination with a policy of targeting interest rates without altering the targets frequently enough, and allowing base drift to occur, led to double digit inflation in the mid 1970s and then again at the end of the decade. This inflation caused severe economic disruptions in several markets, and a huge decline in the real values of bonds and equities. In addition, rising inflationary expectations during the decade meant that at each cyclical peak, nominal interest rates were higher than they had been at the previous economic peak.

By the end of the decade the American public was throughly fed up with the inflation, so they opted for a change in political leadership by voting President Jimmy Carter out of office. The new president, Ronald Reagan, won in part because he promised to reduce inflation. This goal was accomplished, but at the cost of a recession that by several measures was the worst the United States has experienced since the Great Depression.

CHAPTER 5

■■■

Regulation Q

An Act to provide for the safer and more effective use of the assets of banks, to regulate interbank control to prevent undue diversion of funds into speculative activity, and for other purposes.
— Preamble to the Banking Act of 1933, H.R. 5661, 73rd Congress, Session I, June 16, 1933

During the worst years of the Great Depression the United States suffered three separate waves of bank failures. Each episode proved worse than the one before; during the first wave in 1930, 1,350 banks suspended operations; during the next wave in 1931, 2,293 banks did so; and during the final round in early 1933, the number was 4,000 (Federal Reserve Board of Governors 1943, 283). These bank failures were a major reason why the Depression in the United States was so long and severe.

During the 1931 wave of failures several members of Congress became understandably distressed with the problems in the banking industry and initiated changes they hoped would stabilize the situation. These efforts were led by Senator Carter Glass of Virginia and Representative Henry Steagall of Alabama who cosponsored the Banking Act of 1933. This act is better known as the Glass-Steagall Act, and it became law in June, 1933.

The logic underlying Glass-Steagall was that a major reason why so many banks had failed was because they had been taking on too much risk and engaging in cutthroat competition. While these arguments were later shown to be erroneous, at the time many legislators firmly believed them to be true. In the mind of Senator Glass the risk-taking was centered in the practice of banks underwriting security issues, which is called investment banking. This is the risky (and very profitable) business of selling new issues of stocks and bonds while guaranteeing a price to the issuing firm. The cutthroat competition among banks was supposedly taking place in the form of 'rate wars' where banks competitively bid up their deposit rates to attract deposits, but by doing so reduced their profitability and increased their risk of failure.[1] Furthermore, it was argued, in order to pay the higher rates on deposits, banks acquired risky assets so they could earn higher returns. This behavior placed them in precarious positions with respect to the secure value of their assets.

Another alleged cause of the problems in the banking industry revolved around the fact that banks in large cities paid higher deposit rates than rural banks. Because of this rate differential, the claim was made that urban banks attracted deposits from rural areas. Some people contended that urban banks loaned out these funds for use in stock market speculation. Thus, the rate differential between urban and rural banks was supposedly a factor in the stock market boom during the 1920s and the ensuing crash in 1929. There were also claims that stock market speculation and instability had come at the expense of agricultural loans in rural areas (Lash 1987, 96).

The Glass-Steagall Act attempted to stabilize the banking industry by forcing banks to reduce their risk exposure, and eliminating their ability to compete through deposit rates. As a way to get banks to reduce their risk exposure, the act prohibited banks from underwriting securities. This action changed the structure of the industry by separating commercial banking from investment banking. The act also made it more difficult for banks to engage in competitive bidding on deposit rates by declaring that banks which were members of the Federal Reserve system could no longer pay interest on checking accounts, as well as allowing the Federal Reserve to set maximum rates member banks could pay on time and savings deposits. This change had the effect of creating a banking cartel by not allowing banks to compete on deposit rates. In addition, the act worked to stabilize the banking industry by introducing federal deposit insurance in the hope that it would preclude further panic-driven deposit withdrawals and subsequent bank failures. This feature of the act was especially successful as the United States has never experienced a nationwide wave of bank panics since 1933. The act also strengthened the powers of the Federal Reserve by giving them tighter regulatory control over banks, as well as establishing the Federal Open Market Committee to determine monetary policy for the U.S. economy as a whole.

This chapter focuses on the deposit rate regulations and their impact on the U.S. economy. While the prohibition of interest payments on checking accounts caused some problems, far worse were the difficulties ultimately caused by the ceiling rates on time and savings deposits. These rate regulations, which the Federal Reserve called Regulation Q, caused severe disruptions in the banking and savings and loan industry years later, were instrumental in generating severe boom-bust cycles in new home construction during the 1960s, 1970s, and early 1980s, raised home prices higher than they otherwise would have been, and turned out to be highly discriminatory against low-income Americans. These deposit rate ceilings represent yet another example of a well-intentioned policy of economic control that eventually had very perverse unintended effects.

5.1 Regulating Deposit Rates

> *No member bank shall, directly or indirectly by any device whatsoever, pay any interest on any deposit which is payable on demand...*
>
> *The Federal Reserve Board shall from time to time limit by regulation the rate of interest which may be paid by member banks on time deposits, and may prescribe different rates for such payment on time and savings deposits having different maturities or subject to different conditions respecting withdrawal or repayment.*
>
> *—Banking Act of 1933, H.R. 5661, 73rd Congress, Session I, June 16, 1933, pp. 181 & 182.*

> *We do not believe that it is wise or necessary to regulate further by law the rate of interest that may be paid on deposits. From the standpoint of competition of member banks with non member banks, the former would be put at a decided disadvantage with such regulations in force.*
>
> *—Edward Elliott, Chairman of the First National Bank of Los Angeles, and W.R. Williams, Vice President of the Bank of America (San Francisco) in a joint statement delivered on April 2, 1932 to the Senate Committee on Banking and Currency (72nd Congress, Session I) during the hearings on the bill that became the Banking Act of 1933.*

The Glass-Steagall Act applied the interest rate restrictions to banks that were members of the Federal Reserve system. These restrictions consisted of a blanket prohibition against paying interest on checking accounts, as well as ceiling rates on time and savings deposits which would be determined by the Federal Reserve. The early protests over deposit rate regulation revolved around the fact that the rate ceilings only applied to banks that were members of the Federal Reserve system; nonmember banks were exempted. The hearings on the act are filled with comments similar to the one above by the California bankers: by restricting rates paid by member banks and exempting nonmember banks, member banks would be placed at a competitive disadvantage and may lose deposits to nonmember banks paying higher unregulated rates.

The problem the bankers referred to was alleviated somewhat two years later by the Banking Act of 1935. This act dictated that the interest rate regulation would extend to all banks with federal deposit insurance which effectively covered most of the banking industry. The Federal Reserve set rates for member banks while the Federal Deposit Insurance Corporation (FDIC) was given the authority to set rates at insured banks that were not members of the Federal Reserve System. Both the Federal Reserve and the FDIC set the same rates for identical classes of deposits. However, the 1935 Banking Act did not extend the deposit rate regulations to the thrift industry, which consists of mutual savings banks, savings and loans, and credit unions.[2] Ceiling rates weren't extended to thrifts until 1966. Yet despite eventually extending the regulations to virtually all depository institutions, the basic point the California bankers had raised back in 1932 was still a valid one that would come back to haunt the U.S. economy decades later: if interest rates on one class of financial assets are regulated while rates on another class are not, the potential exists for major shifts in how people hold their financial wealth. Glass-Steagall turned the banking industry into a cartel, *but it did not protect the cartel from outside competition.*

The potential problem was that market interest rates earned on financial assets outside of the banking system might rise above the Regulation Q ceiling deposit rates. If this happened, depositors (who were able to) would withdraw their deposits and instead buy assets earning higher, unregulated returns. This outflow of funds from depository institutions is called financial disintermediation and it would occur because depository institutions subject to Regulation Q were unable to offer higher deposit rates to compete for funds. If market rates were only slightly higher than the Regulation Q ceiling rates, regulated banks could try to make up for the lower rates they paid by adding more branches, making their buildings nicer, offering more amenities, and so forth. But if the difference between the Regulation Q rates and market rates became wide enough, the outflow from regulated institutions would become a flood regardless of any non-pecuniary attempts to stop it.

A mild version of this process occurred during the mid 1950s. After World War II the maximum rate banks could pay on savings deposits and time deposits with maturities of six months or more was 2.5 percent. This rate only applied to banks because at that time Regulation Q did not apply to the thrift industry. Until the early 1950s this ceiling rate was well above the market rate, and the growth rate of deposits at both banks and savings and loans were very similar to each other. But the Korean War inflation of the early 1950s pushed up interest rates so that by 1953 the rate paid by savings and loan institutions was above 2.5 percent. In other words, the Regulation Q rates became binding. As a result, from 1954 to 1956, time deposits at savings and loans grew at an annual rate of 15.6 percent while time deposits at banks rose at a rate of just 3.6 percent (Friedman and Schwartz 1963, 666). The Regulation Q rate was raised to a maximum of 3.0 percent on January 1, 1957 which allowed banks to more effectively compete with savings and loans. Deposit growth changed markedly as a result: from December 1956 to June 1958, time deposit growth was 13.0 percent at banks and 12.5 percent at savings and loans. The situation proceeded smoothly until 1966 which is when the first serious disruptions began.

5.2 Depository Institutions Before Deregulation

Before proceeding with our story about deposit rate regulation, we pause to describe depository institutions as they existed prior to the deregulation that occurred during the 1980s. The industry was much different from what it is today.

During the 1950s and 1960s a typical American household held their liquid financial assets in banks and thrifts. A commercial bank was, and still is, in the business of taking relatively short term deposits, in particular checking accounts and time and savings deposits, and issuing commercial and consumer loans. These loans are normally to businesses for expansion, or to households to finance purchases of durable goods such as automobiles.

Savings and loans and mutual savings banks were developed to provide funds for homebuilding. In fact, many of these financial institutions were originally started by real estate agents and building contractors trying to stimulate business (Simpson 1981, 158). As a result, thrifts traditionally held the bulk of their interest earning assets in home mortgages, so the industry has historically been a major lender to the homebuilding industry. Thrifts obtained their funds by attracting time and savings deposits. They were barred from offering checking accounts because that business was considered too risky when holding such illiquid assets as home mortgages.

Since the public always held their checking accounts at banks, it would be more convenient to have time and savings deposits there too. Thus, for thrifts to induce depositors to bother with accounts at two separate institutions, they had to offer deposit rates on time and savings deposits that were slightly higher than those offered by banks. Thrifts were able to pay higher rates because their interest earning assets (mortgages) were longer term, and thus earned higher rates, than the assets of commercial banks (commercial and consumer loans).

Assets held by banks and thrifts typically earned interest at rates that were fixed over their maturity. Fixed-rate loans were prevalent because inflation and interest rates had, for the most part, been low and stable for several years. As a result, banks saw no need to issue variable-rate loans. Thus, if a bank issued a three-year loan at 3.0 percent interest, the bank would earn that rate regardless of the behavior of market rates over the term of the loan. Over that same three-year period, however, deposit rates could vary as long as the Regulation Q ceiling rates were not binding.

Savings and loans and mutual savings banks were in an especially vulnerable position if interest rates rose because of the standard long-term home mortgage in existence after the mid 1930s. In response to the collapse in the real estate market during the Great Depression, the federal government created the Federal Housing Administration (FHA) to insure home mortgages. The FHA worked to standardize home mortgages, and as a result of that agency's efforts the typical home mortgage became a thirty-year loan at a fixed interest rate. Also, in those days the institution that originally issued the mortgage (the originator) usually held it during its entire term to maturity. Today, originators often sell mortgages to other institutions in the secondary market, but that was not commonly done prior to the late 1960s. So if a savings and loan issued a thirty-year mortgage at, say, 4.0 percent, then the issuer was usually stuck with that mortgage and its 4.0 percent rate for thirty years regardless of the behavior of market interest rates during that period.

The widespread existence of fixed rate loans explains why the financial health of the depository industry, but especially thrifts because their assets were primarily thirty-year mortgages, was critically dependent on interest rate *stability*. Depository institutions issued loans at fixed rates that were above the rates they paid on their deposits, and as long as interest rates were stable, they would enjoy a stable, positive interest margin. In fact, this was the case from the mid 1930s until the 1960s; while interest rates fluctuated during that period, they did so within a very narrow range when judged by the standards of the 1970s and 1980s. For example, from 1936 to 1965 the rate on a three-month Treasury bill moved above 4.0 percent just once.

In the event of a dramatic rise in market interest rates, banks and (especially) thrifts would be placed in a troublesome position. Their difficulties would arise from two sources. First, rates they would have to pay on deposits would rise relative to the rates earned on assets, thus their profitability would suffer. The second problem would come about if the rise in market rates was large enough to push them above the Regulation Q ceiling rates. Depository institutions would lose deposits as people withdrew their savings and time deposits and used those funds to purchase bonds or other financial assets paying market interest rates. This action could generate negative profits for the depository institutions even if they still had a positive interest margin because their assets might contract by so much that the interest earned on them did not cover their total costs.

In this case where market rates rose above the Regulation Q ceiling rates, the Federal Reserve in charge of administering Regulation Q, as well as the banks that lobbied the Federal Reserve, would be caught in a Hobson's Choice: damned if you do, damned if you do not. If the Federal Reserve raised the Regulation Q rate and allowed banks and S&Ls to pay market rates to retain deposits, those institutions interest margins would shrink, and perhaps become negative because they would have to pay higher rates on deposits, while still holding those fixed rate loans. Banks would be better able to deal with this situation than thrifts because banks hold shorter-term assets than thrifts. In any given year a relatively large proportion of banks' loans mature, allowing them to re-loan those funds at the higher market rates. Thrifts, however, would only have a small proportion of thirty-year mortgages mature in any given year. As a result, the profit squeeze on thrifts could be severe, in fact, some such highly leveraged firms could quickly go bankrupt.

The other choice is unattractive as well. If the Federal Reserve decided to keep the Regulation Q deposit rates below market rates to preserve depository institutions' positive interest rate spread, then the depository institutions would lose deposits. Depository institutions would have to reduce their assets, and a credit crunch would result where new loans and mortgages became difficult to obtain. Banks and thrifts would not have funds to lend out, so purchases that are typically financed with credit, such as houses and automobiles, would be severely curtailed. Some of the worst effects would show up in the housing sector because virtually all home purchases are made on credit. The result would be a severe reduction in home building which, for reasons we discuss next, harms the American public.

5.3 Some Facts About The Housing Cycle

Construction of new homes is a major industry in the United States. For example, in 1990 about 1,200,000 new single family dwellings were built, which are what we would normally think of as houses (as opposed to mobile homes and apartments).[3] That year, the home building industry employed about 670,000 workers, which accounts for around 2.0 percent of total employment in the United States (U.S. Department of Labor 1991, 42). The value of new homes built in 1990 represented about 2.5 percent of GDP.

An important feature of home building is the volatility of its cycle. Figure 5.1 shows the number of new housing starts from 1946-1996. What stands out in this figure is the extreme volatility-- the most dramatic boom-bust in the series occurred during the early-to-mid 1970s when seasonally-adjusted housing starts went from an annual rate of 1.08 million units in January 1970, to 2.48 million units in October, 1972, an increase of 130 percent over a span of thirty-three months. Then the series collapsed, down to 904,000 units by February, 1975. During that bust, employment in the industry fell by more than 200,000 workers which represents around 10 percent of the entire decline in U.S. employment during the 1973-1975 recession (U.S. Department of Labor 1991, 42). In other words, about one out of every ten workers who lost their jobs during that recession worked in the business of constructing new homes. In addition, workers in industries dependent on new home building, such as lumber, home furnishings, and appliances suffered cuts in both hours and employment as well.

Why is home-building subject to such violent fluctuations? There are several reasons, but the two most important are the stock-flow aspect of housing, and the role of interest rates. The stock-flow refers to the fact that the stock of existing housing in the United States is huge relative to the flow, which is the number of new homes built each year. The 1990 Census of Housing reports the existence of roughly 66 million single family dwellings in the United States (U.S. Department of Commerce 1992, 16). Therefore, the 1,200,000 new ones built that year represent just under 2.0 percent of the total stock. Keep in mind that those new houses were not all net additions to the housing stock because during any year a certain number are torn down or become uninhabit-

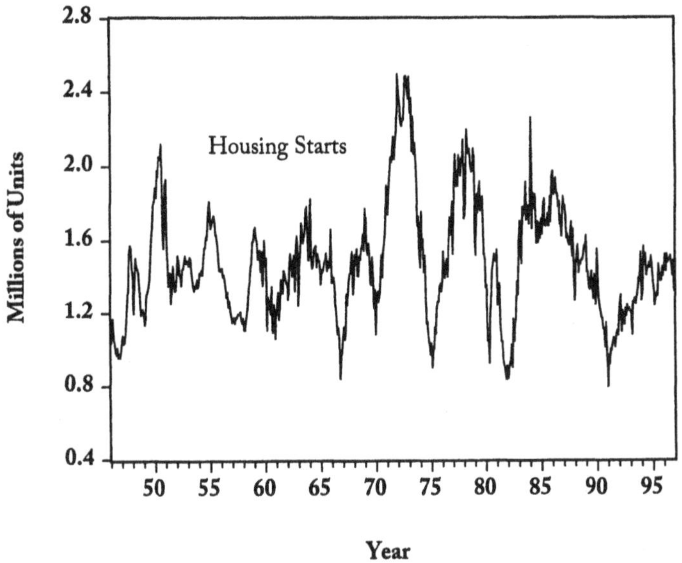

Fig. 5.1 Housing Starts, 1946 – 1996

able. Hall and Taylor (1997, 318) contend that a "reasonable" estimate of the depreciation rate of houses is 2 percent, so if we use that number the housing stock of the United States fell slightly 1990 because the number of new ones built (1.2 million) was less than the number that wore out (.02 x 66 million = 1.3 million). Normally this is not the case, but the

U.S. economy suffered a recession during 1990 so the number of new homes built was below average.

The large stock - small flow situation in housing generates instability in the following manner. Let's use the 1990 Census figures and assume that the demand for single family units that year was 66 million. Let's also use the 2 percent depreciation rate which means that about 1.3 million homes were torn down that year or deteriorated to the extent that they were no longer occupied. If the demand for houses was constant during 1990, then to maintain a stable housing stock the home construction industry would have had to produce 1.3 million units to replace the ones that wore out. Now suppose that the following year the demand for houses rose by 2.0 percent, perhaps because financing costs fell and many families could afford to move from apartments into houses. A 2.0 percent rise in the demand for houses means the U.S. public wants to live in 67.3 million houses (66 million x 1.02). Since the home building industry has to produce 1.3 million just to maintain the same housing stock, that many houses have to be built plus another 1.3 million to raise the stock up to 67.3 million. In other words, a rise in the demand for houses of just 2.0 percent causes the number of new houses built to rise by 100 percent! Thus, a relatively small change in the demand for houses causes a very large change in the production of new houses.[4]

The second major reason why the production of new houses is unstable involves the effects of changes in interests rates. Since a standard house in the United States fetches a price that is several times a typical family's income, virtually all home purchases are made with credit. Buyers usually make a down payment of 20 percent of the purchase price, and borrow the remaining 80 percent in the form of a home mortgage. Since the amount being borrowed is so large, a seemingly small change in the mortgage interest rate can cause a significant change in the mortgage cost. For example, suppose that someone purchased a $100,000 home by making a down payment of $20,000 and borrowing $80,000 for thirty years. If the rate on the mortgage is 7.0 percent, then the monthly payment would be $532.24. If the mortgage rate rose to 8.0 percent the monthly payment rises to $587.01. So a 1.0 percentage point rise in the mortgage rate raises the cost of the mortgage by $54.77 per month, or 10.3 percent. In this way, seemingly small changes in mortgage rates can have a large impact on borrowing costs and, therefore, the demand for housing.

At the same time, the supply of housing also depends on interest rates. Since many building contractors finance construction with borrowed funds, higher interest rates raise their costs and reduce their willingness to produce new houses. This will be true even if the builder did not borrow and instead paid all of the costs with internally-generated funds because the interest rate represents the opportunity cost of the materials and labor they buy.

Therefore, interest rate fluctuations impact both the supply and demand for housing, and do so in the same direction. If interest rates rise, the demand for housing falls as does the supply of new houses. When interest rates fall, more houses are demanded, and more new ones are built. The interest rate's influence on the supply and demand of houses, in combination with the large stock-small flow situation, are the primary reasons why new home construction exhibits a high degree of volatility.

The fact that new-house construction follows a volatile cycle imposes costs on American society. The major cost is inefficiency which refers to producing at a cost above the minimum cost. The housing cycle causes houses to be produced in an inefficient manner because the volatility raises costs which are passed on to buyers in the form of higher prices.

Why does the building cycle raise costs? Hendershott and Villani (1977, 77-83) identify three main causes. First, during boom periods when large numbers of new homes are produced, prices of materials such as lumber, drywall, wiring, windows, and insulation rise along with demand. In addition, since workers are in short supply, their wages rise, as do the number of overtime hours worked at a 50 percent premium.

Second, since building contractors know that production is unstable, they produce new houses in a more labor-intensive manner than would otherwise be the case. During a decline in demand, home-builders find it more cost-effective to get rid of labor (just lay off the workers and stop paying their wages) than to lay off capital (because the firm owns the capital and incurs an opportunity cost when it is not employed). Therefore, building contractors produce new homes using more labor and less capital than is economically efficient. In other words, instead of producing prefabricated homes in factories with machines and assembling them on-site, home builders are more likely to assemble almost the entire home from materials delivered to the building site.[5]

The third way the housing cycle raises the cost of producing new homes is by raising workers' wages above the level they would be in the absence of the housing cycle. Virtually any carpenter can tell you that employment in the homebuilding industry is unstable. There are periods of feast when they can pick their job and get plenty of overtime hours, as well as times of famine during recessions when they are laid off for months on end because there are few jobs available. In addition, many of them are itinerant workers, regularly moving to regions of the country where jobs exist. As compensation for this employment instability, workers in the home building industry receive a wage premium, earning higher wages than they would if employment was stable.

In sum, the existence of the Regulation Q interest rate ceilings which were often binding between 1966 and the early 1980s made house construction considerably more volatile by causing financial disintermediation out of the thrift institutions that were the primary source of financial capital to the housing sector. This severe housing cycle made home prices higher than they otherwise would have been, and caused severe disruption to workers in housing and its ancillary industries.

5.4 Hitting the Ceiling

> *Net acquisitions of residential mortgages decreased by 25 percent in the first two quarters of 1966. This reduction occurred despite signigicant Government aid: the Federal National Mortgage Association purchased nearly $4½ billion of mortgages (annual rate) during the period, and the Home Loan Banks provided funds to offset deposit losses of savings and loan associations. In the third quarter, only $9.4 billion (annual rate) went into residential mortgages— more than 40 percent below the amount provided a year earlier. The net flow into home mortgages from savings and loan associations was virtually zero. The result of all this was the marked decline in residential construction.*
> *—Council of Economic Advisors (1967, 57).*

An important feature of the period from 1966-1981 was the upward ratcheting of interest rates. During those years rates cycled up and down several times, but did so with a definite upward trend. Interest rates behaved this way because inflation was following the same pattern as policymakers kept trying to exploit the short run Phillips curve relationship, creating economy-wide boom - bust cycles. Since interest rates contain an inflation premium, as inflation ratcheted upward so did interest rates.[6] This pattern is clearly seen in figure 5.2 which shows the yield on three-month Treasury bills and the maximum rate banks could

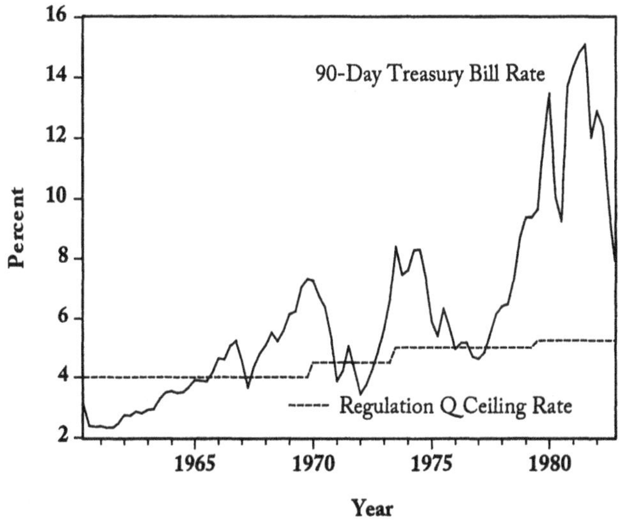

Fig. 5.2 Yield on 90-Day Treasury Bills and the Regulation Q Ceiling Rate

pay on savings account under Regulation Q from 1960-1982.

A three-month Treasury bill is a close substitute for a federally-insured savings deposit at a bank because both are liquid and risk-free. The major difference between the two is that while an individual can open a savings account with a very small sum, during the 1960s Treasury bills carried a minimum face value of $1,000. The Regulation Q ceiling became binding in 1966 when the T-bill rate rose to just over 5.0 percent while banks could pay only 4.0 percent on savings accounts. This gave banks' depositors an incentive to withdraw their savings accounts and buy T-bills instead (assuming they could afford them). At the same time, the rise in market interest rates placed thrifts in a poor position because the (unregulated) rates they had to pay on deposits in order to retain them rose, while they were still holding those long-term, fixed-rate home mortgages earning relatively low rates.

Congress responded to the thrift industry's plight by passing the

1966 Interest Rate Adjustment Act which extended the ceiling deposit rates to thrifts. The idea was that placing ceilings on thrifts' deposit rates would allow those institutions to maintain their profitability by lowering their costs. Also, the act allowed thrifts to pay up to three-fourths of one percentage point higher interest on savings accounts than banks could. This was their compensation for not being able to offer the same services as banks, such as checking accounts. In a move designed to further aid the thrifts, the Federal Reserve and FDIC *lowered* the ceiling rate on *bank* time deposits under $100,000 from 5 ½ to 5 percent.

This 1966 episode of market rates rising above the ceiling deposit rates created a credit crunch which had a major impact on homebuilding. Figure 5.3 shows the difference between the yield on a 90-day Treasury bill and the Regulation Q rate on savings deposits at banks, and new housing starts. The interest rate differential is plotted on the bottom of the diagram and you can see that the Regulation Q ceilings first became binding near the end of 1965. By the summer of 1966 T-bills were yielding over 1.0 percentage point more than savings accounts at banks. Savings account balances during 1966 peaked in March at $166.1 billion, then fell to $162.8 by October.[7] This deposit outflow resulted in restrictive credit conditions, with funds for new housing severely

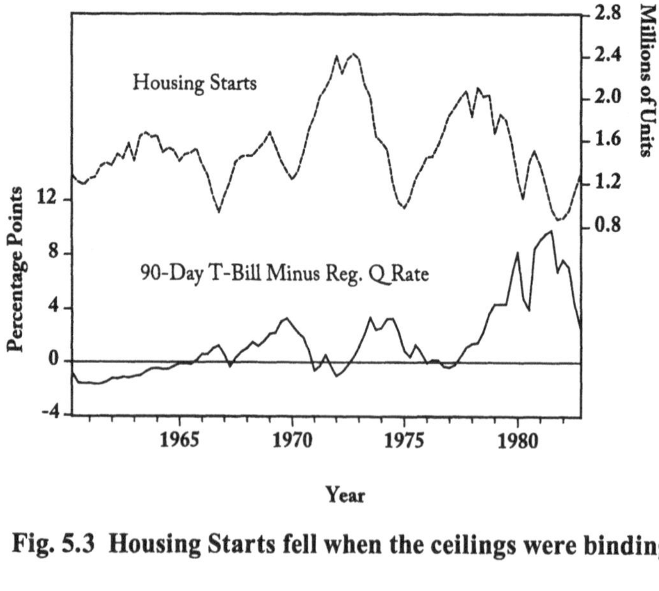

Fig. 5.3 Housing Starts fell when the ceilings were binding

curtailed. The credit crunch was further exacerbated by the fact that several states had usury laws in place which set maximum rates banks and thrifts could charge for loans, including mortgages. When market rates rose above the usury rates, lenders were unwilling to issue loans at below-market rates. In addition, both the Federal Housing Administration (FHA) and Veterans' Administration (VA) maintained ceiling rates on mortgages they insured. Housing starts dropped precipitously during 1966, from an annual rate of 1.4 million units in March to 843,000 by October, which is an enormous decline over so brief a period. This drop in housing starts helped cause a decline in overall U.S. economic growth that year, from 6.4 percent during 1965 to 2.6 percent in 1966.

The Federal Reserve, "startled and shaken by the brush with apparent disaster," (Wojnilower 1980, 288) pursued an easy monetary policy in late 1966, and by doing so drove market rates below the Regulation Q ceiling rates. As a result, funds flowed back into savings accounts and the housing market rebounded. This situation proved only temporary, however, because when the economy recovered, inflation and nominal interest rates resumed their upward climb. By mid 1968 the spread between the T-bill rate and the Regulation Q rate was as large as it had been in 1966, and during 1969 it reached nearly 4.0 percentage points. Again, the public responded by reducing their deposit inflow into banks and thrifts, and again the housing market collapsed, although not as severely as it had during 1966. According to Weintraub (1982, 85-88) the thrift industry was better prepared to deal with the problem in 1969 than it had been in 1966. In particular, thrifts aggressively marketed new types of accounts that could pay slightly higher rates than were available on regular savings accounts. In addition, the Federal Home Loan Banks were much more active in lending to thrifts to help make up for the slowdown in deposit growth. The situation was further aided by the fact that the Regulation Q rates were raised in 1970. In order to keep corporate deposits, the ceiling rate on large ($100,000 or more) short-term certificates of deposit was raised from 5.5 to 6.25 percent in January 1970, and then eliminated a few months later.

Market rates fell below the ceiling rates again in 1971, the result of an expansionary monetary policy initiated by the Federal Reserve in June 1970. That month the Penn-Central Railroad defaulted on its commercial paper, and the development shook financial markets. There was genuine fear that other companies would default on their debt as well. The Federal Reserve responded by increasing bank reserves at an annualized rate of 25 percent during the next three months. This action drove short term rates below the Regulation Q ceiling deposit rates. A rapid inflow into depository institutions occurred, and housing starts rose dramatically.

However, market rates did not stay below the Regulation Q rates for long. The economy cycled up again, taking inflation and short term interest rates along with it. By 1972, T-bill rates were once again above the ceiling deposit rates. Home building busted, this time severely. The ensuing recession knocked market rates below the ceiling rates from 1976-1977, but after that they climbed again and the situation eventually reached the point of absurdity. By 1979 the T-bill rate was nearly 10 percentage points higher than the Regulation Q ceiling rates. This margin was surpassed in 1981 when T-bill rates hit 15 percent, while depositors could earn no more than 5.25 percent on savings accounts at banks. The deposit outflow, from thrifts in particular, was enormous. Savings deposits at thrifts peaked in May 1978 at $278.2 billion. By July, 1982 they had fallen to $183.9 billion. During 1980 mutual savings banks were experiencing negative profits in the aggregate, and the savings and loan industry was in the same situation by the first half of 1981 (Carron 1982, 12). Many thrifts were on the brink of insolvency.

5.5 The Financial Industry's Response

During the period being discussed, there were several developments that worked to lessen the problems caused by Regulation Q. However, while these changes alleviated the problems somewhat, and likely kept the U.S. depository industry from experiencing massive failures, they were patchwork solutions. The major source of the problems, Regulation Q, wasn't completely eliminated until 1986.

One change which occurred in May 1973 was the removal of deposit rate ceilings on certificates of deposit of $100,000 or more. This move was designed to allow banks and thrifts to retain their corporate accounts. Another modification was the "wild card experiment" that took place from July 1973 to November 1973 where depository institutions could offer certificates of deposit in small amounts with maturities of four or more years at rates exempt from Regulation Q. Another important change was the introduction of interest bearing checking accounts in New England which began in 1972. These negotiable order of withdrawal (NOW) accounts were finally offered nationwide in 1981.

Still another important change occurred in 1975 when savings and loans in California started offering variable-rate mortgages.[8]

Another source of relief for depository institutions was the establishment of a secondary market for mortgages. This market allowed banks and thrifts to sell their fixed rate mortgages (at a discount) and free up the funds to invest at higher rates. The practice of selling mortgages to federal agencies had been in existence since the 1930s, but it became considerably more common during the 1960s. The Federal National Mortgage Association (FNMA, or "Fannie Mae") was already in existence, and in 1968 the federal government established the Government National Mortgage Association (GNMA, or "Ginnie Mae"). These organizations sell securities and then use the proceeds to purchase home mortgages from depository institutions. Beginning in the late 1960s, when market interest rates rose above the rates banks and thrifts earned on home mortgages, depository institutions could unload those mortgages by selling them to the government-backed organizations.

While these changes helped prevent the situation in the banking and thrift industries from turning into an absolute disaster, another change occurred that probably had more to do with the eventual deregulation of the depository industry than anything else. In 1972 Merrill Lynch, a large New York brokerage firm, created a hugely successful financial innovation: the money market mutual fund (MMMF). Mutual funds, where the purchaser buys shares in the fund and the proceeds are used to purchase financial assets such as stocks and bonds, had been around for years. With the MMMF, Merrill Lynch sold shares (priced at $1 per share) and used the proceeds to buy short-term financial instruments such as commercial paper. Shareholders were paid dividends which were at market interest rates. What really set the MMMF apart from other mutual funds was that shareholders were issued checkbooks and allowed to write checks on their shares as a method of redeeming them! In other words, the MMMF served as an interest-bearing checking account that paid market rates. It wasn't subject to deposit rate ceilings because Merrill Lynch was not a bank, thrift, nor was its MMMF covered by federal deposit insurance.

The growth of money market mutual fund balances was enormous, especially in the late 1970s when market rates rose so far above the Regulation Q rates. Bank and thrift depositors withdrew huge amounts from banks and thrifts and used the funds to purchase shares of MMMFs.

Year	MMMFs
1973	$0.1 billion
1974	$1.7 billion
1975	$2.8 billion
1976	$2.5 billion
1977	$2.6 billion
1978	$6.7 billion
1979	$34.8 billion
1980	$63.4 billion
1981	$152.4 billion
1982	$185.2 billion

Source: Federal Reserve Bank of St. Louis, FRED.

The MMMF was a development that the depository industry simply could not ignore because the public was funneling billions of dollars of potential deposits into shares of MMMFs. The cartel established by the Glass-Steagall Act of 1933 had to be broken up by deregulating deposit rates, or there would be a bloodbath of failures and defaults in the bank and thrift industries.[9]

5.6 The Short End of the Stick

Not only did the Regulation Q ceiling rates cause economic difficulties by exacerbating the housing cycle and raising the cost of home ownership, they had another pernicious effect: they were discriminatory against the poor. Prior to the 1980s deregulation of the banking and thrift industries, poor Americans were relegated to placing their liquid financial wealth in savings accounts and time deposits at banks and thrifts because accounts at those institutions had low minimum balance requirements. About the only other short-term liquid assets available were Treasury bills which carried a face value of $1,000. At prices in that range they were available to some lower income Americans, but certainly not all.[10] When the MMMFs came along, they required minimum purchases of a few thousand dollars, so that option was unavailable for many low income people as well.

When market rates rose above the Regulation Q rates in 1966, the poor were placed in an unfortunate situation. If they had around $1,000 and were willing to tie those funds up for at least ninety days, they could buy a Treasury bill and earn market rates. However, if they did not have the necessary amount, or wanted the greater liquidity of a savings account, they were stuck earning below-market rates at banks and thrifts. Mayer (1982) says that Federal Reserve officials recognized this pernicious aspect of the deposit rate ceilings, but were also aware of the depository industry's clout in Congress.

When market rates rose above the Regulation Q rates again in 1969-1970, people were withdrawing enough funds from banks and S&Ls and purchasing Treasury bills that the depository industry lobbied the U.S. Treasury to help reduce the deposit outflow by making T-bills less affordable. But if the Treasury raised the price of T-bills, even more Americans would lose the opportunity to earn market interest rates. Alternative solutions would have been to assist lower income Americans by keeping the face value of Treasury bills at $1,000 (or perhaps even lowering the amount!), or urging depository institutions to lobby the Federal Reserve and FDIC to raise the Regulation Q rates. Which choice did the Treasury make? Did they help the poor, or help the banks and thrifts? Need we ask?

In 1970, the U.S. Treasury raised the face value of Treasury bills to $10,000 which is what it still is today. Treasury officials based their decision on the assumption that market rates would be above the Regulation Q rates only briefly, so lower income Americans would be harmed, but not for a prolonged period. Of course, things did not turn out that way: interest rates rose even further above the ceiling rates in the years that followed. So the Treasury's decision to raise the face value of T-bills tenfold turned out to be a figurative slamming of the door in the face of the poor who lost dearly in the form of interest not earned.

How much interest income was lost? Pyle (1974) estimates that over $5 billion was lost from 1968-1970, and Taggart and Woglom (1978) report $20.1 billion over the period 1970-1975. During 1978-1982, a rough estimate of lost interest income on just savings accounts can be obtained by taking the amount held in savings accounts at banks and thrifts and multiplying it by the difference between the ninety-day T-bill rate and the Regulation Q rate. This results in an estimate of $104.4 billion. Who gained this interest income not earned? The managers and shareholders of the depository institutions that did not have to pay market rates.

Therefore, the Regulation Q deposit rate ceilings, originally instituted in 1933 on the basis of the flawed logic that competitive bidding of deposit rates had been a major cause of the banking disaster of 1930-1933, went on to cause major disruptions in the U.S. economy years later.

They helped generate volatile housing cycles during the 1960s, 1970s, and early 1980s which were an important source of macroeconomic instability. They also raised house prices above what they otherwise would have been. In addition, deposit rate ceilings bilked lower income Americans out of billions of dollars of lost interest income which they surely could have used. Regulation Q also caused major disruptions in the depository industry that took years to get settled. In short, placing ceilings on deposit rates was a policy of economic control the United States would have been much better off without.

CHAPTER 6

■■■

Wage and Price Controls in Action

The...decision to impose [wage and price controls] was politically necessary and immensely popular in the short run. But in the long run I believe that it was wrong. The piper must always be paid, and there was an unquestionably high price for tampering with the orthodox economic mechanisms.
—Richard M. Nixon (1978, 521).

The use of economic controls moved a major step forward on the evening of Sunday, August 15, 1971 when President Richard Nixon announced a ninety-day freeze on all U.S. wages and prices as part of his New Economic Policy.[1] The program was extended in varying forms before finally expiring on April 30, 1974. Wage and price controls were supposed to hold down inflation while aggregate demand was stimulated in an effort to reduce unemployment. However, it turned out that this policy was based on the miscalculation that the U.S. economy had a large amount of excess capacity at the time. In reality, the U.S. economy was operating near capacity. As a result, the aggregate demand stimulus drove output well above the full employment level which resulted in a major buildup of inflationary pressures. But with controls in place, prices could not fully adjust to bring markets into equilibrium, so shortages developed. When the controls were finally lifted, the shortages disappeared, but prices shot up. Thus, the wage and price controls just delayed the inflation somewhat. However, in the case of petroleum products the price controls were extended for several more years which caused recurring shortages that were a major problem. In the end, Nixon's system of controls accomplished little beyond creating needless economic disruption.

6.1 It's Politics, Not Economics

Freezing wages and prices can't do any good...but it can't do too much harm so long as the period isn't longer than 90 days. I can sympathize with the President. He's been under tremendous pressure to do something about the economy.

You know, it's really extraordinary the snow job the

> *Democratic politicians and the Democratic economists have accomplished.*
>
> *They've...persuaded the American people that our country is in a very bad economic state. It's not true. The economy is operating at a high level.*
>
> *They've also persuaded the American people that the recovery from the business recession is sluggish, not slow. Not true. The recovery pace is no worse than the pervious four recession recoveries.*
>
> *Also, they have persuaded the American people that no progress has been made in reducing the rate of inflation. Not true. The inflation rate has been reduced from more than 6 percent to 4 percent.*
>
> *—Milton Friedman's reaction to the wage and price freeze announced on August 15, 1971 ("Friedman Declares Freeze Won't Work."* Chicago Tribune *August 16, 1971).*

In order to understand why wage and price controls were imposed, it is necessary to examine U.S. economic conditions in mid 1971. Today, most anyone looking over the 1971 economic data would conclude that the U.S. economy was in pretty good shape. However, at the time many did not view the situation that way.

Inflation and unemployment were major issues during 1971. During the first half of the year, the GDP deflator inflation rate was 5.1 percent while the unemployment rate averaged 5.9 percent. While these rates would have been applauded just a few years later, at the time they were viewed as high. To see why, consider the annual average unemployment and GDP deflator inflation rates from 1966-1971:

Year	**Unemployment Rate (%)**	**Inflation Rate (%)**
1966	3.8	2.9
1967	3.8	3.1
1968	3.6	4.3
1969	3.5	4.7
1970	4.9	5.4
1971	5.1	5.9

Source: Council of Economic Advisors (1997, 306 & 346).

The 5.0-plus rates of inflation and unemployment experienced during 1971 were relatively high compared to what had been the case a few years before. The public had grown to expect unemployment rates below 4.0 percent, and inflation in the 3.0 - 4.0 percent range. Another cause for concern was the fact that from January to August the unemployment rate was stuck at around 6.0 percent. It was 6.1 percent during August, the month the wage and price freeze was announced.

The Nixon administration was acutely aware of the public's concern over the economy. Various options were discussed, including some sort of controls. Arthur Burns, who at the time served as an economic advisor to President Nixon, urged the president to use jawboning tactics to hold down wage increases.[2] However, Nixon opposed that tactic. Since he considered the inflation to be the result of government policies, he thought it hypocritical for him to ask labor unions to accept lower wage increases. He rejected direct wage and price controls as well: "Rationing, black markets, regimentation-- that is the wrong road for America" (Nixon from De Marchi 1975, 299).

As time passed, the political pressure to impose controls grew. In August 1970 the Democratic-controlled Congress passed the Economic Stabilization Act which authorized the president to freeze wages, prices, salaries, and rents. Meanwhile, Nixon's economic advisors were paying close attention to labor union contracts being negotiated in several industries, especially construction. During 1970, average negotiated wages and benefits rose 8.9 percent, while in the construction industry it averaged an astounding 19.6 percent in the first year of contracts. These huge wage increases for construction workers took place despite the fact that the unemployment rate in the industry rose from 6.8 percent in 1969.III to 12.3 percent in 1970.III (De Marchi 1975, 325).[3]

Advocates of wage and price controls were arguing the nonmonetary view of inflation-- that these large wage increases were generating a "cost push" to inflation, a process where workers negotiated large wage increases and firms simply passed on the higher costs in the form of higher prices. They claimed that the root cause of the problem was high expected inflation, which resulted from the buildup in actual inflation that dated to the mid 1960s. In effect, they were arguing that higher expected inflation had caused a rightward shift in the Phillips curve. Wage and price controls were viewed as a way to reduce expected inflation which, if successful, would shift the Phillips curve left. In theory, a demand stimulus applied while wage and price controls held down both actual and expected inflation would cause inflation and unemployment to fall simultaneously.

By early 1971, there was intense pressure on President Nixon to "do something" about the economy. The presidential election campaign was heating up, the public was dissatisfied with the economy, and Nixon's economic policies were being criticized by his potential Democratic opponents in the upcoming 1972 election. In addition, Arthur Burns, now the chairman of the Federal Reserve Board of Governors, was publicly calling for wage and price controls. A Gallup poll taken in January 1971 indicated that 62 percent of respondents favored their use (Rockoff 1984, 201). On several occasions Nixon publically appealed for restraint in setting wages and prices, but he continued to resist formal controls. In March 1971, the pressure on Nixon rose another notch when the metal-can industry agreed to a labor contract that raised wages 9.0 percent per year. Many business leaders, along with the *New York Times* were now calling for controls.

Nixon finally relented, and decided around August 1st to impose a system (De Marchi 1975, 342). However, he had not chosen a date to announce the plan. The impetus to institute the program was the drain on the U.S. gold stock associated with the breakdown of the Bretton Woods system which reached its climax around the middle of August. Being a politician, Nixon tended toward bold moves, so on August 15th he announced the wage and price controls as part of his New Economic Policy, which included closing the gold window and allowing the dollar to depreciate. Thus, he initiated the death throes for one system of economic controls, that being the Bretton Woods system of fixed exchange rates, but imposed new controls in the form of a wage and price freeze.

6.2 The Big Mistake

> *The basic premise of the price-wage control system is that the inflation of 1970 and 1971 was the result of expectations...built up during the earlier period, beginning in 1965, when there was an inflationary excess of demand. Since there is no longer an excess of demand, the rate of inflation will subside permanently when this residue of the previous excess is removed. The purpose of the control system is to give the country a period of enforced stability in which expectations...will become adapted to the fact that rapid infla-*

tion is no longer the prospective condition of American life. When that happens controls can be eliminated.
—Council of Economic Advisors (1972, 108).

The critical error policymakers made in 1971 was to assume that unemployment rates in the neighborhood of 6.0 percent indicated that a large amount of excess capacity existed. While this is easy to see in hindsight, at the time it was not widely recognized. The U.S. economy had maintained unemployment rates of around 4.0 percent during the 1960s, so many believed that an unemployment rate in that range was attainable without a major inflation acceleration.

The unemployment rate was rising because of trends at work during the late 1960s and early 1970s.[4] In particular, large numbers of baby boomers (those born between the mid 1940s and early 1960s) were entering the labor force. Young people have higher unemployment rates than older workers because they possess fewer skills and less work experience. Therefore, as large numbers of young people entered the labor force, the aggregate unemployment rate rose. In addition, millions of women without much work experience were also entering the labor force. Furthermore, as U.S. involvement in the Vietnam War wound down, over a million veterans returned to the labor force during 1970-1971 (Council of Economic Advisors 1972, 109). While these factors were recognized at the time, the magnitude of their impact on the unemployment rate was underestimated. Thus, unemployment rates of around 6.0 percent were considered high. Ironically, the trend of rising unemployment continued for several more years, and during part of the 1980s many U.S. politicians and policymakers would have gotten down on their hands and knees for a 6.0 percent unemployment rate.

The U.S. economic situation during the early 1970s is illustrated in figure 6.1 which plots real GDP and Gordon's (2000) estimates of the natural (or full employment) rate of output from 1968-1974. The 1960s economic boom drove output well above the full employment level, and it stayed there until the 1969-1970 recession pushed GDP back towards, and eventually below, capacity. Note that the 1969-1970 recession was primarily a movement back toward the natural rate of output, so it did not result in a major decline in measured inflation. A significant disinflation would have required levels of output well below the natural rate; the 1969-1970 recession simply was not severe enough to accomplish that task.

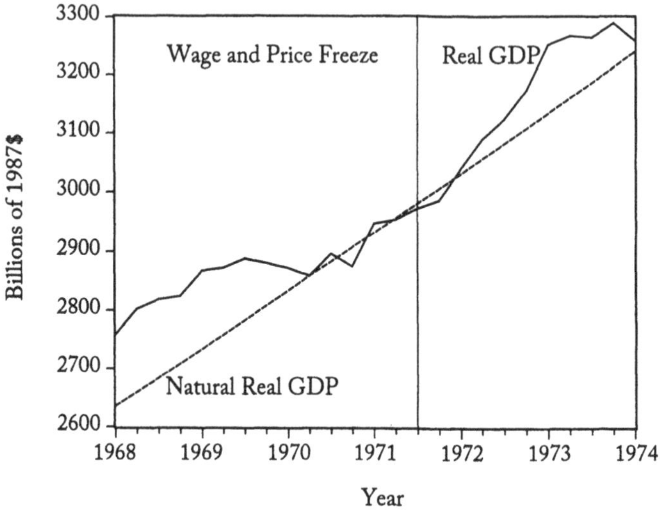

Fig. 6.1 Real GDP and the Natural Rate of Output

As a result, even a modest demand stimulus during 1971 would have been enough to drive output above capacity and cause accelerating inflation. The demand stimulus was carried out through a combination of expansionary monetary and fiscal policies. Figure 6.2 shows the annualized growth rates of the M2 measure of money from 1970.I - 1974.III. The Federal Reserve raised the monetary growth rate in June 1970 in response to the Penn-Central railroad's default on their commercial paper. Money growth stayed in the double digit range throughout 1971 and 1972, and by late 1972, the economy was producing well above the full employment level. Fiscal policy was stimulative as well, especially from late 1971 to mid 1972 because government spending rose significantly.

The New Economic Policy expanded aggregate demand through additional channels as well. Closing the gold window and allowing the dollar to depreciate against foreign currencies placed upward pressure on U.S. import prices. In addition, imports were subject to a 10 percent surcharge. Thus, import prices rose while prices of domestically-produced goods were frozen by price controls. In other words, relative prices changed in favor of domestically-produced goods and against imported goods. This change reduced the U.S. demand for imports, and raised demand for domestically-produced goods. In the auto industry, the effect was especially significant because not only were prices of

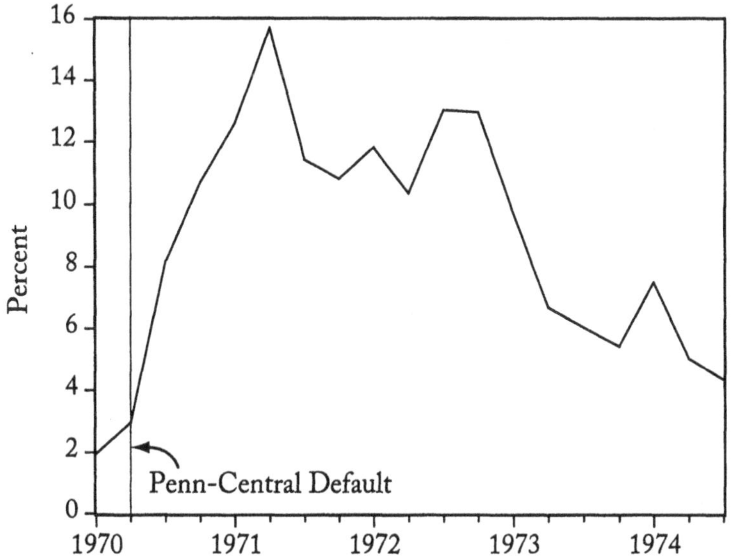

Fig. 6.2 M2 Growth, 1970.I – 1974.III

domestic cars frozen for ninety days, the New Economic Policy also eliminated the 7.0 percent excise tax on them. Sales of domestic autos boomed: before the policy was announced 1971 U.S. domestic auto sales were running at an annual rate of 8 million units, then during September and October rose to an annual rate of more than 10 million units (Council of Economic Advisors 1972, 102).

In sum, the combination of expansionary monetary and fiscal policies, along with price controls and the dollar depreciation, caused rapid aggregate demand growth during the early 1970s. Nominal aggregate demand rose 8.2 percent during 1971, 10.1 percent in 1972, and another 11.6 percent in 1973. The result was a major economic boom: real GDP rose 3.3 percent in 1971, 5.4 percent in 1972, and 5.7 percent in 1973.

6.3 The Reality of Wage and Price Controls

> *The following example illustrates some of the problems, and some of the fun, of administering price controls...[AFL-CIO President] George Meany had charged on television that the number of matzoh balls in Mrs. Adler's matzoh ball soup*

had been reduced from four to three, with no corresponding change in price. C. Jackson Grayson, the head of the Price Commission, checked with the executives at Mrs. Adler's and, on learning that they denied the charge, sent his staff out to buy matzoh ball soup. Some thirty cans were opened to reveal four matzoh balls in each. The following Sunday, on the program "Face the Nation," Grayson waited for the appropriate moment and then, holding aloft a can of soup he had been concealing, he proclaimed the truth about Mrs. Adler's matzoh balls!
—Hugh Rockoff (1984, 228).

If I had a thousand toilets to sell, I'd be King of Denver.
—Frank Jagodzinski, manager of a plumbing supply firm in Denver, Colorado ("More and More Scarcities: Who is Feeling the Pinch" U.S. News and World Report *September 3, 1973, 15).*

Several studies have investigated the affects the wage and price controls had on the U.S. inflation rate from 1971-1974, and a general consensus has emerged: the controls didn't have much impact on measured inflation other than to delay it somewhat.[5] During the first several months the controls were in effect, they kept measured inflation slightly below what it would have been otherwise. However, as the controls were weakened and eventually eliminated, the measured inflation rate caught up to reflect the true extend of the demand stimulus. Thus, the wage and price controls had no long-run impact on inflation.

Even when the controls were in force, they were not very effective at holding down inflation. There are several reasons why. First, the system was relatively weak in the sense of having a small amount of resources devoted to the actual operation of the program. Nixon pledged to keep the bureaucracy running the system small, and it was. The Cost of Living Council was established to control the overall program, while the Office of Emergency Preparedness was charged with running the daily operations. The Internal Revenue Service was responsible for enforcement. According to Rockoff (1984, 221), the government's cost of operating the price controls amounted to just 1.1 percent of the size of the U.S. Postal Service's budget. No more than a few thousand government employees were ever directly involved with the program (Cagan 1979,

163). In contrast, administering the price controls in place during World War II involved 60,000 paid employees, and volunteers numbering in the hundreds of thousands. Since the Nixon administration devoted so few resources to the program, compliance was largely voluntary. This approach worked fairly well during the first months the program was in force because it was so popular. However, as the controls lost public support, compliance increasingly became a problem.

Another reason why the controls were ineffective was because widespread debasement of product quality occurred. The rules dictated that sellers could not raise product prices above ceiling levels, but, without strict enforcement, producers could lower the quality of their products as a way to reduce costs and maintain profit margins. The Nixon controls era is littered with examples of this process in action. Many gasoline stations converted from full-service to self-service. The price of gasoline did not change, but the quality of the overall product clearly declined. Another example occurred in the lumber industry. A board that's called a two-by-four isn't really 2" x 4"; supposedly that is the dimension before it is planed smooth, but the planing process shaves off wood so the final board is smaller, usually 1 3/4" x 3 3/4". When price controls were in effect, lumber manufacturers must have been planing boards extra smoothly, because the average size of dimension lumber fell to about 1 5/8" x 3 5/8".

These are just two examples out of thousands. Books were printed on lower quality paper, the number of coats of paint on new autos and household appliances was reduced, plastic was substituted for metal in various products, low cost filler was added to bubble gum, and on and on it went. The measured inflation rate did not reflect the quality debasement taking place, but the true inflation rate did.

Another reason why the price controls were weak was because illegal trading could take place on the black market at equilibrium prices. It is not clear just how pervasive this phenomenon was when the Nixon controls were in place, but it certainly occurred. There are reports that restaurants paid above-ceiling prices for beef, and construction firms paid black market prices for concrete and steel. There are also reports of cattle being shipped to Canada, then imported back into the United States. Since the cattle were imported, their prices were not subject to the controls.[6]

Price controls combined with the demand stimulus taking place generated shortages that had to be rationed out. One common method of rationing scarce products was through queue pricing, which means waiting to purchase a good or service. Perhaps the most famous example of this process was the gasoline lines-- drivers lined up and waited, sometimes for hours, to buy gas. Home construction was held up by shortages of plumbing fixtures, especially toilets. Commercial buildings worth millions of dollars experienced construction delays due to shortages of steel reinforcing bars costing just a few thousand dollars per building.

The existence of queue pricing meant that buyers were paying prices that were, in many cases, substantially higher than the listed prices. Consider, for example, the gasoline lines. When motorists finally reached the pump they bought gas at the controlled price, but what about the value of their time spent waiting in line, the gasoline burned while waiting, and the general frustration of dealing with the situation? The true price paid, which includes all of the costs involved in the transaction, was far higher than just the price per gallon listed on the pump. In other words, price controls may have held down the measured inflation rate, but they did not control the true inflation rate.

6.4 Phase What?

> *When I saw the price on chicken I got mad. Then I got scared. Then, I grabbed the three that were left before somebody else got them.*
> *—A supermarket shopper in California ("Meat Shortage: When Will it End?"* U.S. News and World Report, *August 13, 1973, 15).*

The wage and price controls were ultimately divided into four phases. The initial ninety-day freeze on wages and prices was called Phase I, and during this period the only products exempted were raw agricultural products because their prices were notoriously volatile, and finished imports and exports because their prices could not be controlled. Phase I garnered widespread public support because the public felt relief from the inflation. In addition, the wage and price freeze was in effect for just ninety-days, so no major shortages developed.

The clothing industry was one of the few problem areas during the Phase I. In fact, this case illustrates some of the difficulties with price controls. During the ninety-day freeze, the new fall fashions were being introduced. By the rules of Phase I, the price of an item such as a woman's wool skirt was supposed to be the same as the price of a wool skirt sold the previous fall. However, in the absence of rigorous administration there was difficulty determining the price of items sold the year before. Plus, fashions change from year-to-year, meaning that in many cases the new skirts were not identical to the ones sold the year before. For these reasons, the price freeze was ineffective in the clothing industry, in fact, clothing prices rose faster during Phase I than they had been during the six month period prior to the freeze (Rockoff, 1984, p. 206). However, for the economy as a whole, prices and wages were virtually unchanged during Phase I.

Phase I expired on November 14, 1971, and Phase II went into effect. This was the longest of the four phases, lasting until January 11, 1973. Phase II allowed wage and price increases, but only in moderate amounts. Firms could raise prices to cover cost increases, but price hikes that raised profit margins above what they had been during a base period were not allowed.[7] As was the case during Phase I, raw agricultural products were exempted, along with exports and imports. Wage increases of up to 5.5 percent were allowed, when fringe benefits were included the limit was 6.2 percent.

The inflation rate was fairly stable during Phase II, in large part because the economy was operating near capacity during the first half of 1972. Annualized CPI inflation, which was 1.9 percent during Phase I, rose to 4.8 percent during the first three months of Phase II because there was some "catch up" taking place. During the remainder of Phase II annualized CPI inflation was 3.4 percent. The inflation rate during 1971 had been 3.3 percent.

According to Cagan (1979, 165-168), the most successful feature of Phase II was that it reduced expected inflation which helped hold down collectively-bargained wage increases. For example, negotiated wage increases for construction workers averaged 6.0 percent during 1972, well below what it had been the previous two years. In addition, during 1972 just 20 percent of workers under new wage agreements received more than a 9.0 percent pay hike during the first year of their contracts.

Phase III began in January 1973 and lasted until June. It consisted of a general loosening of controls: mandatory compliance was dropped, except in the food processing industry, construction, and health care. Established guidelines for all other industries were similar to the rules of Phase II. It was during Phase III that the price controls began to lose public support. The problem was an overheated economy, largely the result of the expansionary monetary growth that began in 1970. According to Gordon's (2000) estimates, the U.S. economy reached full employment during the first quarter of 1972, and was well above full employment by the end of that year and during all of 1973. As a result, inflation began to accelerate, significantly during the first quarter of 1973 which just so happened to be when Phase II ended and Phase III began. The public blamed the inflation problem on the fact that Phase II had expired, but in reality the overheated economy had much more to do with the inflation buildup.

Prices of a wide array of products rose rapidly during Phase III, but food prices attracted the most attention. The food component of the CPI, which had risen 4.7 percent during all of 1972, rose dramatically in the early months of 1973: 2.1 percent in January, 1.9 percent in February, and another 2.6 percent in March. The public was angry, focusing much of their verbiage on meat prices. By early April, hamburger meat cost 20 percent more than it had during Phase I, the price of ham had risen 26 percent, the price of veal was up 17 percent, and lamb prices had increased 12 percent.[8]

One reason why food prices rose so rapidly was because the demand for food was increasing along with income. Even though food is a necessity, household spending on it rises along with income.[9] This rise in income and the demand for food was not confined to just the United States; economies around the world were booming which drove up the world demand for food. In fact, this is an unusual feature of the world economy during the early 1970s: virtually every country experienced a major expansion.[10] Using the G-7 industrialized countries as examples, during 1972, real GDP growth rates ranged from a high of 8.7 percent (Japan) to a low of 3.1 percent (Italy). In 1973 the rates ranged from 10.2 percent (Japan) to 5.3 percent (West Germany).[11]

Another reason why food prices rose was because, on the supply side, a number of unusual weather-related incidents during 1972 and 1973 worked to reduce food output. A drought in Asia and the Soviet Union during 1972 reduced world grain output by 3.0 percent. The Soviet Union, and to a lesser extent China, responded by purchasing large quantities of U.S. grain. During July and August of 1972, the Soviets purchased a volume of U.S. wheat roughly equivalent to 30 percent of the average U.S. output during the previous five years (Luttrell 1973, 2). The U.S. Plains states experienced severe blizzards during the winter of 1972-1973 that resulted in the deaths of over 200,000 head of cattle. This factor helped drive up beef prices. The spring of 1973 featured severe flooding in the Mississippi River valley which significantly reduced farmers ability to plant corn, cotton, wheat, and rice, as well as making it difficult to harvest timber.[12] In addition, anchovies, which are an important input into animal feed, disappeared from their normal feeding grounds off the coast of Peru. The cost of animal feeds rose significantly as a result. Also, food processing and marketing costs were rising because of higher labor costs and increased prices of packaging materials.

Americans were long used to enjoying a gradual decline in the proportion of income allocated toward food expenditures, but in early 1973 the proportion was rising. Shoppers went to supermarkets and paid noticeably higher prices than they had just a few weeks before. There were organized meat boycotts; shoppers signed petitions where they pledged to not eat meat two days a week. Demonstration marches in support of these boycotts were held in several cities. Many Americans purchased lower cost substitutes for beef and pork, in fact retailers specializing in horsemeat reported that their sales doubled.[13] The outcry over food prices put pressure on Nixon to once again "do something." Many Democrats in Congress, as well as AFL-CIO President George Meany, wanted another freeze on prices. In March, Nixon responded to the pressure by announcing a freeze on retail prices of beef, pork, and lamb. However, this action just generated shortages because animal farmers responded by withholding their livestock from the market. They were waiting for the freeze to end and prices to rise. American shoppers grew even more frustrated and angry.

On June 18th, Nixon imposed the second economy-wide freeze on prices, just two weeks after the U.S. Secretary of Agriculture said that only "damn fools" would advocate more price ceilings.[14] This one was dubbed "Freeze II," and it froze the prices of all goods and services except rents and raw agricultural goods. This freeze was scheduled to last no more than sixty days. Wages were exempt, but were supposed to follow the earlier guidelines of no more than 5.5 percent annual increases. A few days later Nixon announced an embargo on exports of soybeans and cottonseeds, two important inputs into animal feed. Halting exports of these items was supposed to provide some relief against rising animal feed prices. Soybean prices had more than doubled during the previous six months.

Public support for the price controls collapsed during Freeze II. The economy had become so overheated by the summer of 1973 that the price freeze generated major shortages of several products. The business community opposed the freeze because by fixing prices but not wages, they expected their profit margins to get squeezed. They also contended that lower profits would reduce investment spending. Consumers did not believe the freeze would provide any long-run relief against inflation because they feared (rightfully so) that prices would explode once the freeze was lifted.

The meat shortages grew even worse during Freeze II. Livestock farmers continued to withhold animals from the market. In addition, chicken growers destroyed hundreds of thousands of baby chicks because the high cost of feed made them unprofitable. When shoppers found meat they often bought as much as they could in anticipation of further shortages. Americans' desire to hoard meat resulted in a one-year wait to purchase a deep freezer.

Most food prices were decontrolled on July 12th, and the general freeze was dropped on August 12th. The increase in food prices between July 12th and August 12th was so dramatic that during the sixty days of Freeze II (June 12th through August 12th, 1973) the annualized CPI inflation rate was 12.1 percent, even though food and rents were the only prices not frozen! (Rockoff 1984, 213). Here are the annualized percentage wholesale price increases of selected food products for the year ending August 15, 1973:[15]

Wheat	195 %
Corn	133 %
Soybeans	168 %
Steers	55 %
Hogs	102 %
Broiler Chickens	153 %

Source: Luttrell (1973, 3).

Phase IV began on August 12th when the general freeze was lifted. By this time the Nixon administration viewed the controls as a dismal failure. They had not checked inflation noticeably, the public no longer supported them, and shortages had become a serious problem. Thus, the purpose of Phase IV was to gradually remove the controls which was done on an industry-by-industry basis. At the outset, several industries, including public utilities, lumber, and copper scrap, were decontrolled. Then gradually, one industry after another was freed from the system with the notable exception of petroleum.[16] Ironically, during Phase IV the controlled industries were monitored much more closely than had been the case under Phase III.

The great experiment with wage and price controls finally ended on April 30, 1974 when the Economic Stabilization Act expired. As a final tally, here are the annualized rates of change of the CPI and nominal wages during the various phases of the Nixon controls:

Period	CPI	Wages
Phase I (8/71-11/71)	1.3 %	4.5 %
Phase II (11/71-1/73)	3.5 %	8.8%
Phase III (1/73-6/73)	8.7 %	3.6 %
Freeze II (6/73-8/73)	12.1%	3.0 %
Phase IV (8/73-4/74)	9.6 %	6.8 %

Source: Rockoff (1984, 213).

CHAPTER 7

■■■

Energy Crisis, Act I: Price Controls, Import Quotas, and the Oil Embargo

Our American energy crisis is a counterfeit crisis thrust onto the American people by a politicized elite who have more ambition than common sense.
—Antony C. Sutton (1979, 2)

The worst gas line I waited in lasted three hours. The line crossed a driveway to an apartment complex, and the cars in line were keeping the driveway clear. A woman drove out of the apartment complex and cut in the line. Immediately, a man jumped out of one of the cars she'd cut in front of. He went over to her car and opened the door and beat the tar out of her. Everyone who saw it happen was so angry at the woman that no one made a move to help her.
—N. Ardizonne, as told to the author.

Looking back on the 1970s, few problems experienced that decade were more absurd than the so-called energy crisis. Major hikes in energy prices occurred, along with shortages of petroleum products and natural gas. The most-publicized manifestation of these shortages were the infamous gasoline lines where motorists queued up, sometimes for hours, waiting for an opportunity to purchase gasoline. Naturally, tempers grew short and a few people were actually shot to death when arguments broke out because people had cut in line. The whole affair was incredibly wasteful and inefficient because in the aggregate Americans spent an enormous amount of time waiting in lines, and burning scarce gasoline while they waited. The really amazing feature of the shortages and gasoline lines, and pretty much the entire energy crisis for that matter, was that it could have been avoided. It was the result of government policy bungling in the form of oil import quotas designed to keep out cheap foreign oil, followed by price controls on natural gas and petroleum. As such, the energy crisis was created by the government of the United States of America.

7.1 Price Controls on Natural Gas

> *One might think it difficult to find a market that has been more thoroughly distorted by regulation than the crude oil market, but this is not the case. The natural gas market has been even more systematically deformed, disfigured, and wrenched out of shape as a result of a longer period of even more perverse price controls than ever existed for crude oil.*
> *—James M. Griffen and Henry B. Steele (1986, 298).*

> *Fedders Corp. said it recently had to close for several days two appliance plants in Illinois, each employing about 1,600 workers. The plants' natural gas service was interrupted...*
> *—"Warmer Weather Alleviates Fuel Shortage But Cold Spell Would Hit Big Users Again."* The Wall Street Journal, *December 21, 1972*

To help understand how the government ended up regulating natural gas prices and creating shortages, it is useful to examine the industry's history. Commercial natural gas production dates to the early 1800s when producers ran small pipes from gas wells or plants that manufactured gas from coal, and distributed it within towns. It was primarily used for home cooking and lighting. In the early days it was not an important energy source because its use was restricted to local areas. The technology to transport major quantities over long distances did not exist.

Advancements in pipeline technology during the 1920s and 1930s allowed natural gas to become an important energy source. The development of both high-tensile steel and electric welding made it possible to build large, long, air-tight pipelines that could move major amounts of gas at high pressure. In addition, more powerful compressors were developed to push the gas through the pipes. As a result, during the 1920s and early 1930s pipelines were built between the gas fields of Louisiana, Texas, and Oklahoma, to the population centers in the Northeast, Great Lakes States, and California.

Once in operation, several states argued that these pipelines constituted a natural monopoly. They correctly maintained that the high fixed costs of building a pipeline resulted in a situation where it made economic sense to have just one pipeline serve an area. This argument was used as the justification to regulate pipeline prices. However, in a series of court cases during the 1920s, these state regulations were ruled unconstitutional by the U.S. Supreme Court on the grounds that they interfered with interstate commerce. Thus, interstate pipelines remained unregulated, although several states regulated prices of intrastate gas.[1]

During the 1930s, Congress received numerous complaints about questionable practices by pipeline companies. Independent gas producers claimed they could not sell their gas to pipeline companies that were also operating gas wells or involved in joint ventures with other gas producers. When pipeline companies did buy from independent operators, there were complaints that they paid prices that were too low. Meanwhile, at the other end of the pipeline, gas users argued that they paid prices that were too high. There were also claims that pipeline companies diverted gas away from producing-states (because their prices were regulated by their own state governments) and toward the unregulated interstate market where prices were higher. As evidence that this was true, West Virginia had the most severe shortages at the time, even though it was a major gas-producing state. (Browne and Syron 1976, 46). In addition, many blamed rising gas prices in the interstate market on the monopoly pipeline companies.

Congress responded to these complaints by directing the Federal Trade Commission (FTC) to study the issue of natural gas pipelines. The FTC released their report in 1935, and it concluded that the pipelines were natural monopolies and should be regulated.

This report helped persuade Congress to pass the 1938 Natural Gas Act. This law gave the newly-created Federal Power Commission (FPC) the authority to set rates that pipeline companies could charge for transporting gas across state lines. This part of the act made economic sense because the pipelines were natural monopolies. However, an important aspect of the act is what it did not do: provide third parties with access to pipeline facilities (Pierce, 1988, p. 6-7). In other words, it did not allow gas producers or users to insist that pipeline companies transport the gas for them. Instead, pipeline companies could require gas producers to sell them the gas, then transport and re-sell it.[2] Another problem with the act was that it did not address the case of companies that operated interstate pipelines and produced gas. Companies that do both and possess a monopoly pipeline have an incentive to practice transfer pricing where the pipeline 'pays' a high price for the gas to its subsidiary (and earns the monopoly profit on the unregulated gas well), and then transports the gas to users through the regulated pipeline and charges users a monopoly price.

This issue of companies that both operated pipelines and produced gas was at the heart of the 1947 U.S. Supreme Court case *Interstate Natural Gas Co. v. FPC* where the court ruled that the Federal Power Commission could regulate gas prices that pipeline companies paid to their gas-producing subsidiaries. This ruling raised concerns among independent gas producers that FPC regulation of their gas prices was next, so they lobbied Congress for a permanent exemption. A bill passed in 1950 stating that independent gas producers' prices could not be regulated by the FPC. However, President Truman vetoed the bill, "based on reasoning that continues to mystify economists" (Pierce 1988, 7). Truman apparently thought that a gas shortage would develop in the future, and that price controls would alleviate the problem!

The independent producers' worst fears were confirmed in 1954 when the Supreme Court ruled in *Phillips Petroleum v. Wisconsin* that the FPC should regulate sales between independent gas producers and pipeline companies. A majority of the Court felt that the 1938 Natural Gas Act required the FPC to regulate all field sales of gas bound for interstate commerce. The following year Congress passed another bill exempting independent gas producers from FPC regulations, but President Eisenhower vetoed it. He apparently supported the intent of the bill, but vetoed it because a senator who had opposed it changed his mind and provided the decisive vote in favor after receiving a large payment from a gas producer (Pierce 1988, 8). Thus, Congress' second attempt to exempt independent gas producers from price regulations failed.

So due to the efforts of Congress, the Supreme Court, and the White House, the Federal Power Commission ended up regulating natural gas prices at the wellhead. Initially, the FPC tried to determine ceiling prices for each gas producer based on their historic cost of drilling for, and producing, gas. However, this system was problematic because of the sheer number of cases involved. Cases were put on hold, and the backlog eventually numbered in the thousands. In an effort to expedite the process, in 1961 the FPC changed to a system where they divided the United States into different producing regions, and specified ceiling prices for each one. These ceiling prices were supposed to be based on average production costs, but determining these costs and prices would take several years. Instead, the FPC established interim rates based on past average transaction prices in each region. These prices were put in place and stayed essentially frozen until 1971.

The ceiling prices set in 1961 were close to the equilibrium prices at the time, so it took a number of years before serious market disruptions occurred. In fact, from the end of World War II to the early 1970s, the natural gas industry could only be described as a major success story. Demand growth averaged about 6.5 percent per year, and $17 billion was spent constructing a system of pipelines that transported gas to all of the lower forty-eight states. The proportion of total U.S. energy consumption accounted for by natural gas rose from 13 percent to 33 percent (Federal Power Commission 1972, 319). Users were attracted to it because it was a cheap, clean energy source.

By keeping gas prices constant during the 1960s, the FPC was implicitly assuming that production costs had remained stable. However, this was not true: drilling costs rose as new gas sources became more difficult to find, and costs were also being driven up by the inflation taking place during the decade. With the federal government regulating natural gas prices, the interstate market was now more regulated than the intrastate market, and prices of intrastate gas rose relative to prices of interstate gas. Natural gas was increasingly being diverted for use within the states where it was produced, and away from the interstate market. At the same time, price controls were having a noticeable impact on exploration for new gas: total gas reserves peaked in 1967 and declined thereafter (Browne and Syron 1976, 46). Also, new gas discoveries that did take place were often committed to the intrastate market instead of the interstate market.

Market imbalances began to appear in the late 1960s, and became noticeable shortages by the early 1970s. In an effort to stimulate development of new reserves, the Federal Power Commission raised the ceiling prices of interstate gas in 1971. However, the price increases were small, so the shortages of interstate gas persisted and then worsened because consumption was still being encouraged thanks to price controls. Here are the nominal and real ceiling prices of a thousand cubic feet of south Louisiana onshore gas from 1960-1972:[3]

Year	nominal price	real price
1960	$0.212	$0.224
----	------	------
1967	$0.212	$0.212
1968	$0.212	$0.207
1969	$0.212	$0.199
1970	$0.212	$0.192
1971	$0.260	$0.228
1972	$0.260	$0.218

Source: Browne and Syron (1976, 47). The real price is the nominal price divided by the consumer price index (CPI).

The 1971 hike in the ceiling price raised the real price, but high U.S. inflation during 1972 brought the real price back down. In fact, the real price in 1972 was below the level in 1960. The small increase in the ceiling price was a completely inadequate solution to the problem. What was necessary was either a much more substantial rise in the ceiling price, or better yet, complete deregulation of wellhead natural gas prices.

As time wore on, the shortages worsened. Demand continued to grow because the expanding world economy raised the demand for energy products. Keeping gas prices artificially low stimulated demand even further. In addition, the role of natural gas was enhanced by the heightened awareness about environmental issues which culminated in the passage of the Clean Air and Water Quality Improvement Acts in 1970. Natural gas is a much cleaner burning fuel than coal and oil, so the move towards improved air quality caused a shift toward natural gas, especially in the electrical-generating industry where gas use rose 37 percent from 1967-1972. Meanwhile, supply growth stagnated because the price controls discouraged the search for new gas supplies. The situation deteriorated to the point that proven reserves in the lower forty eight states dropped 10 percent from 1967-1970. A 1972 Federal Power Commission report (1972, 319) states that 95 percent of proven gas reserves were committed to existing sales contracts. In other words, only a small proportion of proven gas reserves were available to commit to new customers or add volume to existing customers. The natural gas boom that had been going on since the end of World War II was coming to a screeching halt, thanks in large part to price controls.

In 1972, two members of the Federal Power Commission announced that they favored the elimination of price controls on natural gas (De Marchi 1981, 414). They were hardly alone: the vast majority of energy economists recognized that federal wellhead price controls were detrimental. There were widespread calls for decontrol.

Why did Congress not take the logical step to end the natural gas shortages by simply eliminating the price controls? The answer is that, as usual, politics won out over economic reasoning. Natural gas price controls were a regional issue pitting southern gas-producing states (Louisiana-Texas-Oklahoma) against gas-consuming states (the Northeast and Great Lakes region). Decontrol would have allowed gas prices to rise, which in turn would have caused a transfer of purchasing power from gas consumers to gas producers. For this reason, politicians from southern states tended to favor deregulation, while northern interests, led by organized labor and liberals, opposed it. Due to their greater numbers, the northern interests won out.[4]

Therefore, a system of stagnant price controls on natural gas managed to create an artificial shortage of an energy source which is abundant in North America, burns clean, and is easy to transport once pipelines are in place. This shortage created all sorts of distortions in the U.S. economy, the costs of which are impossible to determine. Some firms relocated to gas-producing states so they would have reliable service. There were service disruptions to industrial users that led to temporary plant closings. New homes could not get hooked up to gas service. The United States actually began importing liquified natural gas (LNG) from abroad at a cost "perhaps five to ten times the going rates" (Tussing and Barlow 1984, 91). In sum, the natural gas price controls were a complete failure; they not only created all sorts of economic distortions, they also managed to ruin the growth of a promising U.S. energy source as well. And if that's not a sad enough litany, there's more: the problems grew even worse during the late 1970s.[5]

7.2 Distortions in the Oil Market

> *In 1959 the situation was that foreign oil was cheap and plentiful; domestic oil was, relatively speaking, expensive and scarce. So what did we do? We kept out the cheap plentiful oil and we encouraged domestic oil by imposing a quota on the*

> *amount of oil that could be imported from abroad...*
>
> *Now comes 1973 and what happens? Foreign oil becomes scarce and expensive; domestic oil becomes, relatively speaking, cheap and available. So what do we do in the full wisdom of the government? We impose a tax on the production of domestic oil and give a subsidy to importing the expensive, scarce foreign oil. If you could think of more perverse policies, you have a better imagination than I have.*
>
> *—Milton Friedman (1978, 147-148)*

7.2.A Import Quotas

To better understand how the United States ended up with an oil crisis and fell victim to the Organization of Petroleum Exporting Countries (OPEC), it is useful to have some background on U.S. energy policy towards the petroleum industry. It turns out that OPEC probably would not even exist if the United States had avoided certain policy moves during the late 1950s.

The United States began extracting oil and using it as an important energy source in the 1860s.[6] In fact, the commercial development of oil resources was partly the result of the substitution effect in action. Prior to the formation of the petroleum industry, Americans illuminated their homes by burning whale oil in lamps. However, excessive whale hunting reduced the supply of whale oil, so its price increased. This, in turn, generated demand for lower cost substitutes. Kerosene, which is a petroleum derivative, filled the role.

The petroleum industry grew rapidly during the late 1800s as more and more petroleum products were burned in lamps, used as stove oil in areas of the country where wood was unavailable (e.g., West Texas), and in railroad signal lamps. However, it wasn't until the early 1900s when the internal combustion engine became widely used that the industry took on major importance. The use of petroleum products accelerated during World War I when large numbers of airplanes and diesel-powered submarines were built. Then, during the 1920s the automobile became a staple of American life.

Throughout this period the United States produced enough petroleum to satisfy domestic needs, plus export some to Europe. Over time, however, growing U.S. demand caused larger and larger proportions of U.S. output to be consumed domestically. As U.S. exports declined,

European demand was increasingly met by imports from Middle Eastern sources (which began producing in the early 1900s). By the 1940s, U.S. domestic oil production no longer satisfied domestic demand, so imported oil began entering the country in sizable amounts.

An inherent problem in the petroleum industry is over-pumping oil wells. Oil well owners have an incentive to pump out oil at rates faster than is optimal because the oil may extend beneath their neighbor's land. The owners want to pump the oil and claim it as their own before their neighbor does. This behavior causes problems, however. One is that pumping the oil out quickly lowers the pressure in the well which can reduce the total amount of oil that is recovered over the life of the well. Another problem is that recovering oil involves pumping out water which is often polluted. This polluted water was often dumped onto the land or into streams. A third problem is that the incentive to over-pump can lead to overinvestment in oil wells.

In an effort to control these problems, states set up systems of prorationing, where oil well operators were told what proportion of their maximum efficient rate of production (MER) they could produce each month.[7] The idea was to ensure that oil was recovered, but not too quickly. States had different systems, but the essence was that state commissions used various criteria to determine the maximum efficient rate of output from wells, and then used estimates of monthly oil demand to determine what proportion of wells' MERs could be produced each month. For example, in 1948 Texas (which produced a large proportion of total U.S. output) allowed oil wells to produce at 100 percent of their MERs. The next year, because of lower estimates of demand, just 65 percent of MERs were allowed. The federal government sanctioned this system by passing a law in 1935 stating that oil produced above the amounts set by state rules could not be sold across state lines.

While the impetus for the prorationing system was to control production by reducing the incentive to overproduce, an important side effect was to maintain U.S. oil prices above prices elsewhere in the world. During the 1950s the price of a barrel of domestically-produced crude oil ranged between from around \$2.50 to \$3.00 per barrel.[8] Meanwhile, oil was available from the Middle East at much lower cost. According to Griffen and Steele (1986, 106-107), during the late 1940s and early 1950s, production costs in Saudi Arabia were about \$.10 to \$.20 per barrel, plus taxes owed to the Saudi government of around \$.50 per barrel. Since there were no restrictions on importing oil into the United States, a company like Chevron that operated in Saudi Arabia could produce a barrel of oil there for about \$.70 (including taxes), ship it to the United States, and sell it at a market price of around \$2.50.[9] Not surprisingly, these high profit margins caused a dramatic increase in U.S. petroleum imports from the Middle East.

The importation of low cost Middle Eastern oil put a squeeze on U.S. independent oil producers. They did not operate in the Middle East, so they lacked access to low-cost foreign oil. The demand for their relatively expensive oil was falling, so they began abandoning unprofitable wells and cutting back on drilling for new oil. U.S. domestic oil production declined as a result. By the mid 1950s, the financial squeeze on domestic producers had become severe, so they teamed up with U.S. coal producers to lobby Congress for protection from cheap imported oil. President Eisenhower responded by imposing voluntary import restrictions on oil in 1956, but this approach failed to stop the decline in domestic oil production. So in 1959 he invoked mandatory restrictions on oil imports at levels below those of 1957 and 1958. The scheme was later altered so that east of the Rocky Mountains, imports could be a maximum of 12.2 percent of that region's domestic output, while west of the Rockies, the import quota was the difference between estimated demand and estimated U.S. and Canadian production in the region.

These oil import quotas caused the United States to produce and consume more domestic oil than would have been the case otherwise. In fact, critics called the policy "drain America first," a reference to the fact that using up U.S. reserves at a faster rate would make the country more dependent on foreign sources in the future. In addition, the import quotas harmed U.S. consumers by raising energy prices above what they otherwise would have been.

7.2.B The Formation of OPEC

> *The birth of OPEC was viewed as an unimportant event, given only a four-inch, single-column account on one of the back pages of the New York Times.*
> *—James M. Griffin and Henry B. Steele (1986, 110).*

The U.S. import quotas had a great deal to do with the formation of OPEC. Middle Eastern governments taxed profits earned by international oil companies on production inside their country. These taxes were based on the difference between the posted price and the production cost. The posted price, which is the oil companies' asking price, should not be confused with the transaction price, which is the price actually paid. This distinction between posted and transactions prices is an important part of the story about OPEC.

Attracted by the high profitability of oil production, several hundred small companies were formed after World War II and began drilling for oil in various parts of the world. Within a few years, the major international oil companies faced significant competition from these smaller firms. In 1950, the seven major oil companies produced 98.3 percent of the world's oil output, but by 1957 their share had dropped to 89 percent (Griffin and Steele 1986, 106). Increased world production pushed down the transactions price of a barrel of Saudi Arabian crude, from about $2.20 in 1947 to $1.70 by 1950. In 1950, prices were officially posted in the Middle East for purposes of determining taxes, and the posted prices were roughly equal to transactions prices. Transactions prices remained fairly stable for the next several years.

The situation began to change in 1957, however, when an economic recession in Europe and the United States reduced the demand for oil. Transactions prices fell in 1957, and then declined even further in 1958.[10] Despite falling transactions prices, the oil companies maintained the same posted prices (and accepted reduced profits) because they thought the decline in transactions prices was temporary. Another reason the oil companies held posted prices constant was because there was always the implied threat that countries they operated in would nationalize their oil industries. Keeping posted prices stable meant that tax revenue to the oil-producing countries' governments did not decline significantly.

The world petroleum supply kept rising during the late 1950s, so prices didn't rebound as the international oil companies had hoped. Their profit margins continued to get squeezed, so in February, 1959 they finally lowered posted prices. The next month, the U.S. oil import quota was imposed which caused U.S. demand for imported oil to fall, so foreign oil prices continued their downward slide. That summer Venezuela—which had been a major oil exporter to the United States and was thus badly harmed by the import quota—proposed to other oil-producing countries that they meet in Cairo, Egypt to form an Organization of Petroleum Exporting Countries (Barber 1981, 254-255). The impetus for the countries to actually meet and form OPEC occurred in

August, 1960 when the international oil companies cut posted prices again. OPEC was formed a month later.

Originally, the organization had just five members: Venezuela, Saudi Arabia, Kuwait, Iran, and Iraq. Several other countries joined during the ensuing years, and by 1971 all the major oil exporting countries except Canada had joined. OPEC's goal was to set the world price of oil and maintain it by allocating production quotas among member countries. Yet during OPEC's early years this was virtually impossible to achieve because of disagreements among members as to what the price should be. In addition, excess production capacity existed in the United States and Canada, which meant that any output shortfalls from OPEC could be made up by North American producers. Also, there was plenty of transport equipment available around the world, so if one country (or group of countries) tried to withhold oil production, other producers could make up the shortfall and ship it where needed.

During the 1960s and early 1970s several factors worked to enhance OPEC's position as a cartel. First and foremost, the world's demand for oil grew rapidly. Economic output boomed during the 1960s which caused the demand for petroleum in the noncommunist world to roughly double. This expansion in oil consumption continued during the early 1970s, especially in the United States as the economic growth rate soared and price controls on petroleum products which encouraged consumption were in force beginning in 1971. U.S. oil consumption rose 20 percent just from 1969-1973 (Cochrane and Griepentrog 1981, 694). Several factors, many associated with the economic boom, caused this huge rise in demand. The natural gas shortage led home builders to install furnaces that burned oil instead of gas. Also, both the number of, and average size of, automobiles on U.S. highways increased. Air travel expanded which raised aviation fuel usage. The dramatic increase in petroleum consumption caused excess capacity in the U.S. and Canadian oil industries to decline to the point of being virtually nonexistent by 1971.

Other factors working in OPEC's favor included the fact that the Suez Canal, which is an important shipping lane for oil tankers traveling between the Persian Gulf and the Mediterranean Sea, had been closed since the 1967 Arab-Israeli War. OPEC's position was also enhanced by their own lack of excess capacity; while the Middle Eastern countries held huge oil reserves, demand had grown so rapidly during the late 1960s and early 1970s that their productive capacity barely kept up with demand.

Thus, by late 1971 OPEC was in a very strong position. If they cut oil production to drive up prices, the complete lack of excess production capacity elsewhere in the world would make it virtually impossible for other countries to make up the shortfall in the near term. In addition, with price controls in place in the United States, even if world oil prices went up, ceiling prices took away the incentive to develop new domestic sources. So OPEC held all the cards, but did not play them until October, 1973.

7.3 The Oil Embargo

> *At a classically chic diplomatic dinner in a stately residence on Washington's Embassy Row...the conversation flowed as easily as the vintage French wine. The guests, all elegantly dressed, were a sprinkling of the capital's elite...The host...was Ardeshir Zahedi, Iran's Ambassador to the U.S. There was a pearl-sized gray caviar from the Caspian, of course. But the most remarked-upon item was the menu itself: it was lavishly printed on oversize imitation American dollar bills, British 5 [pound] notes, Swedish crowns and twelve other currencies. And dessert might have symbolized the grand new wealth of an oil power: a chocolate mousse topped by a miniature money tree, festooned with artificial gold coins.*
> —*"Trying to Cope with the Looming Crisis."* Time, *October 14, 1974.*

Despite a colder than normal winter that helped generate widespread fuel shortages and temporary plant closings, the U.S. economic boom continued during 1973:I. Annualized output growth was 9.5 percent that quarter, but inflation was rising.

This high U.S. inflation presented problems for OPEC. Their petroleum revenue source is taxes paid by international oil companies operating in each country, or in cases where the industry was nationalized, from the profits of state-owned companies. These revenues are in the form of U.S. dollars. The difficulty facing OPEC was that the rising U.S. price level reduced the real price of oil. Consider that the price of oil imported into the United States rose just 14 percent from 1960-1972, while over that same period the U.S. GDP deflator rose 42 percent. In other words, the real price of oil fell roughly 28 percent, with much of that decline coming in the late 1960s and early 1970s when U.S. inflation accelerated dramatically.

The oil exporting countries were also harmed by the U.S. dollar devaluation following the collapse of the Bretton Woods agreement in 1971. The trade-weighted dollar fell 7.9 percent in late 1971, and then another 10 percent in early 1973.[11] Following both dollar depreciations OPEC raised oil prices to compensate, but these price hikes did not offset the loss in the value of their existing holdings of dollar-denominated assets. OPEC countries had used many of their "petrodollars" to acquire U.S. Treasury securities, and when the dollar depreciated it reduced the value of U.S. financial assets relative to assets denominated in other currencies.

When these factors are considered, it is not surprising that OPEC was looking for an opportunity to raise their oil revenue. During 1971 they had their big chance because there was no excess capacity in North America, and when President Nixon imposed price controls in August, the incentive to develop new U.S. sources diminished. Even though posted prices were above transactions prices that year, OPEC raised posted prices by 21 percent and the tax rate by about 50 percent. The idea was to capture an increased amount of oil companies profits (Griffin and Steele 1986, 118). The oil companies were left with little choice other than to agree to this change because OPEC threatened to embargo any company that resisted.

The event that led to the embargo occurred in October, 1973 when Egypt and Syria attacked Israel. Tensions in the region had been high for years, with a major issue being the continued Israeli occupation of land they had taken in the 1967 war. Among the territories Israel held as a result of that conflict were the Golan Heights and Sinai Peninsula, which had belonged to Syria and Egypt respectively. On October 6, 1973 Egypt and Syria launched a joint attack on Israel to take back the territories. During the first several days of the war, the Egyptian and Syrian armies experienced success at the expense of the Israelis. A week after the war started the United States announced that it was going to assist Israel by shipping them weapons and supplies.

It happened that two days after the Arab-Israeli war broke out, the Arab members of OPEC were meeting with representatives of the international oil companies to discuss raising posted prices again.[12] The oil companies' representatives were reluctant to agree to such a move, so they requested a two week recess so they could consult with their home offices. While the oil company representatives were gone, the Arab members of OPEC met again on October 16th and simply decided to raise the posted prices by 70 percent, whether the oil companies agreed to it to or not.[13] Such was their power in a time of high demand and no excess capacity.

The Arab members of OPEC announced the oil embargo the following day. They would no longer ship oil to the United States or the Netherlands because both countries were supporting Israel in the war. In addition, oil production would be cut by 5 percent initially, and then 5 percent more each month until Israel withdrew from the occupied territories.

The announcement of the embargo and production cuts set off panic buying. Transactions prices soared above the posted price of $5.12 for

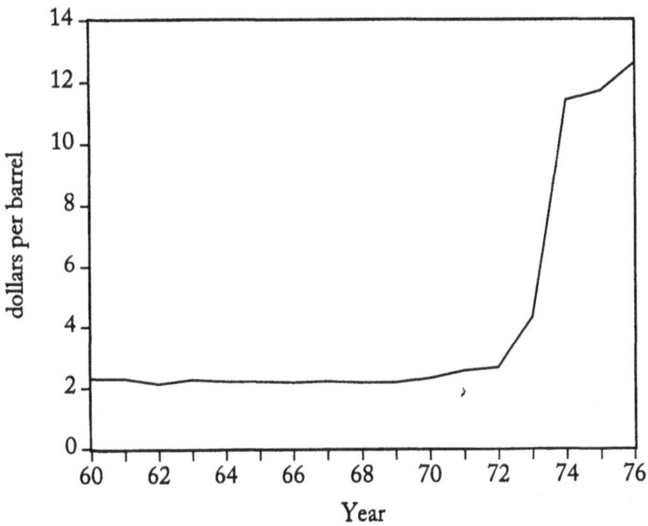

Source: Federal Reserve Board of Govenors

Fig. 7.1 Average Price Per Barrel of Oil Imported Into the United States

Saudi Arabian crude, in some cases barrels of oil were selling in the $15 to $20 range (Griffin and Steele 1986, 120). With transactions prices well above posted prices again, the oil companies were capturing high profits. The exporting countries wanted those profits, so they raised posted prices again, effective January 1, 1974. This time the posted price of Saudi Arabian crude was raised to $11.65. Oil prices had roughly quadrupled over a one-year period, which is shown in figure 7.1.

The price hike caused enormous economic changes. Since the demand for oil is inelastic in the short-run, the price increase was associated with only small reductions in oil usage. As a result, total expenditures on petroleum products soared, and a huge transfer of wealth took place from oil importing countries to oil exporting countries. For example, the value of U.S. oil imports rose from $7.6 billion in 1972 to $24.2 billion in 1973. Saudi Arabia's oil revenue went from $2.7 billion in 1972 to $22.6 in 1974 (Skeet 1988, 241). The share of world financial reserves held by OPEC countries rose from 7.0 percent before the embargo, to 19.0 percent a year later. While consumers around the world were paying significantly higher prices for gasoline, heating oil, airline tickets, and so forth, Saudi Arabian sheiks were treating themselves to virtually any luxury item they desired. Meanwhile, price controls in the United States held the price of petroleum products below their equilibrium prices which resulted in shortages and gasoline lines.

7.4 The U.S. Policy Response: More Controls

One obvious way to help end the energy crisis was to eliminate price controls on petroleum products. Prices would have risen dramatically, but the gasoline lines and other symptoms of the shortages would have disappeared virtually overnight. However, neither Congress nor the White House were willing to decontrol prices because it would have generated huge increased profits to domestic oil well owners. So even though OPEC countries and the international oil companies were reaping the windfall, it was politically unacceptable for domestic oil well operators to do so. Instead, during Phase IV of the price controls, the Nixon administration devised a scheme that was supposed to accomplish two things: protect consumers from petroleum price increases, and stimulate domestic oil production. The system involved classifying domestic oil into three types: old, new, and released. Old oil referred to production from wells that had been in operation up to 1972, and received a ceiling price of $0.35 above the price on May 15, 1973. New oil was defined as oil from an existing well in excess of the amount produced in 1972, as well as oil from new wells. The price of this oil was not controlled. Released oil was a system where for every barrel of new oil a company produced, one barrel of their old oil was released from price controls.

This system was in effect during the embargo. Since controls existed on unreleased domestic old oil, as world oil prices soared, the U.S. price remained below the world price. For example, in early 1974 imported oil cost $12.52 per barrel while domestic oil carried an average price (of controlled and uncontrolled oil) of $7.18 (Griffen and Steele 1986, 287). This artificially-created difference between the prices of domestic and imported oil generated a whole new set of issues, and the attempted solution caused even greater difficulties.

The problems revolved around the refining industry. Under the Nixon price controls, refiners sold their output at a price based on cost plus a profit markup. Refiners that refined price-controlled old oil into gasoline sold it at lower prices than refiners using imported or new oil. This did not present difficulties for refiners as long as the demand for gasoline was high because consumers would first buy the lower-priced gasoline, but if that was not available they would buy the higher-priced gasoline instead. This was the case during the panic buying of late 1973 and early 1974; consumers were buying up all available gasoline and refiners were receiving their profit margins determined under the Phase IV rules regardless of where they purchased their crude oil.

The situation changed, however, when the embargo was lifted in the spring of 1974. The panic subsided, even though prices of imported oil stayed high because OPEC continued to hold down production. Americans quit topping off their gasoline tanks, and instead returned to more normal purchasing patterns. In addition, the U.S. economy was sliding into a serious recession. These factors caused a decline in the demand for gasoline. Suddenly, refiners who used imported oil had problems selling their gasoline because it was priced high relative to gasoline produced by refiners using old oil. Refiners using high cost oil started complaining to the politicians in Washington, claiming they were operating at a competitive disadvantage.

In response to these complaints, Washington bureaucrats created the infamous entitlements system that went into effect in November, 1974. The idea was simple: equalize crude oil costs for all refiners, that way, no group of refiners would have an unfair advantage over their competitors. A system was set up where a refiner who purchased a barrel of high-cost imported oil was "entitled" to a barrel of low-cost, price-controlled oil. To carry out this policy, the Federal Energy Administration (FEA) determined for all refiners a national average ratio of old oil purchased to total oil purchased. For example, during the first month the program was in existence, the ratio was 41.05, meaning that 41.05 percent of oil used by refiners was old oil (Mead 1976, 157). Then each individual refiner's ratio was calculated. If a refiner had a ratio above 41.05, this meant that they used more old oil than the national average. They had to purchase entitlements to the amount of old oil they used in excess of the national average. These entitlements were paid to refiners who used less than the national average of old oil, the amount subsidizing them as if they had purchased 41.05 percent of their oil at controlled prices. The per-barrel entitlement payment was equal to the average price of imported and new oil minus the controlled price of old oil.[14]

This program created all sorts of perverse effects. Subsidizing refiners that imported oil (because they were being paid by refiners using price-controlled oil) reduced the marginal cost of refining a barrel of imported crude, which led to higher levels of imports. In effect, refiners using imported oil were receiving a subsidy that amounted to between $1.60 and $5.16 per barrel, depending on the market price of imports (Kalt 1981, 58). The program also transferred enormous amounts of wealth between refiners; Kalt (1981, 46) estimates that the amounts averaged $21.1 billion (in 1980$) each year from 1974-1979. In addition, the program required a large bureaucracy to operate it, and also created a political interest group (firms that imported oil) with a vested interest in maintaining the system of price controls on crude oil.[15]

7.5 The Energy Crisis (I) in Sum

The energy crisis and all that followed from it largely resulted from misguided policies carried out in the United States. Import quotas were imposed to keep out cheap Middle Eastern oil, so we used up our own domestic reserves and angered our foreign suppliers. OPEC resulted from that error. Then price controls were imposed, first on natural gas, and later on oil as part of President Nixon's wage and price controls program. Consumption was encouraged, while development of new domestic energy sources was discouraged, making the United States even more dependent on foreign energy sources. Then, the entitlements program was imposed which subsidized oil imports. Meanwhile, the Federal Reserve was overstimulating the U.S. economy, creating inflation and dollar depreciation on foreign currency markets which provided the impetus for OPEC to raise world oil prices. The whole affair represents a textbook case of how not to conduct economic policy.

Rising energy costs were instrumental in helping cause a world-wide recession which is described in the next chapter. In the United States, energy costs soared, although not as much as they would have in the absence of price controls. In addition to rising energy prices, Americans suffered the inconveniences associated with shortages. Consumers were forced to wait in line to buy gasoline, there were widespread plant closings because of fuel shortages, and many schools were forced to close temporarily because the buildings could not be heated properly. Meanwhile, just across the border, Canadians experienced high energy costs, but no shortages because they did not have price controls. In fact, the Canadian government ran a radio advertising campaign urging Americans to vacation in Canada. Among other things, the ads said "there's plenty of gas up here."

The American public was understandably upset over the energy crisis and all the problems associated with it. Yet an interesting part of the story is that the public's wrath was not focused on the root causes of the problem: perverse U.S. economic and energy policies that had been in place for decades, along with the more recently-imposed price controls. Instead, their anger was directed at Arabs and the oil companies. The media certainly did not help in this regard; virtually all of the articles about the "energy crisis" in magazines like, *Newsweek*, *Time*, and *U.S. News and World Report* never mention price controls and poor energy policies as causes.[16] The politicians in Washington did not help either: rather than looking in the mirror for the cause of the crisis, many instead blamed the oil companies, claiming they were "ripping off" American consumers. As a result, the focus during the crisis was not on the root causes of the problem, so the perverse energy policies remained in place which is a major reason why the United States had a second energy crisis just a few years later.[17]

CHAPTER 8

■■■

The 1973–1975 Recession

> *The economic outlook for 1974 is a distressing one. Unemployment is going up. Interest rates are at exorbitant levels. Housing is in a state of depression. The energy shortage is causing great disruption, and food prices continue their sharp increases. I don't recall any time since the depression of the 1930s that the American people were so troubled by the state of the economy.*
>
> *—Congressman Wright Patman (D-Texas), Chairman of the Joint Economic Committee of the U.S. Congress (U.S. Congress 1974, 1).*

The perverse economic policies described in the previous chapters were instrumental in causing the recession that took place from November 1973 to March 1975. It was a serious downturn, ranking with the 1981-1982 contraction as the most severe of the post World War II era. GDP fell 4.4 percent, and the unemployment rate peaked at 9.0 percent. Not only was the recession associated with falling aggregate real income and widespread worker layoffs, it was also accompanied by rising inflation which further eroded household purchasing power. For this reason, few American families escaped hardship.

Several policy mistakes caused the recession. The Federal Reserve's rapid monetary growth during 1971-1972 was followed by tight policies that began in mid-1973. These restrictive monetary policies raised short term interest rates above the Regulation Q ceilings, which severely impacted the construction industry. OPEC didn't help either: the October 1973 oil embargo and resulting rise in petroleum prices raised energy bills for American households and firms, and in doing so dramatically reduced the demand for many other goods and services, especially domestically-produced autos. In fact, that industry--along with construction--bore the brunt of the recession and laid off hundreds of thousands of workers. Many of those people went through the demoralizing experience of long-term unemployment.

If the recession had a silver lining, it was that it was deep enough to reduce inflationary pressures in the U.S. economy. In fact, a substantial disinflation did occur from 1975-1976. Unfortunately the opportunity to keep inflation down was squandered because by 1977 the Federal Reserve was once again working to overstimulate the economy. Thus, it's a sad fact that much of the pain Americans went through during the 1973-1975 recession was largely for naught.

8.1 Aggregate Supply and Demand

The 1973-1975 recession was unusual in that inflation rose while output was falling. During virtually every other recession experienced by the United States during the Twentieth Century, the inflation rate fell.[1] This unusual behavior of inflation led economists to focus their attention on adverse supply-side factors as major causes of the recession.

The major supply-side factor that helped cause the recession was the oil price hike that occurred from 1973-1974. Petroleum is an important energy source that is used to heat buildings, produce electricity, and serve as fuel for automobiles, trucks, agricultural equipment, railroads, and aircraft. In addition, it is an important input into the production of chemicals and plastics. Furthermore, petroleum is a substitute for other energy sources such as coal and natural gas. Thus, a rise in the price of petroleum raises the demand for substitutes which causes their prices to rise as well (assuming price controls are not in effect).

Since energy is an input into virtually every production process you can think of, a major rise in oil prices raises firms' production costs. In other words, the quadrupling of oil prices that began in 1973 caused firms' marginal and average cost schedules to shift up. Businesses reduced output and raised prices, the amounts depending on the energy-intensiveness of the production process. In addition, higher energy prices made some physical capital that was especially energy intensive (for example, large gas-guzzling autos at car-rental agencies) economically obsolete. In the near term, the economy-wide aggregate supply schedule shifted to the left, leading to higher prices and less output. Thus, a recession occurred with a temporarily higher inflation rate.[2]

The situation was made worse by additional adverse supply-side factors taking place in the agricultural sector. As mentioned in chapter 6, in 1972 a drought occurred in Asia, the Soviet Union, and the Midwestern United States which reduced world grain output by about 3.0 percent. This drought was partially responsible for the huge increases in food prices that took place during 1972 and 1973. In addition, anchovies, which are an input into livestock feed, disappeared from their normal feeding grounds off the coast of Peru. This event pushed up the cost of livestock feed which raised the price of meat.

Meanwhile, aggregate demand growth was falling as well. The oil and food price hikes not only raised firms' production costs, they also raised the cost of operating a household. American automobile owners incurred large increases in expenditures on gasoline. The cost of heating a home rose, as did electricity prices.[3] Higher food costs drove up the cost of feeding a family. While in the near-term households made efforts to cut their food bill by purchasing lower quality foods, and reduce their energy consumption by turning down the thermostats in their homes and driving less, the decline in consumption of these products did not begin to offset the price increases.[4] So even though real consumption spending fell from 1973-1974, in nominal terms it rose 9.1 percent with nearly half of that increase accounted for by rising nominal expenditures on food and energy products (Council of Economic Advisors 1976, 190). Over time, of course, Americans became much more energy efficient by adding insulation to their houses, installing more energy-efficient furnaces and appliances, buying smaller cars, and so forth, but that took years to occur.[5] But in the near-term, the rise in food and energy prices caused households to spend more on food and energy which left less available for purchasing other goods and services. In this way, the rise in oil and food prices placed downward pressure on aggregate demand.[6]

Restrictive monetary policy was another factor working to slow aggregate demand growth. Monetary policy became contractionary in mid 1973 because the Federal Reserve started trying to reduce the inflation they had helped create during 1971 and 1972. M2 growth, which had been in the 13.0 percent range during 1971 and 1972, fell to 6.9 percent in 1973, and then to 5.5 percent during 1974. Federal Reserve officials, like so many others in government and business, were slow to realize just how severely the economy was contracting, so they kept fighting the rising inflation brought on by the higher oil and food prices. In this way, the Federal Reserve was pursuing a policy of trying to extinguish the rising U.S. inflation, but in doing so they ended up making the recession worse (Poole 1975).

Fiscal policy was contractionary as well. Since prices were rising faster than output was falling, nominal GDP increased which pushed Americans into higher income tax brackets. Despite the fact that the U.S. economy was in a serious economic recession, federal tax revenue during 1974 increased $35 billion, with personal tax receipts rising 15 percent. According to the Federal Reserve these rising tax receipts "largely reflect[ed] inflation" (Federal Reserve Board of Governors 1975, 6). Thus, the progressive income tax--one of our supposed automatic stabilizers--became an automatic destabilizer. Another reason why taxes rose in 1974 was because the base salary subject to social security withholding taxes rose that year from $10,800 to $13,200. On the spending side, although federal purchases of goods and service rose substantially in nominal terms during 1974, in real terms they fell slightly.

Yet another reason why aggregate demand growth fell was because real financial wealth--which is a determinant of consumption expenditures--dropped precipitously. A combination of accelerating inflation, rising interest rates, and falling corporate profits caused such large declines in stock and bond prices that real financial wealth fell an incredible 33 percent from 1973-1974 (Okun 1975, 210).

Thus, the 1973-1975 recession was caused by a combination of reduced growth of both aggregate supply and demand. The fact that inflation rose during the first several months of the downturn suggests that the supply-side effects dominated the demand side effects. The top panel of figure 8.1 shows the behavior of real GDP and Gordon's (2000) measure of the natural rate of output from 1971 to 1975. Output rose well above the natural rate during the economic boom of 1972-1973 which caused the inflationary buildup shown in the bottom panel. Then, the recession began in late 1973 and inflation shot up due to a combination of the oil price hikes that occurred during late 1973 and early 1974, rising food prices in 1973, and the fact that the price controls expired on April 30, 1974. Inflation eventually topped out at over 12.0 percent in late 1974, then declined because the effects of rising food and oil prices had played out. The recession drove output below the natural rate which set off a disinflation that continued until 1977. The unemployment rate rose, eventually peaking at 9.0 percent in the spring of 1975.

As is so often the case when a recession occurs, it came as a big surprise to American firms. Initially, U.S. manufacturers behaved as if the sales decline would be temporary; they continued to produce goods at high rates and allowed inventories to build up. But by mid-1974 it became apparent that the spending decline was going to persist, so firms slashed output and laid off workers in droves. The unemployment rate, which had been 4.8 percent when the recession began in late 1973, rose

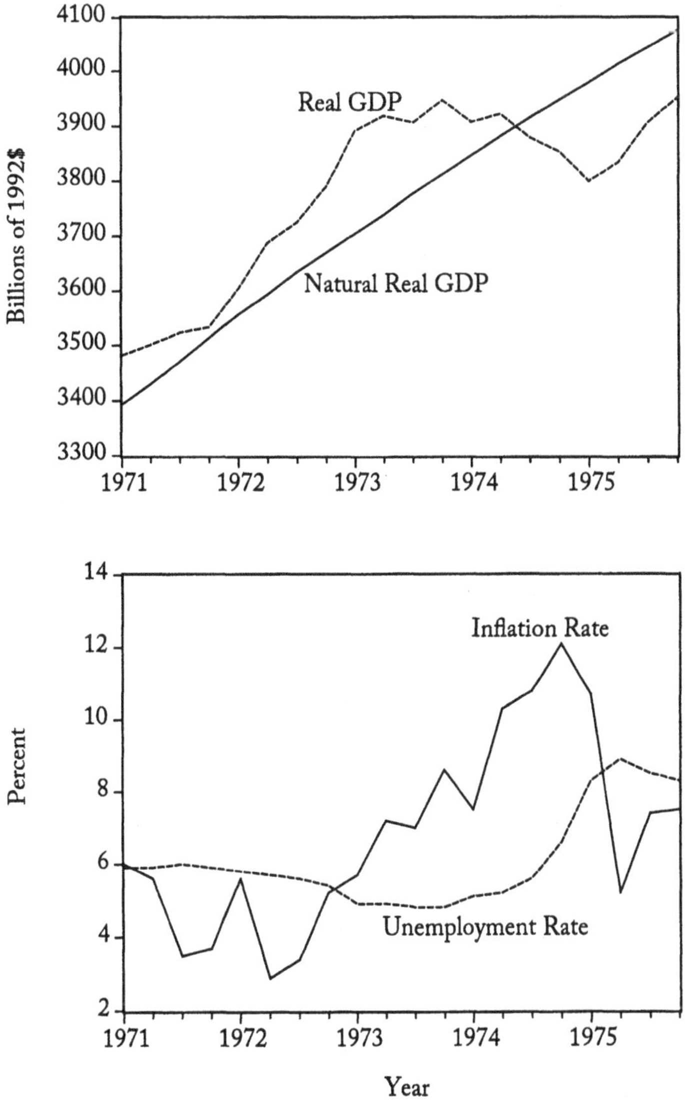

Fig. 8.1 Output, Inflation, and Unemployment 1971.I – 1975.IV

just 0.3 percentage by May 1974. Then, it began to soar:

Month/Year	Unemployment Rate
May 1974	5.1 %
Aug 1974	5.5 %
Nov 1974	6.7 %
Feb 1975	8.0 %
May 1975	8.9 %

Source: Council of Economic Advisors (1976, 199).

Nearly four million jobs were lost during the recession which led to an enormous number of American families being thrown into poverty because of lost wages. Adding insult to injury, the cost of living soared because of rising food and energy prices.

While few escaped the economic misery brought on by the recession, firms and workers in construction and automobile manufacturing bore the brunt of the pain. These two industries are almost always disproportionately harmed during recessions, but their experiences during the 1973-1975 downturn were truly exceptional.

8.2 The Construction Industry

> *First quarter 1975 [housing] starts were at a 991,000 unit seasonally adjusted annual rate, the lowest since third quarter 1946. In that year, this country had 71 million fewer people...*
>
> *Unemployment in the construction industry continues to increase. In May, the construction unemployment rate was 21.8 percent...The residential construction unemployment rate was estimated...to be over 40 percent.*
>
> *—Michael Sumichrast, Chief Economist of the National Association of Homebuilders, testifying before Congress (U.S. Congress 1975, 4-5).*

During the recession the construction industry experienced enormous declines in output and employment. The number of construction workers fell by 1,223,000, and of that number over 200,000 were in homebuilding. This fall in employment indicates only part of the hardship because the problems in construction spread to several other industries whose fortunes were closely tied to it: lumber and other wood products, furniture and fixtures, concrete, drywall, tile, windows, appliances, and a wide array of electrical equipment. Employment declines in construction and these ancillary industries are shown in table 8.1. Taken together, these industries experienced a total job loss of just over two million workers, which is over half the total decline in employment

Table 8.1 - Employment Declines During the 1973-1975 Recession

	Decline in Employment	Dates of Employment Peaks(P) and Troughs (T)
Total Nonfarm Private	*3,774,000*	*12/73(P) - 3/75(T)*
Industry		
Construction	1,223,000	8/73(P) - 3/75(T)
Lumber and Wood Products	220,800	8/73(P) - 2/75(T)
Furniture and Fixtures	116,100	10/73(P) - 3/75(T)
Stone, Clay, and Glass Prod.	120,200	8/73(P) - 3/75(T)
Electrical Equipment	320,200	12/73(P) - 5/75(T)
Tranportation Equipment	321,800	11/73(P) - 2/75(T)

Source: U.S. Department of Labor (1991).

during the recession. When the employment decline in transportation equipment–which is largely automobile and truck production–is included, over 60 percent of the economy-wide decline in private sector non-farm employment is accounted for.

Why was the construction industry hit so hard? One important reason was the huge rise in interest rates that began in 1973. Figure 8.2 shows rates on long-term U.S. government bonds and short-term Treasury bills. Both series rose during 1973 and 1974, especially short-term rates because of higher expected inflation and the Federal Reserve's tight monetary policy that began in 1973. By mid-1973, short-term rates had risen above long-term rates, a familiar sign that an economic slowdown is on the horizon.[7]

The impact of high interest rates on home building is shown in figure 8.3. Short-term rates were above the Regulation Q ceilings by late 1972, but not significantly so. However, by mid-1973 the differential

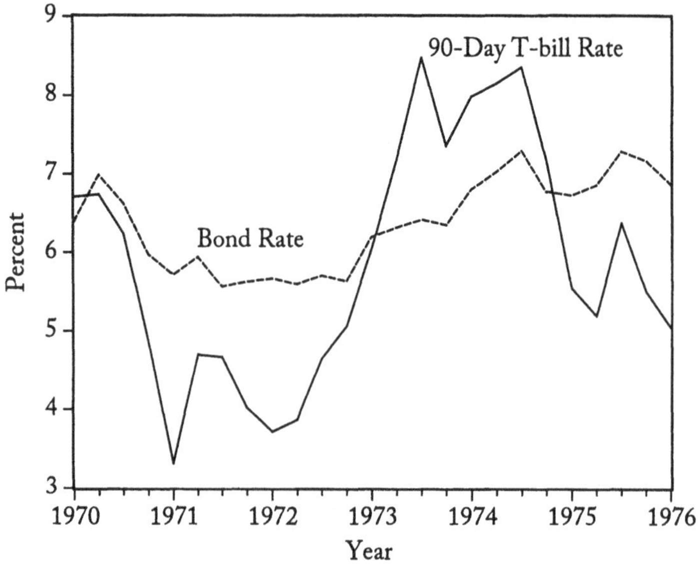

Fig. 8.2 Rates on Long-Term U.S. Government Bonds and 90-Day Treasury Bills, 1970.I – 1976.I

had become large and it stayed high during 1974. Housing starts went into a steady decline, finally bottoming out in early 1975. Housing starts fell from a peak annualized rate of 2.48 million units in January 1973, to a trough of 900,000 units in February 1975.

A considerable amount of construction activity involves building commercial and industrial structures. During the recession, awarded-construction contracts measured in millions of square meters of floor space declined 71 percent (U.S. Department of Commerce 1984, 74). Meanwhile, inflation-adjusted spending on new structures fell by about 25 percent.[8] These declines were caused by high interest rates, a shortage of financing thanks to Regulation Q, plus the fact that falling output reduced the demand for new buildings. Low corporate profits during the recession also worked to reduce construction. One industry that suffered a particularly severe profit squeeze was electrical generation. A combination of rising input costs in the form of higher energy prices,

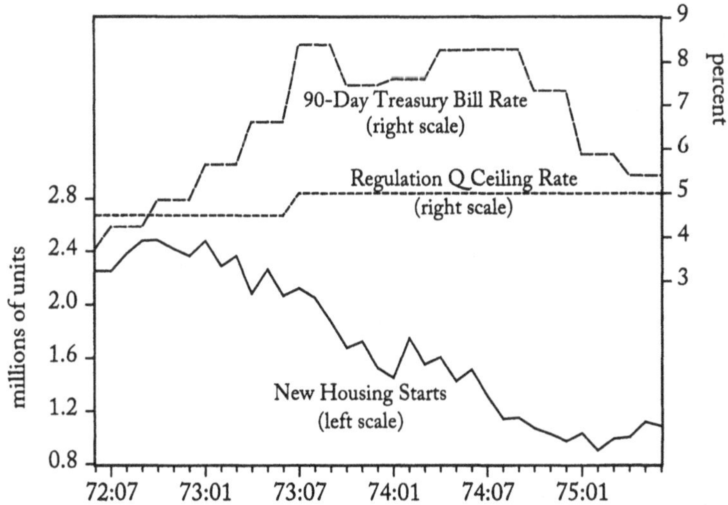

Fig. 8.3 Housing Starts and Interest Rates, 1972–1975

flat demand for electricity as people tried to conserve, and an inability to raise electricity prices because of regulatory impediments, caused a huge reduction in profits. Many industry construction projects already underway were stretched out, and several future projects were canceled (Council of Economic Advisors 1975, 39).

The construction industry was also harmed by major increases in building costs taking place at the time. One major source of rising costs was higher wages paid to construction workers. Due in large-part to labor agreements negotiated during the early 1970s economic boom, average weekly wages paid to nonresidential construction workers rose 17 percent from 1973-1975 (U.S. Department of Labor 1991, 45). Construction costs were also driven up by rising prices of many building materials. Several materials had been in short supply when the price controls program was in effect, so when the controls expired on April 30, 1974, their prices soared.

8.3 The U.S. Auto Industry: Layoffs by the Thousands

> *All last week the bad news mounted. The auto industry reeled from a new model sales rate 35.8 percent below last November's already somewhat depressed pace. Ford and*

> *Chrysler announced massive new layoffs for this month. Automakers now plan to close at least 14 assembly plants and put as many as 230,000 production workers, clerks, accountants and executives out of work before Christmas, and about 20% of General Motors' 500,000 employees will be idle in January.*
> *—"Gloomy Holidays--and Worse Ahead." (*Time, *December 9, 1974, 30).*

The U.S. auto industry was decimated by the recession. From 1973-1975, spending on domestically-produced motor vehicles plummeted, causing production to fall from 12.7 million units in 1973 to 9.0 million in 1975, a 34 percent decline.[9] Sales fell even faster than output, so inventories piled up. The auto companies responded by laying off an enormous number of workers. Employment in motor vehicle and equipment manufacturing fell by 287,300 workers during the recession, and average weekly hours of those production workers who managed to keep their jobs fell from forty-three to thirty-eight (U.S. Department of Labor 1991, 331 & 333). In Michigan, a state whose economic fortunes are heavily dependent on the health of the automobile industry, many were describing the situation not as a recession, but as a depression.

There are four major reasons why the demand for new autos (and other consumer durables for that matter) declined so severely:

(1) According to Okun (1975), the most important reason was the fall in aggregate income and wealth. For the first time since World War II, annual real disposable income declined, by 2.7 percent from 1973-1974. Since automobiles are a luxury good, and the purchase can usually be postponed, the demand for new cars fell proportionately more than income. The huge decline in real financial wealth brought on by falling values of stocks and bonds also played a role in the drop in demand.

(2) American consumers bought 1973 models in very large numbers, so sales in 1974 were probably going to be lower even in the absence of a recession. The 1973 models sold exceptionally well, partly because it was a well-known fact that the 1974 and 1975 models were going to have additional federally-mandated safety and anti-pollution equipment which would add several hundred dollars to their prices. There was widespread acknowledgment among auto industry analysts that price increases on the 1974 and 1975 models were a significant cause of the poor sales.[10]

(3) The oil price hike also played a role. Rising petroleum prices drove up the price of gasoline, although the effect was dampened somewhat by the price controls in place at the time. American auto manufacturers were particularly vulnerable to rising gasoline prices because they specialized in producing large autos that, by today's standards, received poor gasoline mileage. American auto manufacturers focused on producing large cars because they earned higher profit margins on those models than on small cars.[11] The rise in gasoline prices caused the demand for large cars to fall relative to small cars. Foreign manufacturers, who specialized in producing small cars, were well-positioned to reap gains at the expense of domestic producers.

(4) The recession and rising energy prices contributed to a decline in consumer optimism. The University of Michigan's index of consumer sentiment plunged by nearly a third from 1972-1974 (U.S. Department of Commerce 1984, 88). Pessimistic consumers are more likely to hold off purchasing big-ticket items like automobiles.

The decline in domestic new-car sales began a few months after the recession began. The 1974 models (which debuted in September 1973) sold reasonably well until January 1974 which was the same month oil prices peaked. Then the bottom fell out: figure 8.4 shows that auto sales, measured by number of new-car registrations, plummeted during January. By February 1974, new car registrations had dropped by roughly half since the summer of 1973.

Sales rebounded somewhat during the middle of 1974, thanks to intense price cutting by manufacturers trying to reduce their inventories. But the situation deteriorated again in September 1974 when the 1975 models were introduced. They sold poorly from the start, the major reasons being substantially higher prices on these new models and the continuing decline in household income and wealth. Yet, as was the case the previous year, despite falling sales domestic producers continued to manufacture large numbers of cars. This time the result was even more severe: inventories piled up so fast that by December Chrysler held a stock of unsold autos equaling 120 days worth of sales. In other words, if Chrysler completely halted production, at prevailing sales rates it would have taken the company four months to sell off their inventory. Ford and General Motors had similar problems, although not as severe as Chrysler's. In December, manufacturers finally realized that the 1975 models were not going to sell anywhere near as well as originally anticipated, so they slashed output and laid off a huge number of workers.

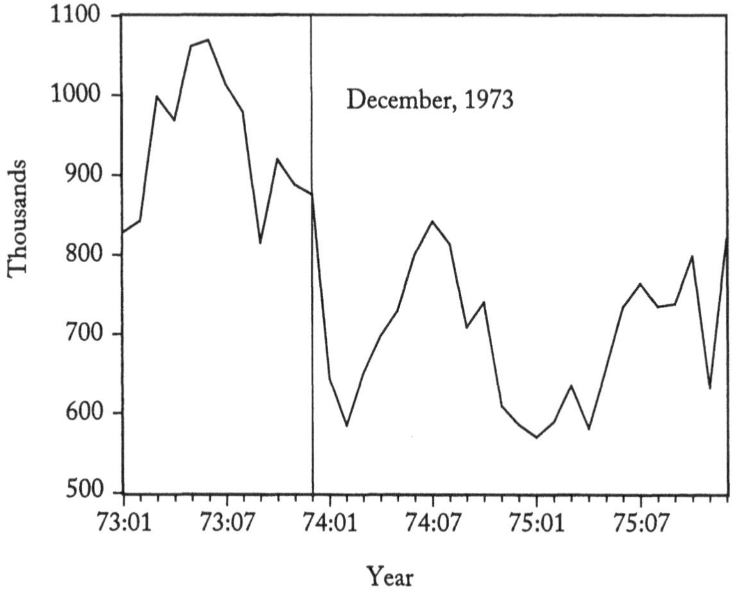

Fig.8.4 New Car Registrasions, 1973–1975

Figure 8.5 shows monthly employment in motor vehicle and equipment production during 1973-1975. Employment dipped in early 1974 when oil prices peaked, but then rebounded during the summer along with auto sales. But beginning in December, employment plunged, by about 200,000 workers over the next three-months. Many auto plants were completely shut down for several consecutive weeks, and the national recession deepened.

8.4 Gas Guzzlers and Imports

The 1973-1974 hike in oil and gasoline prices caused problems for U.S. auto manufacturers that, in some ways, they never recovered from. High gasoline prices led many U.S. consumers to consider (in many cases for the first time) buying small, fuel efficient, imported cars. Foreign producers specialized in producing these vehicles because European and Asian cities have less room for parking than American cities do, plus gasoline taxes overseas are much higher than in the United States.[12] These imported cars were very fuel efficient, but the down-side to ownership was that they were cramped, fairly slow, and fared poorly

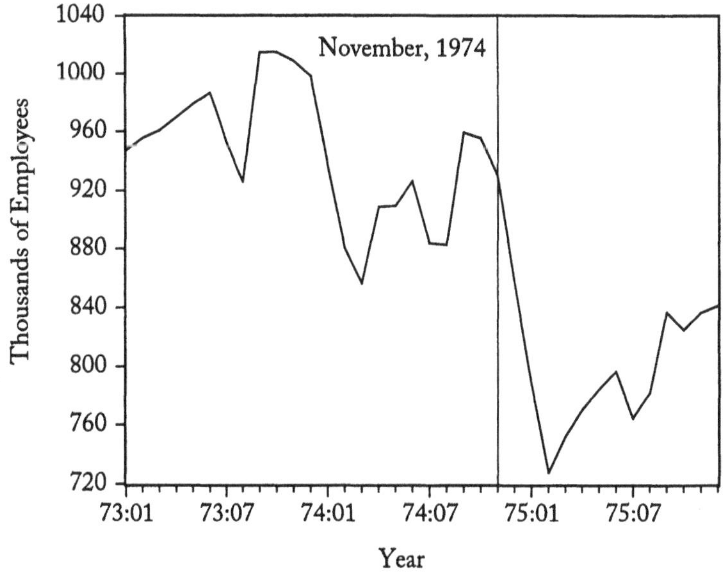

Fig. 8.5 Employment in Motor Vehicle Equipment Production, 1973–1975

in crashes with larger vehicles.

Meanwhile, the domestic vehicles being produced at the time were huge. Perhaps the monument to the 1970s gas guzzler was the 1974 Cadillac Elderado. It was nearly nineteen and a half feet long, over six and a half feet wide, and weighed 5,388 pounds. It came equipped with an enormous 500 cubic-inch, eight-cylinder engine.[13] While official gasoline mileage ratings were not calculated for cars at that time, the Elderado probably averaged around eight miles per gallon. Although the Elderado is an extreme example of a gas guzzler, many cars being produced at the time were not much smaller. The regular-size Chevrolet, which was one of the best-selling models at the time, was over eighteen and a half feet long, weighed 4,318 pounds, and equipped with a 350 cubic inch, eight-cylinder engine. It averaged around fourteen miles per gallon.[14] This regular-size class of autos suffered the largest percent sales decline: from 1973 to 1974 sales fell 51 percent.

While the recession was associated with declining demand for cars of all sizes, in relative terms small car sales held up much better than large car sales. Compact car sales fell just 8.0 percent from 1973-1974. Meanwhile, sub-compacts were in such high demand that two-year-old used models were selling at above their original list price (Snyder 1976, 23). If U.S. automakers had been concentrating on producing more small cars when gasoline prices rose, their fortunes might have turned out considerably better than they actually did. However, they had largely ignored the small car market, despite the fact that it was growing due to trends towards smaller families and multi-vehicle households. Adams and Brock (1995, 79-80) contend that U.S. producers didn't aggressively meet this demand because they were engaging in oligopolistic behavior. No firm wanted to be the first to focus on producing small cars because if they did, the other firms would follow by producing and marketing their own small cars. This outcome would have caused overall industry profitability to decline because increased small car sales would have come at the expense of large car sales. U.S. automakers did develop some smaller cars during the 1960s, but Adams and Brock describe their efforts as "halfhearted and dilatory" (1995, 80). This weak attempt was taking place in the United States despite the fact that U.S. auto manufacturers were aggressively developing and marketing small cars overseas to compete on foreign producers' home turf.

U.S. automakers' focus on large cars prior to and during the 1973-1975 recession led to a significant increase in market penetration by imports, and the domestic industry has been in serious competition with foreign producers for U.S. market share ever since. Owners discovered that these cars were well-manufactured and reliable, so demand continued to grow after the recession ended, even though gas prices leveled off and domestically-produced cars became smaller and more fuel efficient. Imported autos' share of new car registrations in the United States rose from 14.6 percent in 1972 to 18.3 percent by 1977 (Motor Vehicle Manufacturers Association 1978, 245). From 1976-1983, imports' market share averaged 21 percent.[15]

8.5 Sharing the Blame

When it occurred, the 1973-1975 downturn was the worst U.S. recession since the Great Depression. Consumers' real purchasing power fell for the first time since the 1930s, roughly four million jobs were lost, real wealth plummeted, and Americans had to deal with major inconveniences brought on by the energy crisis. Virtually every American household was adversely impacted by the economic disruptions and poor macroeconomic performance.

There are plenty of people to blame for the recession. To name just a few among the long cast of characters, Arthur Burns and his colleagues at the Federal Reserve deserve criticism for overstimulating the economy in 1972, slamming on the monetary brakes in 1973, and then making the ensuing recession worse by hitting the brakes even harder in 1974 in an effort to reduce the inflation they were largely responsible for. Richard Nixon and his economic advisors can be blamed for instituting price controls in 1971; those economic controls had many pernicious effects, including keeping inflation artificially low during 1971, 1972, and 1973, only to be followed by the inevitable "catch up" afterwards. In addition, the price controls created all sorts of shortages and economic distortions, including reducing the incentive to explore for oil in the United States which made the country more dependent on foreign sources of petroleum. Also, the Nixon administration prolonged the energy crisis and set the stage for a repeat performance a few years later by extending the price controls on petroleum products when the general price controls expired on April 30, 1974. We can also point fingers at President Eisenhower, members of Congress, and the domestic oil producers who were responsible for imposing restrictions on foreign oil imports in 1959. That law caused the United States to use domestic oil first instead of consuming cheap imported oil. The law also made foreign oil producing countries angry enough to get together and form OPEC. We should also mention the array of characters responsible for the price controls on natural gas which created artificial shortages and helped make us more dependent on foreign energy sources. And let's not forget the people responsible for creating and administering Regulation Q, the economic control that helped cause the huge declines in business construction and homebuilding during the recession.

These are just a few of the many who were involved in what was truly a group effort. They were responsible for badly designed economic policies that culminated in a very serious recession with the loss of millions of jobs. Incredibly, history would repeat itself just a few years later when another serious bout of economic instability occurred, caused by essentially the same set of factors that brought on the 1973-1975 recession.

CHAPTER 9

■■■

The Energy Crisis, Act II: The Moral Equivalent of War (MEOW)

> *A number of the policy issues that arose in 1977-1979 had parallels in the events of 1971-1976. This coincidence gave policymakers a golden opportunity to show how much they had learned from the bitter experience of the Great Stagflation. The opportunity was squandered.*
> *—Alan S. Blinder (1979, 213).*

The economic calamity that occurred during the mid-1970s–the sharp rise in oil prices coming on top of an overstimulated, inflationary economy–was repeated a few years later. To quote the great baseball player Yogi Berra, it was "*deja vu* all over again" because the underlying causes of the problem were the same. Price controls were still in place on U.S. energy products, and the Federal Reserve was once again overstimulating the economy. Thus, the U.S. economy was doomed to a repeat performance of falling output with rising inflation. One good piece of news, however, is that the 1980 recession that followed the 1979 oil price hike wasn't as severe as the 1973-1975 version. However, since price controls were still in place on petroleum products, the oil price hike caused another round of shortages. An additional piece of bad news is that the 1980 downturn was too short and mild to significantly reduce inflation. It took another, much deeper recession in 1981-1982 to accomplish that task.

U.S. energy problems were an ongoing issue during the 1970s. When Jimmy Carter assumed the presidency in January 1977, he inherited the mess left behind by the failed policies of the Nixon and Ford administrations. However, rather than solve the problems by removing price controls on energy products and reducing the degree of economic control over the sector, Carter declared the "moral equivalent of war" (dubbed MEOW by his critics), and, among other things, attempted to 'solve' U.S. energy problems by creating a new cabinet-level Department of Energy that would enforce even more economic controls. Today, while the controls on energy are largely gone, the U.S. Department of Energy still exists and serves as a monument to the failed energy policies the United States government pursued during those difficult years.

9.1 An Overheated Economy

> *I took office a couple of weeks ago in the middle of the worst economic slowdown of the last forty years.*
> *—President Jimmy Carter, in a speech delivered on February 2, 1977. At the time, the U.S. economy was in its twenty-second consecutive month of expansion.*

> *Why...did Mr. Carter think the country was in a depression when he took office? Whatever answer is given to this question, it does not reflect well on the President...*
> *Probably the best answer is that Mr. Carter was simply listening to the wrong people. There was no shortage of people to tell him that he had arrived just in the nick of time, and that, if he adopted their particular programs, the Republic would indeed be saved.*
> *—George and Joan Melloan (1978, 85-86).*

March 1975 marks the end of the 1973-1975 recession. The oil price hikes were over, inventories were down, and monetary growth had increased slightly during the final months of 1974. Aggregate demand was also stimulated somewhat by the passage in March 1975 of the Tax Reduction Act which legislated temporary tax cuts of $23 billion. However, since the tax cuts were temporary, most economists argue that their impact on aggregate demand was relatively small (Gordon, 1980, 154).[1]

The expansion continued during 1975 and 1976. Table 9.1 shows that by 1975:II output was growing at healthy rates and inflation was trending down. However, by the second half of 1976, output growth had slowed and inflation was rising. By 1976:IV when the presidential election took place the inflation and unemployment rates were both around 7.0 percent.

The economy was a major issue during the 1976 presidential election campaign. On the campaign trail, challenger Jimmy Carter hammered away about the high interest rates prevailing at the time, and the U.S. economy's performance during incumbent president Gerald Ford's term in office. Carter repeatedly referred to his "misery index"

Table 9.1 - Annualized GDP Deflator Inflation Rate, Real GDP Growth, and M1 Growth, 1975-1979

Period	inflation rate (%)	real GDP growth	M1 growth (%)
1975:I	9.8	-9.1	2.8
1975:II	6.2	4.6	6.1
1975:III	8.8	7.4	7.3
1975:IV	7.3	5.2	3.3
1976:I	4.6	7.7	5.3
1976:II	5.1	1.5	6.4
1976:III	5.7	1.4	4.4
1976:IV	6.9	4.1	7.7
1977:I	6.8	5.8	9.1
1977:II	7.8	6.7	7.0
1977:III	4.8	5.6	6.8
1977:IV	7.1	-0.8	8.4
1978:1	5.8	2.7	7.6
1978:II	9.6	12.6	8.8
1978:III	7.2	3.1	8.1
1978:IV	8.1	4.7	7.1
1979:I	9.0	0.1	4.9
1979:II	8.8	0.4	7.3
1979:III	8.1	2.4	13.6
1979:IV	8.0	0.7	4.5

Source: Council of Economic Advisors, various issues.

which was formed by adding the rates of unemployment and inflation. This misery index was an effective campaign tool because by historical standards it was high during 1976. Here are the unemployment rates, CPI inflation rates, and misery index from 1970-1976:

Year	Unemployment Rate	Inflation Rate	Misery Index
1970	4.9%	5.9%	10.8%
1971	5.9%	4.3%	10.2%
1972	5.6%	3.3%	8.9%
1973	4.9%	6.2%	11.1%
1974	5.6%	11.0%	16.6%
1975	8.5%	9.1%	17.6%
1976	7.7%	5.8%	13.5%

Source: Council of Economic Advisors (1978, 291 & 318).

Although the misery index declined considerably from 1975 to 1976, it was still high during the election year which made it an important reason why Carter won the election.[2] Ironically, when Carter came up for reelection in 1980, he probably wished he had never heard of the misery index because it was used against him with a vengeance.

When Carter took office in January 1977, the economy had been expanding for nearly two years, and would continue to grow until early 1980. Referring back to table 9.1, monetary growth was an important determinant of aggregate demand growth during the expansion. M1 growth rose significantly in the fourth quarter of 1976 and stayed high through 1978. Once again, policymakers were trying to stimulate an economy after it had reached full employment. Excess capacity existed in 1977; unemployment averaged 7.0 percent that year, and CPI inflation without food included was roughly the same as it had been in 1976. However, the situation was different in 1978: for that year the *Economic Report of the President* reports a 1978 benchmark unemployment rate of 5.1 percent, and a GNP gap (the difference between full employment and actual GNP) of $37.8 billion (Council of Economic Advisors 1979, 75). Meanwhile, the unemployment rate averaged 6.0 percent during the year.

In other words, the situation in 1978 was almost identical to the one the country faced in 1972-- the economy was actually at full employment, but policymakers thought considerable excess capacity existed. So they stimulated aggregate demand in an effort to reduce unemployment and eliminate the alleged excess capacity. Virtually nothing had been learned from the experience just a few short years before.

Carter's advisors argued in favor of demand stimulus for another reason as well: the widespread recognition that the 1970s inflation had caused "bracket creep," the process where inflation raises nominal incomes and pushes households into higher income tax brackets. In an effort to reduce the contractionary effects of this "fiscal drag," President Carter pushed for a tax cut in 1978. This bill passed and taxes were cut $25 billion effective October 1, 1978.

Demand stimulus helped cause the economy to boom in 1977 and 1978. However, inflation reared its ugly head again. Figure 9.1 shows the inflation and unemployment rates during 1975-1980. The economic boom caused the unemployment rate to drift down, falling below 6.0 percent during 1978. Current evidence suggests that the natural rate of unemployment was in the neighborhood of 6.0 percent at the time, which is supported by the fact that when the unemployment rate fell below that level the inflation rate accelerated noticeably, reaching almost 10.0 percent in early 1978.

Aggregate demand growth wasn't the only cause of accelerating inflation: adverse supply-side influences were at work as well. One factor that helped push up inflation was a dramatic rise in food prices that occurred during the late 1970s. As was the case in the mid 1970s, meat prices were a big part of the story. The profit squeeze in beef produc-

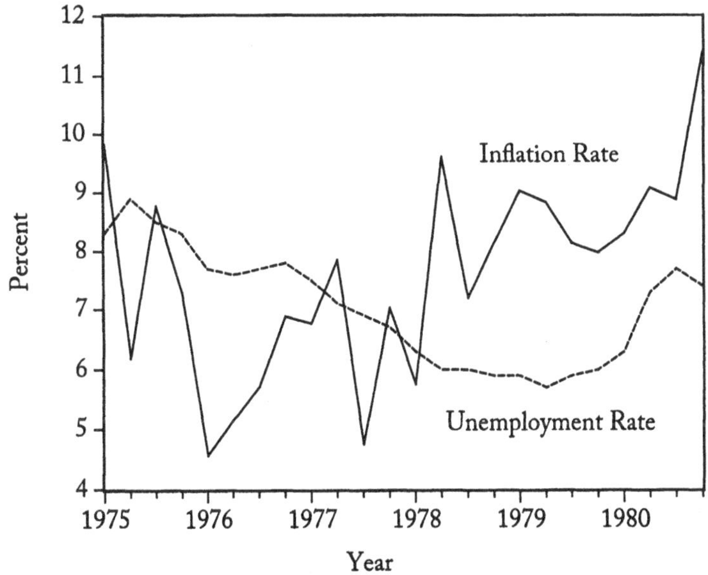

Fig. 9.1 Inflation and Unemployment Rates, 1975–1980

tion during the early and mid 1970s (due in large part to price controls) caused cattle producers to reduce the size of their herds. By the end of 1978, the U.S. cattle herd was 16 percent smaller than its level in 1975 (Council of Economic Advisors 1978, 41). Thus, the supply of beef fell, while the economic expansion raised demand. Largely as a result of rising beef prices, overall meat prices rose 18.9 percent in 1978 (Council of Economic Advisors 1979, 40). Another important contributor to rising food prices was unusual weather in certain parts of the world. A freeze in 1975 severely reduced the 1976-1977 Brazilian coffee crop, causing U.S. retail coffee prices to shoot up 54 percent during just the first six months of 1977 (Council of Economic Advisors 1978, 48). Freezes in 1977 and 1978 also affected citrus crops in Florida, Arizona, and California. As a result of these various factors, overall food prices rose 8.0 percent in 1977 and another 11.8 percent in 1978 (Council of Economic Advisors 1979, 56).[3]

Another supply-side influence at work was legislated increases in the minimum wage. Here are the federally-mandated minimum wage rates from 1977-1981:

Year	Minimum Wage
1977	$2.30
1978	$2.65
1979	$2.90
1980	$3.10
1981	$3.35

Source: Council of Economic Advisors (1978, 177).

The total increase over this period was 46 percent. The rising minimum wage pushed up wages in the aggregate as well. According to the Council of Economic Advisors (1979, 66) the minimum wage hike that took effect in January 1978 raised the U.S. average hourly wage during 1978:I by 0.2 to 0.4 percentage points. Labor costs were also driven up by scheduled increases in the social security payroll tax that took effect in January 1978, and again in January 1979.

In sum, an unwillingness to accept the fact that an economy with 6.0 percent unemployment was fully employed led the Carter administration and Federal Reserve to pursue policies that overstimulated economic activity. Meanwhile, adverse supply-side influences were at work, involving both the weather and policymakers. As a result, by 1978 the U.S. economy was producing well above capacity output, and a major inflation buildup was taking place. It was essentially a repeat performance of 1972-1973. And like that episode, the 1977-1978 version was also followed by a major hike in oil prices.

9.2 The Litany Continues: More Bad Energy Policies

Before discussing the 1979 oil price hike, we pause to describe U.S. energy policies as they evolved after the first energy crisis of 1973-1974. Continued pursuit of economic controls in the energy sector, along with bad macroeconomic policies, laid the foundation for the second oil price hike.

The "energy crisis" in petroleum could have been ended in early 1975 when the Emergency Petroleum Allocation Act was due to expire. The oil industry would have been freed from many of the costly economic controls in place, and the signals provided by market pricing would have eliminated any prolonged market disequilibrium. However, this result did not come about. Instead, President Ford, who favored price decontrol, struggled during much of the year with a Democratically-controlled Congress opposed to decontrol. At the time, few members of Congress wanted to be "in favor" of higher energy prices, so the price controls were temporarily extended while the White House and Congress searched for a compromise. The compromise was finally reached in December when President Ford signed the Energy Policy and Conservation Act. This law extended the price controls on petroleum; the president could propose higher ceiling prices, but they would become operative only if both houses of Congress approved them.[4] Since Democrats controlled both houses, the likelihood of decontrol was virtually nil. One critic of the new law had three different names for it: "the Cold Homes and Dark Factories Act,...the Energy Dependence Act,...[and] the OPEC Relief Act of 1975" (DeMarchi 1981, 506).

Thus, price controls on petroleum (and natural gas) were still in place when Carter assumed office in January 1977. However, rather than try to free the industry from those controls, Carter proposed a massive increase in regulation. He declared the "moral equivalent of war" on U.S. energy problems and in April 1977 announced his National Energy Plan. The proposed plan was based on two underlying ideas. The first was a "limits to growth" mentality, which assumes that no more fossil fuels can be found. Rather than encourage production of energy sources, the plan was to reduce consumption. The second notion was that it was unacceptable to allow energy companies to reap high profits because they controlled a scarce resource (petroleum), the price of which had risen so dramatically back in 1973-1974. There was considerable talk about the "obscene profits" that would result if U.S. oil companies were able to earn the world price (instead of the controlled price) for domestically-produced oil. To a large extent, the American public went along with this argument. Oil companies were held in low esteem during the 1970s. In fact, petroleum executives were the villains of the 1970s, much like bankers in the 1930s, and tobacco company officials during the 1990s.

The main proposals of the National Energy Plan included:[5]

(1) creating a new cabinet-level Department of Energy
(2) raising the federal gasoline tax
(3) imposing regulations and tax penalties to encourage factories and utilities to convert from scarce natural gas and oil to abundant coal
(4) imposing a gas-guzzler tax on new autos that achieved lower than average gasoline mileage
(5) having federal regulators set electricity prices
(6) placing intrastate natural gas under federal price controls
(7) setting energy efficiency standards for appliances
(8) a crude oil equalization tax which would allow oil companies to charge the world price of oil, but pay in taxes the difference between the world price and the controlled price.

This enormous plan was dumped on Congress in April 1977, and, incredibly, Carter told the press a few days later that it would be passed by October 1st.

The plan was controversial to say the least. It was savaged by most economists because it increased rather than decreased regulation of the energy sector. Many environmentalists opposed the plan's incentives to burn coal because it would increase air pollution. Governors of natural gas-producing states were opposed the plan because it applied price controls to intrastate gas.[6] In addition, several industries objected to various facets of the plan. The auto industry opposed the gas-guzzler tax. Among other things, it would have increased the incentive for Americans to buy small imported cars. The chemical industry opposed higher taxes on petroleum because petroleum is a major input into the production of many chemicals. The home-appliance industry objected to setting efficiency standards for appliances. And last but not least, many ordinary Americans opposed the plan because it proposed raising taxes and increasing the size of the government bureaucracy.

The House of Representatives considered the plan first. In a rush to complete their work before the summer recess, the House removed the gasoline tax, but passed the remainder of the plan with only minor revisions. Then, during the summer recess, conditions changed. The country enjoyed an oil glut (which is discussed in the next section), so it was not clear to the public that there was, in fact, an "energy crisis." In addition, President Carter's popularity was declining. So when the Senate reconvened, they proceeded to gut the bill. They removed the gas-guzzler tax, the wellhead tax on oil, reducing the size of several of the user taxes, and rejected federal regulation of electricity prices. The Senate version also included price deregulation of newly discovered natural gas.

President Carter was very unhappy with the Senate's actions. He held a press conference in October 1977 where he warned of "war profiteering" and the upcoming "biggest ripoff in history" by the oil companies if the Senate didn't approve his original plan.[7] In effect, he characterized the situation as a battle between the public and the oil companies, completely ignoring the fact that the energy mess was largely the creation of economic policies put in place by the federal government. The National Taxpayers Union responded with a full page advertisement that ran in major newspapers. It contained a statement signed by several prominent free-market economists who accused the president of "demagoguery," and pointed out that his energy plan as originally conceived would "be the largest peacetime tax increase in history" and would "rip-off the public."[8] *The Wall Street Journal*'s editorial board blasted Carter's press conference by referring to "idiocy by the government."[9]

The final outcome of Carter's National Energy Plan was the National Energy Act of 1978. The bill, "standing about eight inches high" (Cochrane 1981, 584) became law on November 9, 1978. Provisions included creating the Department of Energy, setting federal efficiency standards for appliances, incentives to insulate homes and install energy-saving devices, and government loans to low income families to help them conserve energy. The gas-guzzler tax was included, although it was lower than Carter originally wanted, and power companies were encouraged to convert to coal, but only if it could be done cheaply and without violating environmental laws. As for federal regulation of electricity rates, states were urged to "consider" federal guidelines. Natural gas regulation was extended to both interstate and intrastate natural gas, with no less than seventeen different categories of natural gas. One bright spot in the law was phased-out regulation of newly discovered natural gas, with complete deregulation by 1985.

Thus, what came out of the Carter National Energy Plan was much less regulation than Carter originally requested, but it was more regulation, along with a cabinet-level department to administer those regulations. The opportunity to get the federal government out of the energy business, promote domestic production, and reduce domestic consumption by letting the marketplace operate unhindered had failed. Instead, by keeping price controls in place, the United States remained vulnerable to shortages if another oil crisis occurred.

9.3 The 1977-1978 Oil Glut

The major difference in conditions prior to the two oil price hikes of the 1970s was that while in 1973 oil production was going virtually full tilt around the world and barely meeting demand, in 1977-1978 there was an oil glut The major reason for these abundant supplies in the latter period was increased production from Alaska, the North Sea, and Mexico. Oil had been discovered in all three places prior to the 1973-1974 oil crunch, but turning the fields into big producers took time. The Alaskan oil field had been discovered in 1967, made possible by the development of seismic explosives that could operate at very cold temperatures.[10] Given the frozen seas that far north, it was decided that the best way to transport the oil south would be through a pipeline. However, construction of the pipeline was held up for years, initially because of claims by native Americans, as well as disagreements between the pipeline partners. Then, in 1970 environmentalists won a federal court injunction that blocked construction for another four years. The 1973-1974 energy crisis provided the impetus for the federal government to give the emergency go-ahead to start construction, and by 1978 sizable amounts of oil were flowing from Alaska.

Large oil deposits in the North Sea had been discovered in 1969. However, it took time to develop this source because of the adverse working conditions. Platforms had to be build in a sea where "waves of fifty feet and winds of seventy miles an hour were not uncommon" (Yergin 1991, 669). In addition, the oil companies were drilling in water depths never before tried. Sizable production from the North Sea began in 1975.

Mexico's major oil discovery occurred in 1972. However, Mexico was not interested in becoming an oil exporting country because nationalist feeling dating back to the 1930s dictated that their oil should only be used domestically (Yergin 1991, 666). However, a combination of high world oil prices and a serious Mexican economic crisis that came to a head in 1976 led the Mexican government to focus on increasing oil production and exports. Mexico was exporting sizable amounts by 1976, and the flow continued to increase for several years afterwards.

In the midst of the resulting worldwide oil glut, there was considerable disagreement within OPEC about what action to take on prices. The leading oil price dove, Saudi Arabia, wanted to keep oil prices stable for fear that further increases would abort the economic recoveries taking place in the United States and Europe. The price hawks–Iran and Libya–wanted further price increases, but to do so would have required major cuts in output. As it turned out, prices were relatively stable during 1977 and 1978, largely because Saudi Arabia reduced production to offset the increased supply from non-OPEC sources.

Meanwhile, the demand for oil was growing, but more slowly than it had been earlier in the decade. Demand growth had slowed because the 1973-1974 energy price hikes led to increased conservation efforts. In the United States, homeowners added insulation, turned down their thermostats during the winter, and installed more energy-efficient furnaces and appliances. The average gasoline mileage of the U.S. auto fleet rose as large cars were gradually replaced with smaller cars. The number of lights in commercial buildings was reduced. New jetliners were equipped with engines that burned less fuel than the ones they replaced. The United States was in the process of becoming more energy efficient, and that trend that would continue for several more years. A measure of efficiency is energy consumption per unit of output, where energy consumption is measured in British Thermal Units (BTUs). In the United States during 1972, each dollar of GNP produced was associated with the consumption of 61.2 thousand BTUs of energy. By 1978, each dollar of GNP (in 1972$) was associated with consumption of 54.2 thousand BTUs (Ahrari 1986, 206). This represents a 12.0 percent increase in energy efficiency. Stated another way, U.S. energy usage was expanding 12.0 percent more slowly than output. With respect to oil consumption, from 1972 to 1978, U.S. usage rose 13.8 percent while real GDP increased 20.6 percent (Cochrane and Griepentrig 1981, 694).

Yet despite these conservation efforts, U.S. petroleum imports continued to rise, both in terms of number of barrels and as a percentage of total U.S. consumption. The reason was twofold: rising U.S. demand, and falling U.S. output. Despite the addition of Alaskan oil, the United States was producing less petroleum in 1978 than had been the case in the early 1970s. Depletion of existing fields was part of the reason, but another important cause was the continued existence of price controls on U.S. petroleum products which discouraged production.

9.4 The Second Oil Crisis, 1978-1979

> *There is one simple way to end the energy crisis and the gasoline shortage tomorrow–and I mean tomorrow and not six months from now, not six years from now. Eliminate all controls on the prices of crude oil and other petroleum products. The gasoline lines would melt faster than the snows of winter...*
>
> *This solution would reduce the cost of gasoline to the consumer–the true cost. Prices at the pump might go up a few cents a gallon, but the cost of gasoline today includes the time and gasoline wasted standing in line, and hunting for a gas station with gas, plus the $10.8 billion annual budget of the Department of Energy, which amounts to about nine cents per gallon of gasoline.*
>
> *—Milton Friedman (1979).*

As described in Chapter 4, the 1973-1974 oil price hike was largely the result of two factors. First was the dollar depreciation. Since oil is bought and sold on international markets with U.S. dollars, the dollar depreciation reduced the oil producing countries' dollar-denominated revenues relative to other currencies. Second was the complete lack of excess capacity in the North American oil industry. If other oil-producing countries reduced their output, the United States and Canada did not possess the ability to make up the difference. During the early 1970s, OPEC members discussed reducing output several times, but were never able to come to an agreement until the outbreak of the Arab-Israeli war in October 1973 provided the Middle Eastern members with a common cause to rally around.

The major similarity prior to the two oil price hikes was the falling value of the dollar. The trade-weighted dollar, which stood at 105.3 at the end of 1976 (1973=100), fell to 88.5 by the end of 1978, a decline of 17.3 percent (Council of Economic Advisors 1980, 315). By early 1978 Saudi Arabian officials were complaining so much about the falling dollar that the U.S. Secretary of Energy paid them a visit. He convinced Saudi officials to continue accepting dollars for oil (Ahrari 1986, 218).

The second oil crisis of the decade began on October 31, 1978 when 40,000 Iranian oil workers went on strike as part of nationwide demonstrations against the Shah of Iran. Within a week, Iranian oil production had plummeted from 6 million barrels per day (b/d) to 1.8 million b/d (Ahari 1986, 146). The impact was quickly felt in the petroleum spot market where prices rose substantially. However, the crisis appeared to be short-lived, because the oil workers returned to work in mid November under threats from the Iranian military. Iranian oil production rebounded, and the market stabilized.

However, the relief was only temporary. The demonstrations against the Shah continued, and in December, Ayatollah Rouhollah Khomeini, a longtime critic of the Shah who was living in exile in Paris, called on the oil workers to go on strike again.[11] The workers responded, and by late December Iranian oil production had virtually ceased. Iran stopped exporting oil on December 25, 1978, and even within Iran petroleum products were scarce. In a bizarre twist of events, an American oil tanker was diverted to Iran to deliver oil (Yergin 1991, 681). The decline in Iranian oil output was partially made up by other OPEC countries, but output in the noncommunist countries during the first quarter of 1979 was about 2 million b/d below the level produced during the last months of 1979.

The decline in oil production was about 5.0 percent, yet prices nearly tripled. For example, the spot market price of a barrel of Saudi Arabian light crude was $12.80 in September 1978 which is the month before Iranian production began to decline. By May 1979, the price had risen to $34.50. How could a 5.0 percent decline in output result in such an enormous increase in price?

A major factor causing the huge price hike was panic buying. There was genuine fear that Iran's Islamic revolution would spread to other Islamic oil-producing countries and disrupt oil supplies to an even greater extent. As a result, oil companies began buying heavily to add to their stock of inventories. In addition, consumers started topping off their cars' gas tanks so they would be sure to have plenty of gasoline, even if it meant waiting in long lines. These increased purchases by oil companies and consumers generated an increase in demand equal to 3 million b/d. Thus, the output decline of 2 million b/d was combined with increased demand of 3 million b/d which resulted in a 5 million b/d shortfall compared to what had been the case earlier.

In the United States, gasoline lines reappeared, and once again the reason was price controls. The controlled price of regular gasoline was about $1.00 per gallon, which was several cents below the equilibrium price. Excess demand manifested itself in long lines where motorists waited, sometimes for hours, to purchase gasoline. Some states tried to reduce the gasoline lines with schemes such as alternating the days consumers could buy gas depending on whether their license plate ended in an odd or even number. But these were just half-baked attempts to deal with the problem that had an obvious solution: eliminate the price controls. But politicians opposed this move because it would have created "windfall profits" for the oil companies. Meanwhile, American motorists focused their anger at OPEC and the oil companies instead of where it really belonged: the politicians in Washington D.C. Meanwhile, many of these same politicians were hypocritically joining the chorus of criticism directed at the oil companies.

9.5 U.S. Economic Performance in 1979

> *The fact that the economy did not tip into recession in 1979 has received widespread comment and attention...In 1979, despite rising inflation, restraint on aggregate demand from monetary and fiscal policies, and a huge "oil tax" levied by OPEC, the economy continued to move forward.*
> *—Council of Economic Advisors (1980, 29).*

During the first half of 1979, the consensus forecast among economists was that the United States would slip into a recession later that year. One reason was the fact that a reduction in the monetary growth rate occurred during the first quarter. The growth rate of M1, which averaged 7.9 percent during 1978, fell to an annualized rate of

4.1 percent during 1979:I. A second reason was that despite the fact that taxes were cut in 1978, fiscal policy was actually more restrictive in 1979 than it had been in 1978 as measured by the cyclically-adjusted (full employment) budget.[12] This measure moved from deficit in 1978 to surplus in 1979 (Council of Economic Advisors 1980, 51). The third reason was the adverse supply shock in the form of the sharp rise in oil prices.

Output growth slowed in 1979, but the economy did not slip into a recession. The main reason why the economy continued to grow was because of surges in both consumption expenditures and net exports. Table 9.2 shows the changes in real GNP and the various spending components during 1979. Although businesses ran down their inventories by $11.3 billion, the big increases in consumption spending on nondurables and services, along with rising net exports caused real GNP to keep rising.

Most economists believe that consumption spending increased during 1979 because a rare event occurred that year: the public's expected inflation rate rose right along with actual inflation. Changes in expected inflation often lag behind changes in the actual rate, but not in 1979. The rise in oil prices and accompanying gasoline lines were all too familiar to Americans who had gone through the same experience just a few

Table 9.2 - Changes in Real GNP at Annualized Rates, Billions of 1972$

Period	GNP	Cd	Cnd	Cs	FBI	CBI	G	(X-M)
1978:IV-1979:IV	+24.8	-4.7	+7.8	+15.1	+0.9	-11.3	+5.2	+11.7

Cd=spending on consumer durables
Cnd=spending on consumer nondurables
Cs=spending on services
FBI=fixed business investment (=spending on new plant and equipment)
CBI=changes in business inventories
G=government purchases
(X-M)=net exports

Note: sum of changes in the GNP components do not equal the change in GNP because of rounding.

Source: Council of Economic Advisors (1981, 234-235).

years before. The 1973-1974 oil price hike had helped raise inflation, so the public expected the same thing in 1979. Higher expected prices caused households to increase their spending on goods and services in an effort to beat further expected price increases (Council of Economic Advisors 1980, 30-31). So despite the decline in spending on consumer durables (primarily due to falling auto sales), spending on nondurables and services rose substantially and raised overall consumption spending by a total of $18.2 billion. Auto sales declined because the rise in gasoline prices and accompanying shortages caused a shift away from domestically-produced large cars and toward small imports, as had occurred in 1974.

The second factor that kept the U.S. economy from plunging into a recession during 1979 was rising net exports. They rose $11.7 billion that year, and a big part of the reason was the lagged effect of the dollar depreciation that took place in 1977 and 1978. The falling value of the dollar made U.S. goods cheaper overseas and raised the price of imports sold in the United States. Another factor at work was a surge in grain sales to the Soviet Union due to that country's crop shortfall (Council of Economic Advisors 1980, 46).

Thus, the U.S. economy avoided a recession in 1979. Instead, the American public endured a slow-growth economy characterized by high inflation, and those irritating and wasteful gasoline lines. A recession finally did begin in the first half of 1980 (which is described in Chapter 10), and coming on the heels of the second energy crisis of the decade and the economy's mediocre performance in 1979 was a factor costing Jimmy Carter the 1980 presidential election.

But before we discuss the 1980 recession and the end of the Carter administration, we relate another very important development that took place in 1979: the appointment of Paul Volcker to the chairmanship of the Board of Governors of the Federal Reserve. Volcker was one of the major economic policy figures of his era, and had a huge impact on macroeconomic events by leading the way in eradicating the inflation that had been plaguing the United States since the mid 1960s.

CHAPTER 10

■■■

Paul Volcker at the Federal Reserve

Volcker was selected because he was the candidate of Wall Street. This was their price, in effect. What was known about him? That he was able and bright and it was also known that he was conservative. What wasn't known was that he was going to impose some very dramatic changes.
—Stuart Eizenstat, President Carter's domestic policy advisor, explaining why Paul Volcker was chosen to be chairman of the Federal Reserve Board of Governors (taken from Greider [1987, 47]).

I recognize that monetary policy itself has a particularly crucial role to play, for no inflation can persist without money growth.
—Paul A. Volcker (1978, 62).

During 1979, inflation was a major political and economic issue. CPI inflation averaged 13.3 percent during the year, with prices of virtually all goods and services rising. Among the major contributors to inflation, energy prices rose 25.2 percent, food prices increased 10.9 percent, services' prices went up 11.0 percent, and home ownership costs increased 14.4 percent (Council of Economic Advisors, 1983, 222 & 224). In addition, this rapid U.S. inflation was causing the dollar to continue depreciating on foreign currency markets. The trade-weighted dollar fell 18 percent from 1976-1979, which further contributed to inflation by raising import prices.

A large segment of the American public was upset about the rising prices. Many felt they were moving backwards economically because their nominal wages weren't keeping up with inflation. While this wasn't true for all Americans, it was certainly the case for some. Others did not feel they were moving backwards, but instead thought that their standards of living had stagnated because their nominal incomes were just keeping pace with inflation.[1] On this point they were essentially correct: inflation-adjusted median family income in 1979 was a measly $40 higher (in 1980 dollars) than in 1978 (Council of Economic Advisors, 1982, 261).

In addition, this rapid inflation was imposing major costs on the American public. One of these costs was the inflation tax on money. Currency does not earn interest, and, at the time, neither did checking accounts at banks. Also, time and savings accounts at banks and thrifts were subject to the Regulation Q ceiling rates. High inflation drove up nominal interest rates, but people holding currency, checking accounts, and time and savings deposits could not earn those high rates. Thus, inflation represented a major tax on holding those assets. In an effort to avoid this tax, the public spent considerable time and energy minimizing their holdings of assets not earning market rates, and instead purchasing Treasury bills or shares of money market mutual funds.[2]

High inflation also caused the public to incur transactions costs associated with altering their portfolios of stocks and bonds which were losing value in the high-inflation environment. Due in part to inflation, stock prices fell dramatically; from 1976-1979, the Dow Jones Industrial Average fell 14.3 percent in nominal terms, and 38.6 percent in real terms (Council of Economic Advisors, 1983, 224 & 267). Rising inflation and interest rates also caused bond prices to fall, both in real and nominal terms.

As stocks and bonds lost value, investors shifted to assets whose prices rose along with inflation. These included real estate, gold, silver, and collectibles such as rare paintings, all of which experienced major price increases. To cite just two examples, gold–which was valued at $35 per ounce when the United States closed the gold window in 1971–sold for around $800 per ounce by late 1979. Real estate prices also experienced huge gains: the median price of a home in Southern California rose 25 percent per year during the late 1970s.

There was considerable political pressure on President Carter to "do something" about the high inflation. Not only was the general public upset, the politically-powerful financial industry centered in New York City was furious because inflation was killing the stock and bond markets. So when the chairmanship of the Federal Reserve Board of Governors opened up, U.S. financial leaders made it clear they wanted the vacancy filled with someone they knew and trusted. A logical choice was Paul Volcker, the highly-respected president of the Federal Reserve Bank of New York. President Carter appointed him chairman of the Board of Governors of the Federal Reserve, and he was sworn in on August 6, 1979. He went on to have an enormous impact on U.S. economic events, and in doing so became a genuine "economic hero."

10.1 Paul Volcker

> *[Paul Volcker] is a citizen that our whole state [of New Jersey] is justifiably proud of. His career and his record in the Federal Reserve, in the private sector and certainly the Treasury during the chaotic days of the international monetary crisis in the early 1970's, all these are well known to the committee. That career and record...says that he will be a Chairman of the Fed who is strong, independent and highly respected.*
>
> *In my view, as in the view of many of our European allies, Paul Volcker is the right man in the right job at the right time. And it's not completely New Jersey chauvinism...when I say that he is probably the best appointment that the President has made.*
>
> *—Senator Bill Bradley (D-NJ), introducing Paul Volcker to the Senate Committee on Banking, Housing, and Urban Affairs at the start of his confirmation hearings on July 30, 1979 (U.S. Congress 1979).*

Paul Volcker was born in 1927, the son of first-generation Americans of German descent. He spent his youth in Teaneck, New Jersey before enrolling at Princeton University in 1945. He was awarded his bachelors degree in economics in 1949, and then attended Harvard University for his graduate work. He completed all of the coursework required for the Ph.D. in economics, but never received the degree because he did not finish his doctoral dissertation. During the early years of his marriage he told his wife that "he would never amount to much and would probably wind up working in some dark office as an economist, wearing his green eyeshade and making only $6,000 a year" (Neikirk, 1987, 117).

He spent his working career at the Federal Reserve, the U.S. Treasury, and Chase Manhattan Bank. He started out at the Federal Reserve Bank of New York in 1951 and worked there for five years, first monitoring the British economy, then doing research on U.S. economic issues, and finally at the open market desk placing purchase and sale orders for U.S. government securities. He moved to the private sector in 1956, working as a financial economist with Chase Manhattan Bank in New York. He quit that job in 1962 and moved to the U.S. Treasury where he specialized in international economics. Next, he returned to Chase in 1965, then ended up at the Treasury again in 1969. It was during this second stint at the Treasury that he attracted widespread attention.

Volcker served as the U.S. Treasury's Undersecretary for Monetary Affairs, a position that oversees the Treasury's role in international economic affairs, monetary policy, and government debt. Volcker was a busy man there because the Bretton Woods system of fixed exchange rates was falling apart. He was heavily involved in the 1971 decision to close the gold window and allow the dollar to float. He was also a major player in the negotiations later that year which resulted in the Smithsonian Agreement that essentially ratified the United States' actions in breaking up the Bretton Woods Agreement. Two years later he helped work out the Jamaica Agreement which confirmed the new status quo of floating exchange rates. Because of his work in allowing the dollar to float on currency markets (and therefore depreciate) *Time* magazine (incorrectly) described him as "the only man in history who has officially devalued the U.S. dollar twice."[3]

He left the Treasury in 1974 and taught at Princeton for a year before being named president of the Federal Reserve Bank of New York. He served in that position until the summer of 1979 when he was appointed chairman of the Board of Governors.

Volcker secured a place in history for himself by being the principal architect of monetary policies that broke the trend of rising inflation which had been going on since the mid 1960s. In August 1979, the month Volcker assumed the chairmanship of the Board of Governors, the annualized CPI inflation rate was over 15 percent. In 1987, the year he left the Federal Reserve, the CPI inflation rate was 4.4 percent.

While these restrictive monetary policies broke the inflationary spiral, they also helped cause two recessions, the second of which resulted in the highest U.S. labor force unemployment rate since the 1930s. These tight monetary policies also helped drive interest rates to heights not experienced in the United States since the Civil War. In the midst of this economic instability, the Federal Reserve–and Paul Volcker in particular–received heavy criticism. At one point protesting farmers arrived in Washington D.C. with their farm equipment and proceeded to drive tractors onto the grass in front of the Federal Reserve building. Volcker earned his place in history by having the strength of character to stay with these restrictive policies, believing that in the end he would be vindicated. It turns out he was right.

10.2 New Operating Procedures

> *In the gallows humor of Wall Street, the Federal Reserve's policy shift swiftly became known as Paul Volcker's "Saturday Night Special."*
> *—William Greider (1987, 125).*

After Volcker assumed the chairmanship of the Board of Governors, inflation continued to accelerate and the dollar kept depreciating on foreign exchange markets. Volcker soon reached the conclusion that the Federal Reserve had to pursue a tight monetary policy to get inflation under control. However, given the existing economic environment of high and rising interest rates, a policy of tightening credit conditions while targeting interest rates would have required a huge hike in the federal funds rate, perhaps 4 or 5 percentage points. Such increases would be necessary because tight policies had been put off for so long, allowing inflation to spin out of control. Volcker did not think he could persuade the members of the Federal Open Market Committee (FOMC) to agree to these increases. So as an alternative, he concentrated on persuading his fellow governors–who constitute a majority vote of the FOMC–on the idea of changing operating procedures.[4] Specifically, Volcker wanted to target a monetary aggregate and allow interest rates to adjust to supply and demand conditions, thus serving their role as the market price that allocates the scarce resource of credit. He was proposing a major change because virtually throughout its history the Federal Reserve has conducted monetary policy by targeting interest rates.

In September, Volcker presented his idea to the other Federal Reserve governors who were, for the most part, receptive to it. However, members of the Carter administration initially opposed the plan, but changed their minds after meeting with European financial officials later that month. At those meetings, the German delegation informed the Americans that they would not participate in any moves to support the dollar unless the United States brought its monetary growth and inflation under control.

Volcker called a special meeting of the Federal Open Market Committee on Saturday, October 6, 1979 and presented his plan. The committee approved it, along with agreeing to increase the discount rate, raise reserve requirements on managed liabilities including new time deposits and Eurodollar borrowings, and engage in moral suasion aimed at getting banks to stop lending for speculative purposes. According to Volcker, the FOMC members understood what might result: high and volatile interest rates, and possibly a recession.[5] The decision was announced that evening and it generated an enormous amount of interest. Monetarists–who had been advocating such a policy for years–were especially excited. They wondered if the Federal Reserve was finally coming around to their way of thinking, that the preferred method of monetary control is to target a monetary aggregate instead of interest rates.

The monetarists were disappointed, however, when they found out the next day just what the Federal Reserve intended to do. The open market desk manager at the Federal Reserve Bank of New York explained that they were going to target banks' nonborrowed reserves, and that they "[didn't] plan to be rigid or mechanistic in pursuit of reserve targets" (Melton, 1985, 50). In other words, the idea was to target nonborrowed reserves, but if interest rates fluctuated too widely, they would intervene. So the new operating procedure was really nothing more than federal funds rate targeting with a much wider-than-usual band of tolerance before the Federal Reserve would intervene in the market.[6] The target range for the federal funds rate was changed from 11.25 - 11.75 percent to 11.50 - 15.50 percent.[7]

Once the new policy was in place, the federal funds rate shot up. Figure 10.1 shows the weekly federal funds rate during this period, and you can see that it hit nearly 16 percent just a few weeks after the new operating procedures were announced. Yet despite these high interest rates, the monetary base continued to grow rapidly. Table 10.1 shows the annualized growth rates of the base, M1, and M2 during this period. The base grew faster during 1979:IV than it had during the previous quarter. Yet the monetary growth rate slowed considerably because the money multiplier fell, largely due to the increased reserve requirements.

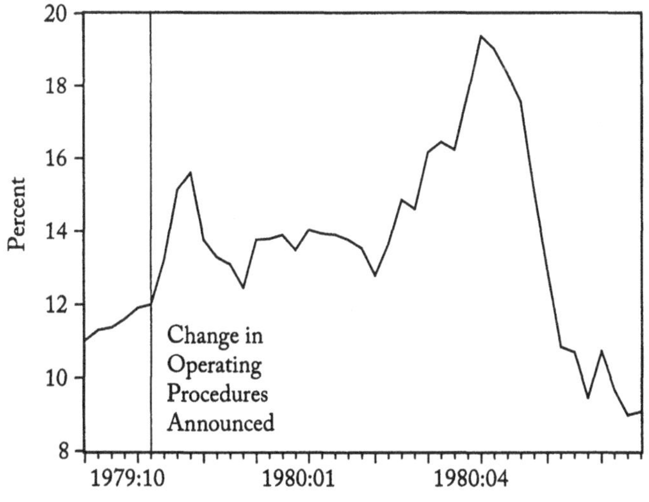

Fig. 10.1 Weekly Federal Funds Rate, 9/5/79 – 6/25/80

Fig. 10.1 Weekly Federal Funds Rate, 9/5/79–6/25/80

Table 10.1 - Annualized Growth of Monetary Aggregates, 1979:I - 1980:IV

	Monetary Base	M1	M2
1979:I	5.9%	4.8%	6.3%
1979:II	4.8%	10.7%	10.2%
1979:III	9.3%	10.1%	10.3%
1979:IV	9.6%	5.3%	7.2%
1980:I	7.6%	5.9%	7.2%
1980:II	5.2%	-2.4%	5.5%
1980:III	9.9%	13.5%	15.5%
1980:IV	10.6%	10.9%	8.1%

Source: Federal Reserve Bulletin, various issues.

10.3 The 1980 Recession

> *The idea was not to make the economy go into the tank--it was supposed to allow the economy to grow but without the credit excesses. Instead, the consumer got it into his head that the government was telling him not to use credit. The darned economy just fell off the cliff.*
> *—Federal Reserve governor Fred Schultz, discussing the credit controls that were imposed in March 1980 (taken from Greider [1987, 187]).*

The combination of the tight monetary policy and high oil prices brought on by the 1979 energy crisis led to the recession that began in early 1980. This downturn is notable for the simple reason that it lasted just six months, making it the shortest recession in U.S. history. Another reason why the recession is interesting is because it was dramatically worsened by the use of economic controls.

The recession began in February, and initially it was fairly mild. In fact, real GDP actually rose during 1980:I because the rise in output during January was greater than the decline in February and March. A major cause of the initial downturn was high interest rates which resulted from both slower growth of the supply of credit and rising demand. Supply growth declined because of the Federal Reserve's restrictive monetary policy. Demand grew rapidly due to fear of further increases in interest rates, plus concerns that the Carter administration would impose some form of credit controls. Business credit rose at an annualized rate of 24 percent between December 1979 and February 1980 (Council of Economic Advisors 1981, 134).

Figure 10.2 shows the yield on 90-day Treasury bills from 1979-1982. During 1980, yields rose from 12.0 percent in January to 15.5 percent in March. These high interest rates helped cause spending declines that were concentrated in the housing and auto sectors. New home construction collapsed because high interest rates raised the cost of building and owning homes. In addition, those high rates went above the Regulation Q ceiling rates which set off another round of financial disintermediation. As a result, new housing starts, which had been running at an annualized rate of over 1.8 million in September 1979, were down to 927,000 by May 1980 (U.S. Department of Commerce 1984, 78). Auto sales fell due to a combination of high interest rates and high gasoline prices associated with the second energy crisis. Nominal spending on automobiles during 1980:II was $15.7 billion below its level the previous quarter (U.S. Department of Commerce 1984, 145). As

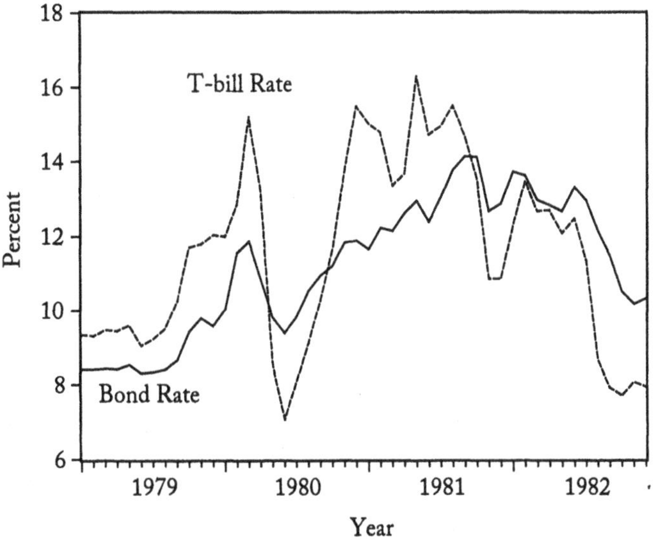

Fig. 10.2 Monthly Yields on 90-day Treasury Bills and Long Term Government Bonds, 1979–1982

was the case in the mid 1970s, gasoline lines (because price controls on petroleum products were still in place) and higher gasoline prices caused Americans to shift spending away from large domestic autos and toward smaller imported cars.

Inflation was still accelerating during the first months of the recession, thanks in large part to the adverse supply-side increase in petroleum prices. The CPI inflation rate, which had been running at around a 13 percent annual rate during the last quarter of 1979, rose to an annualized rate of 18 percent during January and February. Rising energy prices were not the only cause: CPI inflation with energy prices netted out was 12.9 percent during those same two months (Council of Economic Advisors 1981, 134). The Carter administration was becoming very alarmed about inflation, especially with the 1980 election looming on the horizon.

Credit controls as a method of reducing inflation had been under consideration since May 1978 when AFL-CIO president George Meany urged President Carter to impose them. Carter had the authority to do so because the Credit Control Act of 1969 gave the president the power to "authorize the Federal Reserve Board to regulate and control any or all extensions of credit" (Schreft 1990, 27).[8] At the time, however, Carter opposed such a move because he considered them "inefficient, inequitable, and costly to administer" (Carter from Schreft 1990, 28). Instead, he tried to appease Meany by setting up voluntary wage and price standards, but they were widely ignored and had virtually no impact on inflation. During 1979, inflation continued to accelerate and so support for controls grew. In March the Secretary of the Treasury urged Carter to impose them, but he continued to hold out. But as time passed--and inflation soared--more and more members of the administration jumped on the credit controls bandwagon. Also, Carter's major contender for the Democratic nomination, Senator Ted Kennedy, was advocating wage and price controls. Polls indicated that a majority of Americans supported Kennedy's position (Schreft 1990, 32). In February 1980, Carter's advisors finally convinced him they were needed.

Later that month, Carter met with Paul Volcker to discuss imposing credit controls. Volcker opposed their use because he thought they were unnecessary since the economic data suggested that the economy was slowing down. But he agreed to participate in the program because he "found it impossible to resist the...argument that, at a time when the president had publicly supported our [tight monetary] policy...we in the Federal Reserve ought to respect his political judgement that...credit controls were needed" (Volcker and Gyohten 1992, 171).

The credit controls were announced on March 14th, 1980 and consisted of five major changes:[9]

(1) All lenders must maintain a 15 percent reserve on deposit at the Federal Reserve against new credit card and other unsecured lending.

(2) An increase in the marginal required reserve ratio to 8.0 - 10.0 percent on bank managed liabilities with maturity less than one year at all large member banks and branches of foreign banks operating in the United States.[10]

(3) Special deposit requirements of 10.0 percent on additional managed liabilities at nonmember banks.

(4) A 15.0 percent deposit requirement on new money market mutual funds.

(5) A surcharge of 3.0 percentage points on discount borrowing by large member banks.
(6) A voluntary program where banks and finance companies limit total annual loan growth to a range of 6.0 – 9.0 percent.

Most U.S. economists and financial officials considered the credit controls more window dressing than anything else. For example, the prominent economist Otto Eckstein described the controls as "a symbolic gesture" (Eckstein from Schreft 1990, 34). At the Federal Reserve, officials were joking about all the loopholes in the controls, thinking that they would be easily found and the controls bypassed (Greider 1987, 185). For example, requirement (2) could easily be circumvented by offering new negotiable CDs with a term to maturity of more than one year. Virtually all of the restrictions in the credit controls program were riddled with such loopholes.

Yet despite the loopholes, the credit controls produced their intended effect and then some. What no one had counted on was the American public's willingness to support the program. The president of the United States had asked for credit restraint, so it was the patriotic thing to do! Huge numbers of Americans cut up their credit cards and

Table 10.2 - Changes in Real GNP at Annualized Rates, Billions of 1972$

Period	GNP	Cd	Cnd	Cs	FBI	CBI	G	(X-M)
1979:IV-1980:II	-27.3	-22.3	-4.7	+2.2	-23.0	+2.0	+6.6	+9.5

Cd=spending on consumer durables
Cnd=spending on consumer nondurables
Cs=spending on services
FBI=fixed business investment (=spending on new plant and equipment)
CBI=changes in business inventories
G=government purchases
(X-M)=net exports

Note: sum of changes in the components of GNP do not equal the change in GNP due to rounding.

Source: Council of Economic Advisors (1981, 234-235).

mailed them to the White House, the Federal Reserve, and to the banks and finance companies that had issued them. The mail rooms at both the White House and Federal Reserve were innundated with envelopes containing cut up credit cards.

Not only did Americans destroy credit cards, they also dramatically reduced their spending. Instead of buying goods and services, households paid off installment debt. The fall in spending caused real GNP to decline during 1980:II at an annualized rate of 9.6 percent, "one of the most abrupt quarterly declines on record" (Melton 1985, 60). Table 10.2 shows the changes in the components of aggregate demand during the recession. The increases in government purchases and net exports were swamped by the declines in consumer expenditures on goods and fixed business investment. The public's response to the credit controls helps explain the fall in consumption expenditures. With respect to business investment, nearly two-thirds of the decline is accounted for by the collapse in residential construction. The high market interest rates were well above the Regulation Q deposit rates, and far in excess of loan rates specified in several states' usury laws. The result was a severe credit crunch in the housing sector.

The steep decline in output drove down the demand for credit. The Federal Reserve lowered their federal funds target band, but not by enough to keep the money supply from falling. The M1 money stock fell 2.4 percent during 1980:II. Yet despite the falling money supply, the demand for credit declined so rapidly that a huge drop in short-term nominal interest rates occurred. Referring back to Figure 10.2, the monthly average rate on 90-day Treasury bills fell from 15.52 percent in February to 6.99 by June. Meanwhile, long-term rates fell, but by nowhere near as much as short-term rates did which suggests that the economic downturn had a relatively small impact on long-term inflationary expectations. The monthly average yield on long-term Treasuries fell from 11.87 percent in February to 9.40 percent in June.

The economic free-fall during 1980:II put genuine fear into the hearts of Washington policymakers. The credit controls were removed in June, and that same month the Federal Reserve lowered the federal funds target in an effort to ease credit conditions and revive the economy. The money supply began growing rapidly, at annual rates of over 10 percent (see table 10.1). The economy recovered, aided by rebounds in homebuilding and auto sales as both industries benefitted from the huge decline in short-term interest rates taking place. The quick recovery from the recession was a big surprise to the economic forecasting industry; most forecasters expected the recession to continue through the remainder of the year.

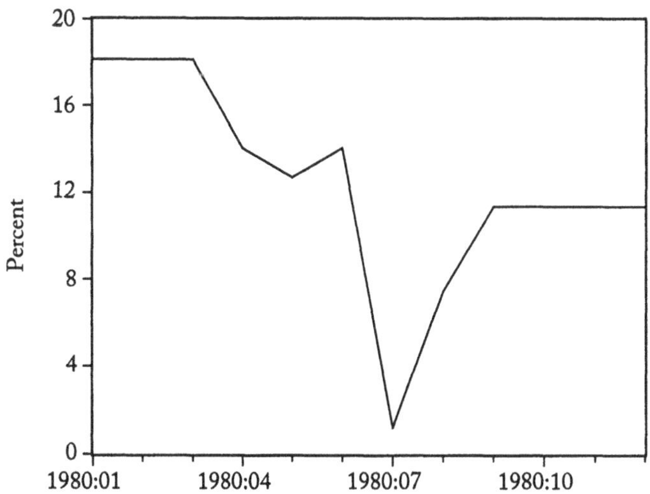

Fig. 10.3 Annualized CPI Inflation Rate, January 1980–December 1980

Unfortunately, this resumption of economic growth was accompanied by rising inflation. Figure 10.3 shows the monthly (annualized) CPI inflation rates during 1980. With the onset of the recession, the inflation rate headed down, and then experienced an enormous drop in July. However, once the economy rebounded the inflation rate promptly shot back up before stabilizing at 11.0 percent. Meanwhile, interest rates rose again, and by the end of the year the T-bill rate was higher than it had been early in the year (see figure 10.2). Clearly, the 1980 recession had been so short that output did not decline enough to significantly reduce actual and expected inflation. It would take a much longer, deeper recession to accomplish that task.

10.4 The Monetary Control Act of 1980

Another event took place in 1980 that eventually had major economic consequences. It was the passage of the Depository Institutions Deregulation and Monetary Control Act (DIDMCA) which President Carter signed into law in March 1980. This act was designed to solve a number of problems in the depository industry, and provide the Federal Reserve with enhanced powers to control the money supply.

One major purpose of the law was to deal with the Regulation Q deposit rate ceilings that had been in place since 1933. As described in Chapter 4, this economic control caused all sorts of problems in the banking and thrift industries, exacerbated the housing cycle, and harmed poor Americans.

Another issue the new law addressed was the thrift industry's desire to diversify their balance sheets. Industry profitability suffered badly during the 1970s because financial disintermediation caused a loss of deposits. Plus, thrifts depended on home mortgages for their interest income. In order to attract and retain deposits, thrifts wanted to be able to offer checking accounts so they would be better positioned to compete with banks. As far as interest earning assets were concerned, thrifts wanted to be able to diversity by issuing more loans for purposes besides home mortgages.

The law also dealt with the Federal Reserve's claim that they were having trouble controlling the money supply because so many banks had dropped out of the Federal Reserve system. During the 1970s banks left the system because inflation and the accompanying higher interest rates substantially raised the cost of membership. This occurred beçause member banks must hold their required reserves as vault cash or on deposit at the Federal Reserve, neither of which earns interest income for the bank. Meanwhile, some states allowed state-charted banks which were not members of the Federal Reserve system to hold their reserves at another bank where they could earn interest on those reserves.[11] In addition, the Federal Reserve's required reserve ratios were often higher than states' requirements. Foregone interest on required reserves was not a major issue for member banks during the 1950s and 1960s when market interest rates were low, but high interest rates during the 1970s made it a major issue. As a result, many banks left the Federal Reserve system so they would be exempt from the Fed's regulations.

Another reason the Federal Reserve felt they were losing monetary control was because thrift institutions were exempt from Federal Reserve regulations. The Federal Reserve thought that their ability to conduct monetary policy would be enhanced if they could exert control over those depository institutions.

In an effort to deal with these issues, the DIDMCA contained several provisions, but the most important were the following:[12]

1. It phased out Regulation Q. Ceiling rates on time and savings deposits would be gradually eliminated, with all deposit rate

regulations gone by 1986.

2. Banks and thrifts could offer Negotiable Order of Withdrawal accounts (NOW accounts), which are interest bearing checking accounts.
3. State usury laws on home mortgage loan rates were repealed, and limitations on usury laws were imposed on business and agricultural loans in excess of $25,000.
4. Thrifts could hold up to 20 percent of their assets in consumer loans, 5 percent in business loans, and 5 percent in student and community development loans. Also, thrifts could offer loans and mortgages at adjustable rates.
5. Federal deposit insurance was raised from $40,000 to $100,000 per depositor.
6. All depository institutions (including thrifts) would adhere to required reserve ratios set by the Federal Reserve. In exchange for imposing this cost on nonmembers, they were allowed access to Federal Reserve services such as discount borrowing and check clearing, at prices equal to those paid by member banks.

This law marks a major step forward in banking deregulation. In particular, the phase-out of Regulation Q and the advent of interest-bearing checking accounts meant that depository institutions could now engage in price competition, not just among themselves, but also with the mutual fund industry. Also, by allowing thrifts to offer checking accounts and diversify their loan portfolios, that industry was placed on a more level playing-field with banks.

There is little doubt that the DIDMCA contributed to economic stability. By removing deposit ceilings, the quantity of funds available to the mortgage market no longer exhibits the extreme volatility that characterized it during the 1960s and 1970s. Of course, homebuilding is still a cyclical industry because the demand and supply of new houses is sensitive to interest rates, plus the large stock - small flow feature of housing. But the funds available to the industry do not dry up when interest rates rise because depositors (lenders) no longer have an incentive to remove them from the mortgage market. In fact, high deposit rates provide an incentive for depositors to lend more to banks and thrifts, who then make additional funds available to the mortgage market which helps hold down mortgage rates. Thus, eliminating Regulation Q has helped stabilize mortgage rates and dampened the homebuilding cycle.

The law also allows low-income Americans to earn market interest rates on deposits at banks and thrifts. No longer are poor Americans frozen out from earning market rates because they lack the amounts necessary to buy Treasury bills or make the initial purchase necessary to buy shares in a mutual fund.

While the law brought about these benefits (and others), it also generated some harmful effects. Deregulation of thrifts' balance sheets, in combination with raising the ceiling on federal deposit insurance, increased the likelihood that managers of thrifts would engage in risky activities.[13] Savings and loans were given license to acquire riskier assets while their depositors' funds were protected by federal deposit insurance. Depositors do not care how thrift managers invest their deposits, because in the worst-case scenario where the thrift becomes insolvent, the depositors are insured. In this situation, if government regulators do not monitor the situation carefully, thrift managers might acquire very risky assets in an effort to pursue high returns, or even engage in fraudulent behavior. Either activity could run the thrift straight into the ground at taxpayer expense because the government insured the deposits. This scenario essentially describes the savings and loan crisis of the late 1980s and early 1990s, which cost U.S. taxpayers hundreds of billions of dollars and ranks as one of the genuine disasters of the 1970s and 1980s deregulation movement.

The 1980 DIDMCA negatively impacted the economy in another way that virtually no one anticipated when the law was passed. By allowing interest-bearing checking accounts, the law raised the return from holding money which caused Americans to wish to hold a larger proportion of their wealth in money balances. An increase in the demand for money causes spending to fall, because it puts upward pressure on interest rates and causes the velocity of money to decline. This was taking place during 1981 and 1982, which happened to be the same time the Federal Reserve was pursuing contractionary policies designed to reduce the inflation that reignited after the 1980 recession. The Federal Reserve's tight monetary policies combined with rising money demand to generate the huge collapse in aggregate demand growth that caused the severe 1981-1982 recession. But before relating that story (in chapter 12), we address yet another major event that took place in 1980 and what followed after it: Ronald Reagan's victory in the 1980 presidential election and the economic policies he pursued upon taking office. His ascendency to the presidency was a watershed event because he advo-

CHAPTER 11

■■■

Reaganomics

I have always thought of government as a kind of organism with an insatiable appetite for money, whose natural state is to grow forever unless you do something to starve it. By cutting taxes, I wanted not only to stimulate the economy but to curb the growth of government and reduce its intrusion into the economic life of the country.
—Ronald Reagan (1990, 232).

Poor U.S. economic conditions were a major factor in costing President Jimmy Carter the 1980 election. The brief recession during the first half of that year did virtually nothing to alleviate long-term inflation pressures, so inflation accelerated again shortly after the recession ended. The CPI inflation rate was 11.0 percent during the last quarter of the year, which is when the election took place. High energy prices were another factor working against Carter.[1] Throw in the Americans being held hostage in Iran, and the result was a triple whammy (inflation-energy crisis-Iran crisis) that cost Jimmy Carter his political hide.

The victor in the election, Ronald Reagan, ran on a platform that largely stressed economic issues. At virtually every stop on the campaign trail, he made essentially the same speech, telling audiences that he wanted to accomplish five goals:

1. Cut taxes
2. Reduce inflation
3. Raise U.S. military capability
4. Reduce the growth of government spending on social programs
5. Continue industry deregulation

This economic policy package was dubbed Reaganomics, and Reagan's efforts to bring it about and what happened afterwards constitute one of the most interesting (and controversial) stories ever in U.S. economic policy. This chapter describes the Reagan administration's economic plan. Chapters 12 and 13 analyze its impact on the U.S. economy.

11.1 Ronald Reagan

> *Historians and intellectuals have a bias towards intellectual politicians that is wholly unfounded. We tend to like people who read and write because that is who we [intellectuals] are. We tend to dismiss too quickly those who do not like to read and write...Reagan is not an intellectual. He did not read very much and wrote almost nothing. There is still a case to be made, however, that he should be regarded as one of the five most important presidents of the 20th century.*
> *—William A. Niskanen (1994, 39).*

Ronald Reagan (b. 1911) followed an unusual road to politics. After graduating from Eureka College in 1932 with a bachelors degree in economics, he first became involved in radio announcing, then acting. His big break in his acting career occurred in 1937 when Warner Brothers' Studio hired him. In the years that followed he appeared in a total of fifty-three movies, his last in 1964 (where he played a gangster in *The Killers*). He also served as host of two long-running television shows, *General Electric Theater* and *Death Valley Days.* While never a major star, he was, none-the-less, a well-respected Hollywood actor.

In 1954, when General Electric Corporation hired him to host *General Electric Theater,* they also paid him to visit their production facilities around the country, "as a kind of goodwill ambassador from the home office" (Reagan, 1990, 127). He worked for the company for eight years, touring GE plants and making speeches to the employees. At first, these speeches were about his movie acting career and television, but over time they evolved into warnings about the danger of government intrusion into the business sector. Reagan's speeches were well received, partly, no doubt, because he was an exceptionally good public speaker. But his audiences also liked the message he was delivering, and before long he was in great demand on the public speaking circuit.

Reagan's political career began in 1966 when, at the urging of a group of wealthy California Republicans, he ran for governor. He won that election, and was reelected in 1970. After leaving the California governorship in 1975, he focused on unseating President Gerald Ford in the 1976 Republican presidential primaries. That campaign was the only genuine failure of Reagan's political career.[2] He ran for the presidency again in 1980, this time emerging victorious, and was reelected for a second term in 1984. Looking back on it, Reagan had an amazing political life: he didn't become involved in politics until he was in his fifties, won four out of the five election campaigns he ran in (all four victories by landslides), and the only public offices he ever held were governor of California and president of the United States. By any standard, it was a remarkable career.

Reagan was a controversial president, in large part because he managed to attain the highest political office in the United States by running on an *anti*-government platform. Reagan's basic message was that he wanted to make the government smaller, and he wanted to accomplish this goal by cutting taxes and spending. In addition, he believed that the government should be much less involved in private economic decisions than was the case at the time. His ideas were very popular among conservatives and many moderates. However, they were diametrically opposed to those held by establishment liberals, and this is one of the reasons they reviled him.[3]

11.2 Cutting Taxes

> *Taxes, when they have grown to a certain height, are a curse equal to the barrenness of the earth and the inclemency of the heavens.*
> *—Adam Smith (1776, 433).*

> *At the peak of my career at Warner [Brothers], I was in the ninety-four percent tax bracket; that meant that after a certain point, I received only six cents of each dollar I earned...The IRS took such a big chunk of my earnings that after a while I began asking myself whether it was worth it to keep on taking work...You don't say "I've got to do more pictures," you say "I'm not gonna work for six cents on the dollar"...*
>
> *If...you reduce tax rates and allow people to spend or save more of what they earn, they'll be more industrious; they'll have more incentive to work hard, and money they earn will add fuel to the great economic machine that energizes our national progress. The result: more prosperity for all—and more revenue for government.*
>
> *A few economists call this principle supply-side economics. I just call it common sense.*
> *—Ronald Reagan (1990, 231-232).*

Reducing income tax rates was one of the most important components of Reagan's economic program. The intellectual underpinnings of the proposed tax cut are called supply-side economics and the Laffer curve. Supply-side economics refers to the idea that reducing income tax rates causes not just the aggregate demand schedule to increase, but aggregate supply as well. Lower tax rates increase consumption (which increases aggregate demand), but also raises saving which leads to higher levels of investment spending. In addition, reducing tax rates raises after-tax wages which increases labor supply by providing an inducement for people to work more. Thus, tax cuts stimulate aggregate supply by raising both labor supply and the capital stock. However, the demand and supply-side effects of the tax cuts would not occur at the same time. Tax cuts would impact aggregate demand fairly quickly because when the public receives more disposable income they will spend some of it. The supply-side effects would occur more slowly because while higher saving would lead to more investment, new capital goods take time to build and install.[4]

Most economists accept the supply-siders' general prediction that a reduction in income tax rates stimulates both aggregate supply and demand. The argument is about the relative strength of the effects. Ardent supply-siders contend that the supply-side effect dominates the demand-side effect, meaning that a cut in income tax rates would cause output to rise while inflation falls. Keynesian demand-side economists argue the opposite: the demand-side effect would dominate the supply-side effect, resulting in more output, but at a higher inflation rate.

Another controversy over Reagan's proposed tax cuts revolved around the predicted impact on the government's budget deficit. The administration firmly embraced the Laffer curve (named after economist Arthur Laffer) which describes a relationship between marginal income tax rates and total tax revenue.[5] The curve is shown in Figure 11.1. The Laffer curve intersects the origin because if the marginal tax rate is zero, the government would receive no revenue. Supply-siders argue that the same is true at a marginal tax rate of 100 percent. If people receive no income from working because it is all taxed away, then no one would attempt to earn taxable income. Instead, people would only work at nontaxable activities such as home production and illegal industry, and then engage in barter. As tax rates fall below 100 percent, people increasingly engage in taxable production, so tax revenue rises.[6] At some (unknown) tax rate, t^*, tax revenue is maximized. If the marginal tax rate is reduced below t*, revenue falls because lower tax rates cause taxable income to rise, but not by enough to offset the tax cut.[7]

In 1980, supply-siders were arguing that the marginal tax rates in place exceeded t*. Thus, reducing income tax rates would generate more revenue. However, this additional revenue would hardly material-

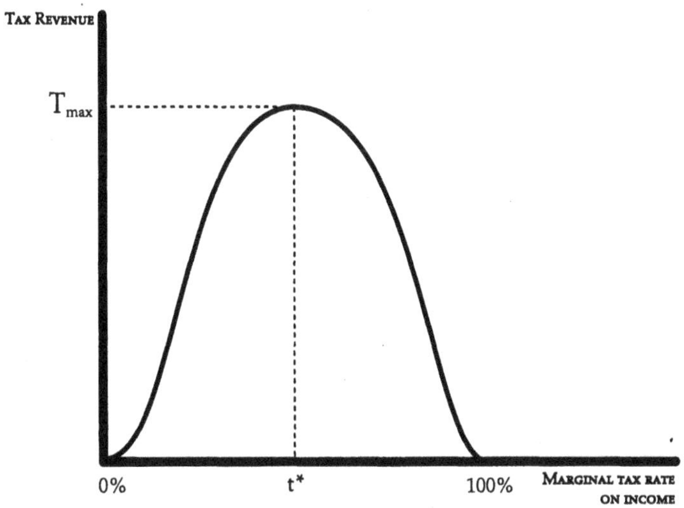

Fig. 11.1 The Laffer Curve

ize overnight, instead the supply-side effects would take a few years to have their full impact. This is because the tax cuts are a long-run economic growth program. In the near term, reducing income tax rates would reduce tax revenues.[8]

As evidence that the Laffer curve exists, supply-siders cite the income tax cuts that took place during the 1920s at the instigation of Treasury Secretary Andrew Mellon, and the 1964 income tax cut originally proposed by President Kennedy in 1962.[9] The tax cuts during the 1920s were followed by expanding budget surpluses, and the 1964 tax cut preceded a large increase in revenue that occurred in 1966. However, in these cases it is difficult to calculate just how much of the additional tax revenue was the direct result of the tax cut, and how much was caused by other factors working to raise taxable income.

The widespread perception during and after the 1980 presidential election campaign was that Reagan and the supply-siders believed that cutting taxes would not expand the budget deficit because higher tax revenue would flow immediately. However, Reagan administration economist Martin Anderson contends that no economist in the administration ever said that. Their argument was that in the near term, "a tax cut would *not lose as much revenue as one might expect*" (Anderson, 1988, p. 152).[10]

The tax cuts became law with the passage of the 1981 Economic Recovery Tax Act (ERTA). This law had several provisions, including reducing the top marginal tax rate from 70 percent to 50 percent, partially indexing income tax rates to inflation in an effort to reduce bracket creep, and cutting the maximum capital gains tax rate from 28 percent to 20 percent. Overall, income tax rates were reduced a total of 23 percent: 5 percent in 1982, then another 10 percent in both 1983 and 1984.[11] Table 11.1 shows the marginal tax rates for a married couple with two workers at various income levels under both the ERTA and as they would have been under the law ERTA replaced. The tax cuts impacted all income levels, and by the mid 1980s tax rates were consid-

Table 11.1 - Income Tax Rates for a Married Couple, Two Workers, 1981-1986

	1981	1982	1983	1984	1985	1986
Income $10,000						
Tax Rate (old law)	18%	18%	18%	18%	18%	18%
Tax Rate (ERTA)	18%	16%	15%	14%	14%	14%
Income $20,000						
Tax Rate (old law)	24%	24%	28%	28%	28%	28%
Tax Rate (ERTA)	24%	22%	19%	22%	18%	18%
Income $30,000						
Tax Rate (old law)	32%	32%	37%	37%	37%	43%
Tax Rate (ERTA)	32%	29%	26%	28%	28%	28%
Income $50,000						
Tax Rate (old law)	43%	49%	49%	49%	49%	49%
Tax Rate (ERTA)	42%	44%	40%	38%	38%	38%

Note: Income levels are in 1979$.

Source: Council of Economic Advisors (1982, 119).

erably lower than would have been the case if the ERTA had not been enacted.[12]

The new tax law also included incentives to stimulate business investment. Most important among these was allowing accelerated depreciation of capital goods. Allowable depreciation schedules were reduced to three or five years for equipment, depending on type. Buildings could be depreciated in fifteen years. Since depreciation expense is a cost to a firm, reducing the number of years to expense an asset means that firms' accounting costs rise which makes their taxable profits lower. Thus, by lowering firms' income tax liabilities, the law reduced the cost of capital in an effort to stimulate investment. Another provision of the law allowed an investment tax credit. Firms could also expense new equipment investment up to $5,000.[13]

These tax cuts were partially rescinded in 1982. The federal budget deficit ballooned that year due to both the recession and the first stage of the tax cuts, so there was pressure to reverse course and raise taxes to try to reduce the deficit. The Tax Equity and Fiscal Responsibility Act reduced the size of the 1981 tax cut by about 25 percent. It closed several loopholes, and increased enforcement. In addition, the new law repealed increases in accelerated depreciation scheduled to go into effect in 1985 and 1986. But importantly, it left alone the reductions in personal income tax rates, and retained the provisions that partially indexed the tax code to inflation. The estimated net impact of the 1981 and 1982 tax laws was to reduce taxes by about $215 billion through 1988 (Boskin, 1987, 66).[14]

The final major tax law passed during the Reagan administration was the 1986 Tax Reform Act (TRA). This legislation came about for a number of reasons. One was the desire to simplify the tax code by allowing fewer deductions and having a smaller number of tax brackets. Another motivation was the fact that some corporations and wealthy individuals were paying either no income taxes, or very small amounts, a fact that grated on the public consciousness. A third issue the law addressed was the fact that existing law treated business investment in structures and equipment differently.

The Tax Reform Act represented a major change in existing tax law. It reduced the number of tax brackets from fourteen (that ranged from 11 to 50 percent) to three: 15 , 28, and 33 percent.[15] While lowering tax rates, the TRA also broadened the tax base by eliminating several deductions. For example, state and local sales taxes and interest paid on consumer loans were no longer deductible. In addition, several tax shelters were closed, for example, individuals could no longer deduct losses on real estate from ordinary income. Such losses could only be deducted against gains from similar activities.[16]

For businesses, the TRA repealed the investment tax credit for equipment, allowed slower depreciation of assets, and reduced the corporate income tax rate from 46 to 34 percent. As with households, the idea was to lower the tax rate while broadening the tax base. At the same time, investment in equipment and structures were to be treated equally. Compared to the existing law, the slower depreciation schedules were expected to raise the cost of capital which would lower investment in the short run (Council of Economic Advisors 1987, 93).

The 1986 TRA was designed to be revenue neutral. The plan was for taxes paid by households to fall, while taxes paid by corporations rose. As a percent of total federal tax liabilities, the amount paid by households was expected to decline 6.6 percent while the amount paid by corporations rose 6.6 percent.

In sum, there were three major tax laws passed during the Reagan administration. Perhaps the most important legacy of these changes is that when Reagan took office, the highest marginal tax rate on income was 70 percent. When he left office it was 33 percent.

11.3 Reducing Inflation

> *Money growth had to be restrained, and consistently restrained over the long run...*
>
> *These policies were the basis of the policies pursued by Paul Volcker...[and they] were understood by Ronald Reagan, without whose support Volcker could not have stood the course through the 1981-1982 recession, at the time and still the most serious U.S. recession since the Great Depression.*
> *–William Poole (2002, 1-2).*

Ronald Reagan didn't control the money supply, so he could not personally reduce inflation. He did, however, make it clear to the Federal Reserve that he supported efforts to maintain what he called "moderate" monetary growth designed to reduce inflation. In effect, he was telling Federal Reserve officials that if they engineered an anti-inflationary monetary slowdown, he would support them. Reagan did not waver from this position. When the going got tough as the resulting recession significantly deepened, he did not criticize the Federal Reserve. Instead, he used the term "stay the course," meaning that if the recession was allowed to run its course, the recovery that followed would feature a much lower inflation rate than had existed before the recession began.[17]

The monetary growth slowdown began in early 1981. The federal funds rate, which had been around 14 percent in November 1980, reached 20 percent in January 1981. Meanwhile, growth of the monetary aggregates slowed markedly which is most noticeable in the monetary base, which is currency in the hands of the public plus bank reserves. This measure grew 8.4 percent during 1980, then rose 4.8 percent in 1981.

11.4 The U.S. Defense Build-Up

> *[U.S. Defense] Secretary Weinberger's call for the revitalization of our defense capabilities does represent a vindication of this committee which has warned for several years that our capabilities were eroding at an accelerating rate while those of the Soviet Union were increasing out of all proportion to their legitimate defense needs.*
> *--U.S. Representative Samuel S. Stratton (D-NY), Chairman of the House Armed Services Committee, lending bipartisan support to the Reagan administration's proposed defense build-up (U.S. Congress 1981).*

During 1980, the proportion of federal spending allocated to national defense was far below what it had been at the height of the Cold War. In 1962—which many consider the peak of the Cold War because the Cuban Missile Crisis occurred that year—49 percent of all federal outlays went for national defense. The proportion stayed high during the 1960s because of the Vietnam War, but then dropped dramatically during the 1970s. Figure 11.2 shows federal defense spending as a proportion of total federal outlays, and you can see that by the mid 1970s when U.S. involvement in Vietnam ended, the proportion had dropped to about 25 percent. The decline continued in the late 1970s as real defense spending fell. The proportion bottomed out in 1980 at just under 23 percent.[18]

The impact on the military was well-documented.[19] Salaries hadn't kept up with inflation which lowered morale. Financial problems were especially acute for U.S. military personnel stationed in Germany who faced high local prices because the dollar had depreciated against the German mark. Quality military personnel were not reenlisting. Some equipment could not be used because of a lack of spare parts. In addition, many of the military's weapons were outdated because only a few new ones had been developed since the 1960s. Meanwhile, the Soviet Union was spending considerably more on their military than was the United States. During the 1970s, the Soviets spent $150 billion more than the United States, and the widespread perception was that the Soviet Union had reached parity with the United States in nuclear weapons, and had an advantage in conventional weapons.

Reagan proposed major increases in defense spending to develop and accumulate new weapons, raise military salaries, and expand the size of the military. Among his priorities were developing the B-1 and stealth bombers, increasing the size of the U.S. Navy to six-hundred ships, and acquiring more nuclear missiles. Reagan felt that increasing both the quantity and quality of the U.S. military would not only bet-

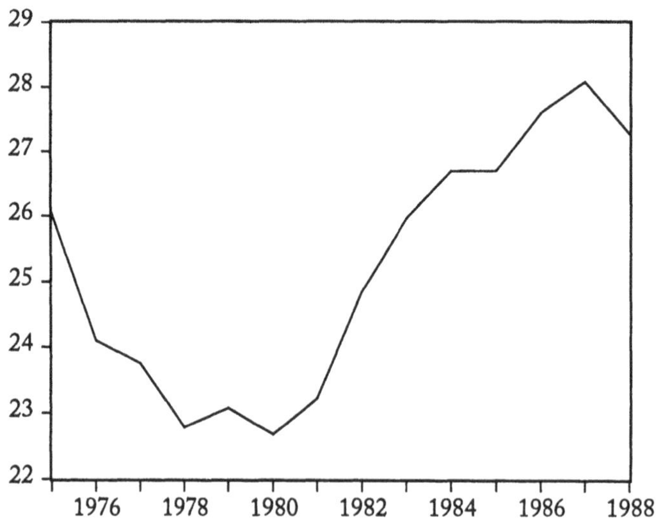

Fig. 11.2 Federal Defense Spending as a % of total Federal Outlays, 1970–1988

ter prepare the United States to handle future conflicts, but also bring about another goal he desired: forcing the Soviet Union to the negotiating table for arms reduction talks. His view was that the United States had "to bargain with them from strength, not weakness" (Reagan 1990, 294).

The resulting defense build-up approved by Congress involved huge increases in federal defense spending. From 1981-1988, real defense spending increased by a total of 77 percent in nominal terms, 43 percent in real terms. Federal defense spending also increased as a proportion of total federal outlays; referring back to Figure 11.2, you can see that after bottoming out at just under 23 percent in 1980, it rose to over 28 percent by 1987. This defense build-up not only provided a major stimulus to the U.S. economy, it also (as Reagan had hoped) helped push the Soviets to the bargaining table for arms limitations talks. In addition, it was instrumental in enabling the United States to successfully wage the Gulf War in 1991.

11.5 Slower Spending Growth

> *The continued growth of real federal spending, at a rate higher than the growth of the economy, was the major failure of Reagan's first term.*
> *—William A. Niskanen (1988, 27-28).*

Reagan's economic plan called for reduced government spending in the form of both spending cuts and slower growth of future spending. However, the general consensus among Reagan administration economists is that this was their area of greatest failure. The spending cuts never amounted to much, and those that did occur met strenuous opposition. The one area where Reagan achieved limited success late in his presidency was in reducing the growth rate of spending. This occurred because the continuing budget deficits made Congress reluctant to legislate major increases in federal outlays. Reagan had, to some extent, "starved the organism." This inability to curb spending, in combination with the tax cuts and the 1981-1982 recession, explain why the budget deficits were so large during Reagan's years in office.

There are two basic reasons why Reagan was unsuccessful in his efforts to cut spending. First was the 1981-1982 economic downturn. As the economy slid deeper into recession, the number of people losing their jobs and ending up in poverty increased substantially. As a result, more and more Americans applied for welfare and unemployment compensation which caused federal outlays on these items to increase substantially. To cite just one example of how this impacted spending, in 1982 outlays for food stamps rose $1.2 billion, even though Congress had approved a $1.7 billion cut (Weicher 1986, 13).

The second reason for Reagan's lack of success had to do with the fact that so much of the federal budget was, in effect, 'off the table' as far as spending cuts were concerned. To see why, it is useful to divide federal spending into two components: entitlements and discretionary spending. Entitlements are "a binding obligation on the part of the federal government, and eligible recipients may have legal recourse if the obligation is not fulfilled" (Schick 1995, 210). The major entitlements are Social Security and Medicare. Discretionary spending refers to outlays provided for by annual appropriation acts. The major discretionary spending item is defense; other components include the budgets for various cabinet-level departments such as Transportation, Agriculture, Commerce, and Interior.

The basic problem facing Reagan (and other recent presidents as well) is that over the past several years the entitlement portion of the budget expanded greatly at the expense of the discretionary share. For example, in the early 1960s, discretionary spending constituted 67 percent of federal outlays. The remaining 33 percent was accounted for by entitlements (26 percent) and interest on the debt (7 percent).[20] During the 1960s and 1970s the entitlements share grew enormously, largely because Medicare was created in 1966, and Social Security benefits were greatly expanded during both the Johnson and Nixon administrations. By the time Ronald Reagan arrived on the scene in 1981, discretionary spending had fallen to 45 percent of federal outlays, while entitlements comprised another 45 percent of the total.[21] Interest on the debt accounted for the remaining 10 percent.

In other words, during Reagan's first year in office roughly 55 percent of total federal outlays were, in effect, untouchable. Interest on the debt could not be reduced, and entitlements were (and are) a political hot-potato because recipients scream loud and clear whenever the issue of cutting benefits is discussed. For example, when the Reagan administration proposed reducing social security benefits for those who retired at age sixty-two from 80 percent to 50 percent of the full benefit amount if they instead retired at age sixty-five, the plan was shot down in the U.S. Senate by a vote of 98-0.

In addition, by advocating a defense build up, Reagan was saying that outlays for defense were going to increase which added another 23 percent of federal outlays to the 'untouchable' portion. This gives a total of 78 percent of total federal outlays that Reagan could not, or would not, cut.[22] This was the unpleasant arithmetic facing his plan; if he was going to reduce spending, it had to come out of the remaining 22 percent of the total. What was this 22 percent spent on? Largely social programs, the environment, and various construction projects such as waste treatment plants and roads. Reducing expenditures on those programs was problematic for the simple reason that every federal program has a constituency. When Reagan made proposals to do so, Congress often balked, or authorized smaller cuts than he wanted.

What ultimately happened was that a few of these programs were cut deeply: sewage treatment plant construction, construction of low priority roads, and the public employment branch of the Comprehensive Employment and Training Act (CETA). Most other programs were impacted, but only to a minor extent. Reagan requested a total of $23 billion worth of spending cuts during fiscal years 1981 and 1982, and Congress approved $15 billion. For fiscal year 1983, Reagan requested cuts of another $1.5 billion, but Congress approved none of them (Schick 1995, 176).

The Reagan administration's inability to cut federal spending is clearly illustrated in Figure 11.3 which shows the patterns of federal spending on national defense, nondefense, and transfer payments from 1960 to 1988. This figure illustrates that the huge growth in government spending that started in the late 1960s was concentrated first in transfer payments, then during the Reagan administration on both national defense and transfer payments. Reagan's only real claim to success in the spending area is that transfer payments grew slower than the overall economy from 1984 to 1988.[23]

11.6 Deregulation

> *My inaugural address [in 1981] ended the ceremonies and we went into the Capitol for lunch with members of Congress and other guests. On the way to lunch, I stopped in a room in the Capitol...and performed my first official act as president: I signed an executive order removing price controls on oil and*

gasoline, my first effort to liberate the economy from excess government regulation.
—Ronald Reagan (1990, 227). Since then, the United States has experienced occasional bouts with high energy prices, but never accompanied by gasoline lines.

The term "government regulation" refers to the rules the government has imposed on business practices. These regulations fall into several categories: restrictions against firms entering an industry, rules on setting prices, specifying which products and services firms can and can not offer, product safety rules, workplace safety rules, environmental restrictions, hiring and firing practices...the list is seemingly endless. Thousands upon thousands of these rules exist.

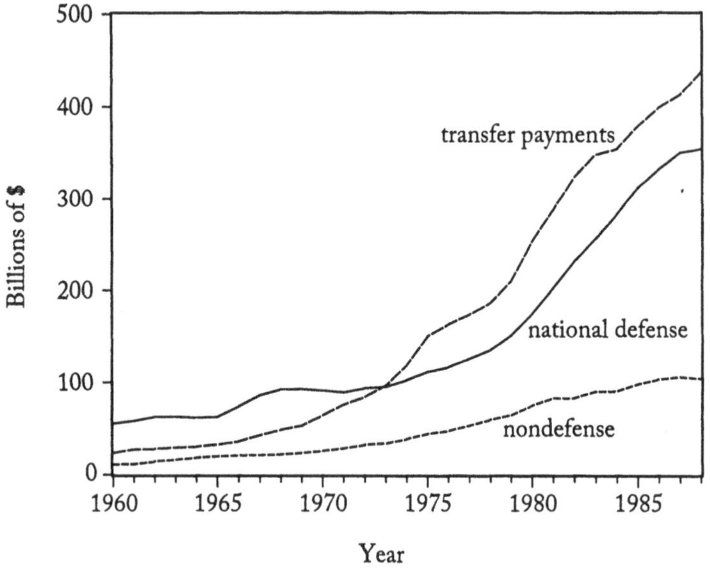

Fig. 11.3 Federal Spending on Defense, Nondefense and Transfer Payments, 1960–1988

These regulations were put in place during three big waves. The first occurred during the late 1800s and early 1900s when the Sherman Antitrust Act was passed and the Interstate Commerce Commission (ICC) and Federal Trade Commission (FTC) were formed. The second wave occurred as part of the New Deal legislation that was enacted during the 1930s. The third wave occurred during the 1960s and 1970s, when the attitude that the government should be more involved in economic decisions was taken to a new level. Two agencies were created at that time that are responsible for many of these rules--the Environmental Protection Agency (EPA) and Occupational Safety and Health Administration (OSHA). This third wave swamped the previous two in terms of numbers of new regulations put in place (Yandle 1986).

The growth of regulation during the 1960s and 1970s is illustrated by the growth of federal spending on, and employment in, regulatory activities. Warren and Weidenbaum (1999, 17-18) estimate that real federal spending on regulatory activities rose from $1.9 billion in 1960 to $10.3 billion by 1980.[24] From 1970 to 1980, the number of full-time equivalent federal employees involved in regulatory activity rose from 69,946 to 121,791.

As the amount of regulatory activity increased, so did complaints by business groups and economists. Excessive regulation became a public policy issue in the fall of 1974 when President Gerald Ford convened a series of summit conferences to discuss the problem of inflation. Conference participants, however, were much more interested in talking about costly regulations than discussing inflation. In fact, at one session, a "petition calling for elimination of numerous regulations was signed by twenty-one out of twenty-three economists" (Yandle 1986, 118). Ford's response was to sign an executive order requiring federal agencies to assess the economic impact of proposed new rules.

The increasingly widespread recognition that there are costs associated with the social regulations put in place by agencies such as the EPA and OSHA led to progress in the area of industry deregulation. During the Ford administration, the securities brokerage industry was deregulated, and the deregulatory process was started in railroads, airlines, and trucking.

During President Jimmy Carter's term in office, the rule about regulatory agencies assessing the economic effects of new regulations was retained, and industry deregulation accelerated. Airlines, trucking, railroads, natural gas, petroleum, and the banking industry were all deregulated during the Carter administration.[25] Part of the impetus for this continued deregulation came from economic studies being publishing in the late 1970s that reported estimates of the costs of regulation. They were providing some fairly astounding numbers, some as high as 5.5 percent of annual GDP.[26]

Reagan's role was simply to continue the deregulatory process. His administration forged ahead with the industry deregulation already under way, and took an active role in deregulating the savings and loan, and cable TV industries. In addition, the Reagan administration continued the policy of requiring federal agencies to assess the economic impact of regulations.

One noticeable effect of deregulation during the Reagan administration was that growth of federal spending on regulatory activity slowed considerably, while employment in regulatory agencies declined. Warren and Weidenbaum (1999) estimate that real outlays on federal regulatory activities rose 17 percent during Reagan's term in office (1981-1989), compared to a gain of well over 100 percent during the 1970s. Meanwhile, employment in federal regulatory activity declined during Reagan's term, from 117,209 full-time equivalent employees in 1981, to 107,017 by 1989.

While economists supported the moves toward deregulation, many were quick to point out that anti-trust implications should not be ignored. Anti-trust is an important consideration because when the government deregulates an industry and allows market forces to work, considerable merger activity may take place among firms in the newly deregulated industry. Problems may arise if firms gobble up their competitors to the point that just a few firms remain. In this case, the ones left might have dominant market power leading to economic inefficiencies in the form of higher prices, and lower quality and quantity of output. The gains from deregulation may be severely reduced, or even canceled out completely.

In the minds of many economists that study deregulation, the Reagan administration's adherence to free markets worked to a fault. Reagan administration officials felt that free markets always generate the optimal result. Thus, mergers and acquisitions within an industry were considered acceptable because it was simply the free market at work. As a result, an enormous number of mergers and acquisitions took place during the 1980s, and the federal agencies in charge of enforcing anti-trust laws approved virtually every single one of them. In certain industries, such as airlines and railroads, large increases in industrial concentration occurred, and years later it is not at all obvious that consumers ended up being big winners.

The airline industry provides an illustration of this point. During the early 1980s, many restrictions on entry into the industry were eliminated, as was government regulation of airline ticket prices. Firms entered the industry, and the increased competition caused prices to fall dramatically. The result was a huge boom in air travel; quantity demanded increased and the airlines purchased many new planes to meet this demand. Over time, however, many of the recent entrants went out of business or merged with the major airlines, so much so, that "fifty airlines disappeared in the first few years after deregulation" (Shepherd and Brock 1995, 251). The mergers and acquisitions continued during the decade, and the Department of Transportation approved all of them. As a result, the industry changed from being competitive in the years immediately following deregulation, to an oligopoly consisting of just a few major carriers by the early 2000s. The effects on passengers are well-known: high ticket prices charged to those living in a city largely served by one airline (for example, Delta customers in Atlanta, Georgia), narrower seats with less leg room, and diminished service.

The results of airline deregulation actually fall somewhere in the middle in the deregulatory success-failure spectrum. Perhaps the most successful deregulation occurred in long distance telephone service. Prior to deregulation it was controlled by America Telephone and Telegraph (ATT). Long distance telephone service was opened to competition during the 1980s, and today consumers have a wide array of competing companies vying for their business. The combination of competition and technological advancements (fiber optics) have caused long distance telephone costs to plummet and service to improve dramatically. Consumers have clearly been big winners.

At the opposite extreme is the experience following deregulation of the savings and loan industry. A combination of freeing S&Ls to invest in assets previously unavailable to them while reducing regulatory oversight of their activities resulted in the Savings and Loan Crisis which came to a head in the late 1980s and early 1990s . Hundreds of S&Ls failed and had to be merged with healthy banks; the bailout cost taxpayers an estimated $350 billion.

11.7 A Change of Direction

Every component of the Reagan's economic program (with the exception of industry deregulation) represented a genuine change in economic policy relative to what had been the case before. Efforts were made to substantially cut taxes, downsize the government, reduce inflation, and expand the military, all of which went against trends that had been going on for years.

The Reagan administration was more successful in achieving some of these goals than others. But it is important to remember the overriding theme of the Reagan administration's efforts: reduce taxes so households can choose how to spend more of their income, downsize the government so it becomes less involved in economic decisions, and remember that private decisions usually generate better outcomes than government decisions. Reagan presented a refreshing message to an American public tired of slow gains in living standards, bracket creep, energy crises with shortages and gasoline lines, and a political climate suggesting that they had better get used to these limitations. He rode that theme to the White House, and then delivered almost all of his program.

The next chapter examines the near-term result of the anti-inflation component of Reaganomics: the 1981-1982 recession. It was the most severe U.S. downturn since the 1930s, but the good news is that caused a major disinflation that set the stage for the huge recovery that followed.

CHAPTER 12

■ ■ ■

The 1981-1982 Recession

> *I've been spending a lot of time putting applications in for work all over the place, and I've concluded that there are a lot more people hunting work than there are jobs. It used to be that when one steel mill slacked off, you could find work at another. But this entire valley is dead. I can't even get a job pumping gas, and believe me, I've tried. Even my wife...can't find a simple waitress job...*
>
> *When I look around at friends from the mill who are getting divorced or losing their homes, I wonder, "Am I next? Is my marriage going to fall apart? Am I going to lose the home I've worked for all my life?"*
>
> *I can't help but be depressed.*
>
> *—John Worrall, an unemployed steelworker from McKeesport, Pennsylvania (1982, 73).*

The monetary slowdown that began in January 1981 helped push the economy into a recession that started in July. Early on, the decline was steep: during 1981:III output fell at an annualized rate of 5.0 percent. Yet despite the severe drop in spending, during the first months of the recession many firms retained workers, thinking the worst would soon be over. However, by early 1982 it became clear that the situation–especially in construction and manufacturing–was not going to improve soon. As a result, millions of workers were laid off, with much of the hardship occurring in and around the industrial Great Lakes region. A huge number of Americans were subjected to the agony of unemployment, poverty, and mental depression. The U.S. unemployment rate soared, peaking in December 1982 at 10.8 percent, the highest recorded since the Great Depression.

Fortunately, this economic misery came with a silver lining. The recession–since it was both long and severe–drove output well below capacity which caused a major disinflation. The annualized CPI inflation rate, which was 10.0 percent during the six-months before the recession began, was down to 3.2 percent by 1983, the first full calendar-year after the recession ended. This major disinflation, plus the fact that the U.S. economy performed so well for so many years afterwards, suggests that we owe a large debt of gratitude to those millions of people who bore the pain of joblessness and poverty during the early 1980s. They were the unfortunate victims of an effort to eradicate the inflation caused by the misguided aggregate demand-management policies of the 1960s and 1970s. They paid a huge personal price for the disinflation that an enormous number of Americans benefitted from afterwards.

12.1 The Collapse In Aggregate Demand Growth

> *This recession is distinguished, above all, by the sharp slowdown in nominal GNP growth that had occurred. The four-quarter growth rate of nominal GNP ending in 1981: Q3 was 12.8 percent, compared with 3.2 percent in the five quarters ending in 1982:Q4. This represents a "cold turkey" slowdown of almost ten percentage points.*
> *—Robert J. Gordon (1983, 3).*

The 1981-1982 recession was caused by a severe decline in aggregate demand growth. Table 12.1 shows the annualized rates of nominal aggregate demand growth, output growth, and inflation from 1980:IV to 1983:IV. Aggregate demand was increasing at rates in the 17 to 18 percent range during 1980:IV and 1981:I, then grew just 3.8 percent in 1981:II. This was followed by a rebound during the next quarter to 12 percent, but then it grew at an average rate of just 1.0 percent over the next six months.

This huge decline in nominal GDP growth had to be reflected in the growth rates of output and prices, and in the near term output experienced the largest decline.[1] This is a typical pattern when aggregate demand growth declines substantially: initially, output growth falls more than inflation does. This occurs since prices exhibit considerable inertia because of rigidities caused by factors such as price contracts, menu costs, and markup pricing in combination with sticky costs. As a result, when demand changes, most of the short-run adjustment shows up in output growth.[2] Then, in the longer-run, prices do the bulk of the adjusting because wages and prices become more flexible over time. This pattern is illustrated in table 12.1: nominal GDP growth fell from 17.5 percent in 1981:I to 3.8 percent in 1981:II, a decline of 13.7 percentage points. During that same period, output growth fell from 7.4 percent to -3.6, a decline of 11 percentage points. Meanwhile, inflation fell just 2.6 percentage points. By the last two quarters of 1982, inflation had declined considerably and output growth increased.

Table 12.1 - Annualized Nominal GDP Growth, Output Growth, and Inflation, 1980:IV-1983:IV

	DPY	DY	DP
1980:IV	18.1 %	7.8 %	10.4 %
1981:I	17.5 %	7.4 %	10.1 %
1981:II	3.8 %	-3.6 %	7.4 %
1981:III	12.0 %	4.7 %	7.3 %
1981:IV	2.7 %	-5.0 %	7.7 %
1982:I	-0.8 %	-6.7 %	5.8 %
1982:II	6.3 %	1.6 %	4.6 %
1982:III	3.7 %	-2.0 %	5.7 %
1982:IV	4.5 %	0.5 %	3.9 %
1983:I	7.7 %	3.8 %	3.9 %
1983:II	12.4 %	8.5 %	3.9 %
1983:III	10.9 %	7.1 %	3.8 %
1983:IV	11.2 %	7.4 %	3.8 %

Note: DPY = annualized growth of nominal GDP
DY = annualized growth of real GDP
DP = annualized GDP deflator inflation rate
DPY = DY + DP

Source: Federal Reserve Bank of St. Louis, FRED.

The collapse in aggregate demand growth was caused by a combination of the monetary slowdown and falling velocity.[3] Table 12.2 shows the annualized quarterly growth rates of M1, M2, their corresponding velocities, and nominal GDP. The low monetary growth rates in 1981:I were offset by rapid velocity growth, so nominal GDP growth stayed high. But in 1981:II , the velocities of both M1 and M2 fell, dragging aggregate demand growth down with them. During the remainder of the recession, either slow monetary growth or falling velocity kept nominal aggregate demand growth low.[4]

The slowdown in monetary growth was a deliberate effort by the Federal Reserve to reduce inflation. However, Federal Reserve offi-

Table 12.2 - Annualized Monetary Growth, Velocity Growth, and Aggregate Demand Growth, 1980:IV-1983:IV

	DM1	DV1	DM2	DV2	DPY
1980:IV	10.9 %	7.2 %	8.1 %	10.0 %	18.1 %
1981:I	4.5 %	13.0 %	7.5 %	10.0 %	17.5 %
1981:II	9.2 %	-5.3 %	12.0 %	-8.2 %	3.8 %
1981:III	0.3 %	11.7 %	8.3 %	3.7 %	12.0 %
1981:IV	5.7 %	-3.0 %	8.8 %	-6.1 %	2.7 %
1982:I	10.4 %	-11.2 %	9.8 %	-10.6 %	-0.8 %
1982:II	3.3 %	3.0 %	9.5 %	-3.2 %	6.3 %
1982:III	3.5 %	0.2 %	9.8 %	-6.1 %	3.7 %
1982:IV	16.1 %	-11.6 %	8.8 %	-4.3 %	4.5 %
1983:I	14.1 %	-6.3 %	20.3 %	-12.5 %	7.7 %
1983:II	12.2 %	0.2 %	10.1 %	2.3 %	12.4 %
1983:III	8.9 %	2.0 %	7.8 %	3.1 %	10.9 %
1983:IV	2.1 %	9.1 %	7.0 %	4.2 %	11.2 %

Note: DM1 = annualized growth rate of M1 money supply
DV1 = annualized growth rate of M1 velocity
DM2 = annualized growth rate of M2 money supply
DV2 = annualized growth rate of M2 velocity
DPY = annualized growth of nominal GDP
DM1 + DV1 = DM2 + DV2 = DPY

Source: Federal Reserve Bulletin, *various issues, and Federal Reserve Bank of St. Louis, FRED.*

cials were as surprised as anyone by the magnitude of the decline in aggregate demand growth and the severity of the economic downturn that resulted. The reason why is because the decline in the velocity of money came as a complete surprise.

The fall in velocity was unexpected because it was completely out of line with recent historical experience. Figure 12.1 shows the velocities of M1 and M2 from 1959-1983. Both series had been following stable paths for several consecutive years, so few economists expected velocity to deviate from those paths. While the fall in M1 velocity is more apparent in the diagram than the decline in M2 velocity, the rates of decline are actually quite similar (see table 12.2). The fall in velocity was not only unexpected, it was also thought to be temporary which led the Federal Reserve to keep monetary growth low during the last half of 1982 (Melton 1985, 62-64). They expected the declines in M1 and M2 velocity to reverse, with both series returning to their longer-run trends. Maintaining the tight monetary policy reinforced the contractionary effects of the fall in velocity and resulted in the huge collapse in aggregate demand growth.

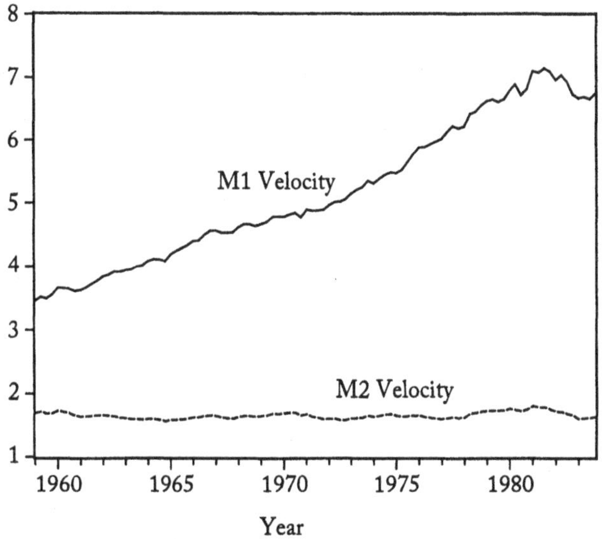

Fig. 12.1 Velocities of M1 and M2, 1959.I–1983.IV

Velocity's unusual behavior presented economists with an important puzzle to solve, and several explanations were provided. Paul Volcker's view is that the fall in velocity was largely caused by the availability of new types of bank accounts made available to the public (Volcker, 1983). Particularly important were the interest bearing checking accounts called Negotiable Order of Withdrawal accounts (NOW accounts) that became available nationwide in 1981. The 1980 Depository Institution Deregulation and Monetary Control Act specified that banks could offer these accounts beginning in 1981.[5] While the rates paid on these accounts were initially fixed below market rates, the point is that the interest rate that could be earned on a checking account went from zero to over 5.0 percent as a result of the new law. Thus, the demand for money increased, causing velocity to fall.[6]

Many economists believe that the advent of nationwide NOW accounts is only part of the story. Other variables that influence the demand for money were also changing at the time, in particular inflation and nominal interest rates. The 90-day Treasury bill rate, after peaking in May 1981 at 16.3 percent, was down to 7.7 percent by October 1982, an incredible decline of 860 basis points over a seventeen-month period.[7] Thus, the opportunity cost of holding money declined substantially which caused the quantity of money demanded to increase. At the same time, financial innovation in the form of more interest-bearing accounts that serve as substitutes for traditional forms of money raised the interest sensitivity of the demand for money (Carlson and McElravey 1989). In other words, the large decline in nominal interest rates during the recession caused an even larger increase in the quantity of money demanded than would have been the case in prior years.[8]

Milton Friedman (1984) argues that increased economic uncertainty caused the decline in velocity. When the public becomes more uncertain about the future, their desire for liquidity increases which causes the demand for money to rise (and velocity to fall). Friedman contends that the extreme volatility of monetary growth (see table 12.2) following the Federal Reserve's 1979 change in operating procedures caused this increase in uncertainty. Thus, Friedman believes the Federal Reserve caused the decline in velocity through their stop-and-go monetary policies during the late 1970s and early 1980s.[9]

Whatever the factor(s) at work, the decline in velocity came as a huge surprise to virtually everyone. As a result, not only was the 1981-1982 recession itself unexpected, its severity astonished many as well. For example, the forecast supplied by the Council of Economic Advisors in the 1982 Economic Report of the President called for real GNP to grow 3.0 percent during the year, i.e., a healthy rate of economic growth. The actual rate during the year turned out to be -2.5 percent, which means the forecast was not only dead-wrong, but also had an enormous error of 5.5 percentage points.

12.2 Regional Depressions

> *The first iron furnace came to Ohio's Mahoning Valley in 1803. By 1875, 21 blast furnaces were producing 250,000 tons of steel annually. By 1925–the whole valley wreathed in smoke*

and flame–production was four million tons a year...

Now, a visitor can drive south from Warren, down through Niles and McDonald, Girard and Youngstown, on to Campbell and beyond to Struthers, and see silent, empty steel mills stretching mile after mile–the Brier Hill complex, the Campbell works, the Youngstown and McDonald works.

It is a necropolis.

—James M. Perry (1983, 1).

I took a gun to myself. I pulled the trigger...I either moved my head–I don't remember. I'm sorry for doing it, because I thought it was a quick way out of this. I got two little kids. The little one said to me..."Daddy, we'll make it."

—Albert Bragg, an unemployed steelworker from New Cumberland, West Virginia, testifying before Congress (U.S. Congress 1982, 49).

By several measures, the 1981-1982 downturn was the worst economic contraction in the United States since the 1930s. Between July 1981 and November 1982, real GDP fell 3.0 percent, industrial production dropped 13.2 percent, and there was a net loss of nearly 3.0 million jobs (U.S. Department of Labor 1991, 1). As firms reduced output and laid off workers, capacity utilization rate hit 69.7 percent, the lowest since the Great Depression (Schinasi 1983, 2).

Not only did the number of people who were unemployed go up, the amount of time they were jobless increased as well. The unemployment rate peaked in December 1982 at 10.8 percent, and in May 1983 the average duration of joblessness was twenty-two weeks, and one-quarter of those unemployed had been jobless for six months or more (Gay and Hedlund 1983, 483). This long-term unemployment caused significant hardship for many people because their unemployment benefits expired. Only about one-third of those unemployed received benefits during the recession, compared to over half during the 1973-1975 recession (Gay and Hedlund 1983, 483).

The recession impacted some industries much more than others. Table 12.3 shows the changes in employment that occurred in various sectors of the economy. As is normal during a business contraction, the output decline was focused in goods production where employment fell by a staggering total of over 3.3 million workers. The vast bulk of that decline occurred in mining, construction, and durable goods production (U.S. Department of Labor 1991, 6).[10] Employment declines during business recessions are usually focused in those sectors, but the number of layoffs during this downturn was extreme. Meanwhile, private service-sector employment increased by about 400,000 workers due to employment gains in retail trade, financial services, and health care (U.S. Department of Labor 1991, 689). When government service employment is included, the number of people working in services rose by more than 800,000.

The huge decline in goods production occurred for several reasons. Construction was adversely affected by the high interest rates at the time, along with the fact that soaring house prices during the 1970s

Table 12.3 Employment Changes in Various Industry Groups, 1981-1982

	Time Period	Change in Employment
Goods Producing	7/81–12/82	- 3,070,000
Mining	9/81–12/82	- 203,000
Construction	8/81–12/82	- 660,000
Durable Goods	6/81–12/82	- 1,900,000
Industrial Machinery	6/81–12/82	- 491,400
Primary Metal	6/81 - 12/82	- 345,200
Fabricated Metal	6/81–12/82	- 273,600
Transportation Equipment	9/81–11/82	- 256,000
Lumber & Wood Products	6/81–12/82	- 110,800
Nondurable Goods	9/81–12/82	- 650,000
Service Producing (including government)	7/81–11/82	+ 858,000

Source: Employment, Hours, and Earnings, United States, 1909-1990, Volumes I & II *(Washington D.C.: U.S. Department of Labor, Bureau of Labor Statistics, 1991).*

made home ownership increasingly unaffordable. From 1970-1982, the average price of a new home (adjusted for quality changes) rose 190 percent, while the CPI rose 143 percent (Freund 1983, 65). This rise in the real cost of homes—in combination with the high interest rates then prevailing—raised the average carrying-cost of a new home from 20 percent of mean household income in the early 1970s, to 40 percent by 1982 (Freund 1983, 66). In addition, demographics worked to reduce demand for new houses because by the early 1980s members of the post WWII 'baby bust' were reaching the age where they would purchase homes. As a result of these various factors, housing starts, which had been above 2.0 million in 1978, declined to 1.06 million during 1982 (U.S. Department of Commerce 1984, 78).

Auto production was adversely affected by falling income, high interest rates, and the fact that the 1979 oil price hike caused American consumers to once again shift their preferences away from large domestically-produced cars and toward small imported autos. Weak sales of new domestic autos spread to the steel industry which was also harmed by the downturn in construction. In addition, U.S. steel producers were no longer competitive in world markets due to the strengthening dollar on foreign exchange markets, and high U.S. pollution-abatement costs. Several large steel plants in western Pennsylvania and eastern Ohio were shut down permanently, resulting in huge numbers of lost jobs. As those workers' incomes plummeted, so did their spending which spread the misery throughout that region of the country.

Regional differences during the recession are shown in table 12.4 which contains the unemployment rates in selected states at the economic trough in November 1982. West Virginia and the Great Lakes states fared the worst. As steel production plummeted, so did the demand for coal, both of which caused severe problems in West Virginia. Automobile production was (and still is) concentrated in the Great Lakes region, so Michigan, Ohio, and Indiana were all harmed by the decline in demand for domestic autos. Within these states, pockets of extreme hardship occurred in communities heavily dependent on particular industries. Communities such as Youngstown, Ohio (steel) and Flint, Michigan (autos) experienced unemployment rates of around 20 percent, similar to the national unemployment measures recorded during the Great Depression.[11]

Some states fared reasonably well during the recession. High petroleum prices benefitted the oil-producing states of Texas, Oklahoma, and Kansas, so employment in that region held up much better than in the Great Lakes states. North Dakota, Nebraska, and Hawaii have small manufacturing bases, so those states avoided major layoffs.

Even though unemployment did not soar in the farm belt, this does not mean that farmers prospered during the recession. In fact, the U.S.

Table 12.4 - Unemployment Rates in Selected States at the Economic Trough, November, 1982

State	Unemployment Rate (%)
West Virginia	17.2
Michigan	16.3
Ohio	13.6
Illinois	12.8
Indiana	12.7
Washington	12.5
Pennsylvania	12.2
Wisconsin	11.5
U.S. National Average	**10.7**
Georgia	8.4
Texas	8.3
Oklahoma	7.8
Virginia	7.7
Kansas	7.1
Hawaii	6.5
Nebraska	6.4
North Dakota	6.2

Source: U.S. Department of Labor, Bureau of Labor Statistics, http://stats.bls.gov.lauhome.htm

agriculture sector suffered greatly. The combination of high interest rates and falling inflation meant that ex-post real interest rates were high. Since, as Greider (1987, 452) notes, "even a modest-sized farm might be carrying $500,000 or more in revolving bank loans in order to operate," high real rates imposed a serious burden on farmers. In addition, because agricultural products are traded internationally, the strong appreciation of the U.S. dollar on foreign currency markets (caused by the high real interest rates) placed downward pressure on food prices.[12] Throw in bumper crops in the United States--which placed further deflationary pressure on farm prices--and the result was a decline in real per-farm family income of 11 percent during 1982 (Council of Economic Advisors 1983, 130). Farmers weren't the only ones experiencing hard times in agriculture regions: farm equipment manufacturers and retailers felt the pain as well. To cite just one example, in 1982 International Harvester Corporation experienced a 31 percent decline in sales, laid off 22,000 employees, and lost $822 million (Greider 1987, 478-479).

12.3 The Good News: Inflation Relief

> *Because wages are the major part of unit costs of production, they are the key to a sustainable deceleration of the underlying rate of inflation.*
> *–Phillip Cagan and William Fellner (1983, 604).*

In the midst of this economic mess, there was some good news: inflation relief. Figure 12.2 shows real GDP relative to Gordon's (2000) natural rate series. Output was near the full employment level during mid-1981, then the recession dragged real GDP well below capacity so that by 1982:IV the output gap was $361 billion (in 1992 dollars). This excess capacity and associated labor force unemployment placed downward pressure on the growth of wages and other costs. Nominal wages, which increased over 10 percent during 1980, were growing at a 6.0 percent rate by the end of 1982 (Gay and Hedlund 1983, 484). Slower wage growth for unionized workers was part of the story, in fact Perry describes the recession as generating "a climate of unprecedented concessions in important union wage contracts" (Perry 1983, 594). Here are the data on wage adjustments in the first year of union contracts during the early 1980s:

	First-year wage adjustments in	
Year	Manufacturing	Construction
1980	7.4 %	13.6 %
1981	7.2 %	13.5 %
1982	2.8 %	6.5 %
1983 *(1st half)*	-1.9 %	1.6 %

Source: Perry (1983, 595).

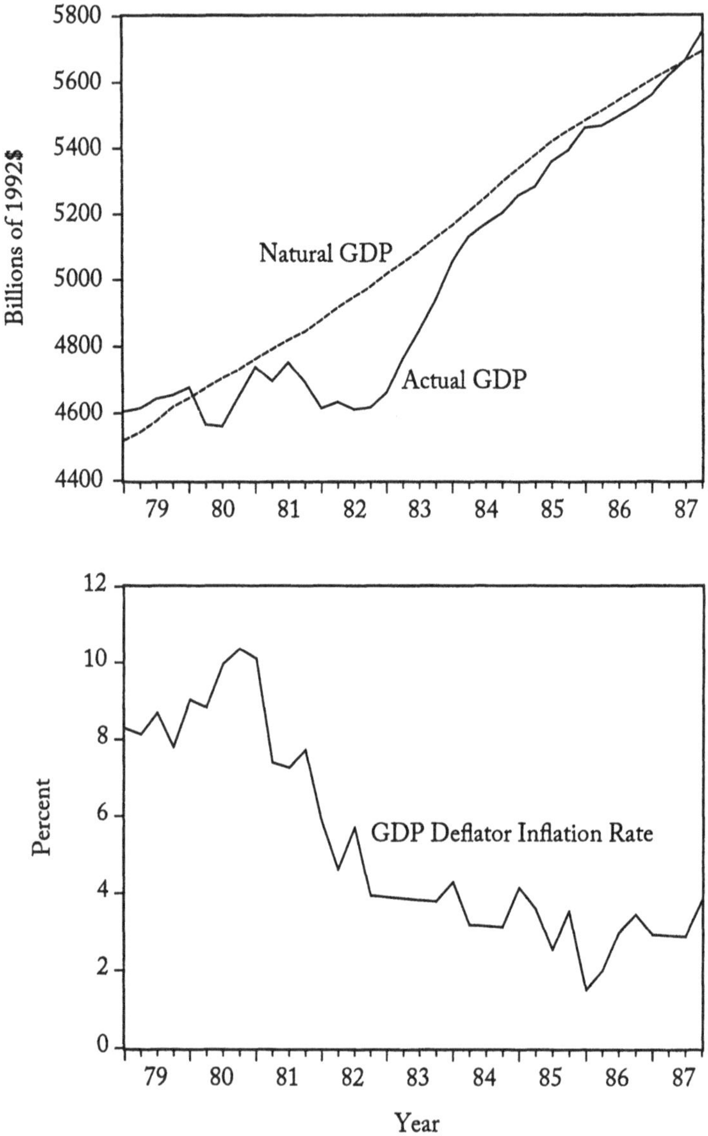

Fig. 12.2 Output Gap and Disinflation

Not only did wage growth decline substantially during the recession, in manufacturing it actually became negative during the first half of 1983. During that same period, Perry reports that "an unprecedented 60 percent of wage adjustments in the construction industry showed [either] no change or [a] decline" (1983, 596).

Meanwhile, even though public sector employment rose in the early 1980s, unionized public employees were relatively undemanding. This may have been because unionized federal workers were served notice that illegal strikes would not be tolerated when in August 1981 President Reagan fired the air-traffic controllers who staged an illegal strike.

Diminished wage growth was a major contributor to the disinflation that occurred. Other factors included pervasive excess capacity in the economy which placed downward pressure on cost increases. In addition, the appreciating dollar on foreign currency markets helped reduce inflation by moderating price increases of imports and domestically-produced tradable goods.[13]

Dotsey and DeVaro (1995) report that the disinflation during the recession was unexpected. This means that inflation fell more rapidly than people thought it would, so ex-post real interest rates were above ex-ante real interest rates. Thus, borrowers ended up paying higher real interest costs than they expected to, while lenders received higher real interest revenue than they expected. The lenders who gained from this unexpected wealth transfer were banks and their shareholders, along with wealthy Americans. Borrowers were the losers, predominately farmers and middle-class households with large mortgage debt.

Disinflation claimed other victims as well. Real estate–which was such a good hedge against inflation during the 1970s–turned out to be a poor investment during the early 1980s. The California housing market–which had been among the hottest in the country during the 1970s–cooled off considerably in the early 1980s. After increasing at double digit rates during the 1970s, the U.S. Commerce Department's quality-adjusted home price index for California rose 4.6 percent in 1981, and then just 2.1 percent during 1982.[14] In some states, home values actually fell. During the recession the house price index for Michigan fell 17 percent, while house prices in Ohio fell 5.0 percent. In virtually every state, the amount of time it took to sell a house rose.

Gold, which had been a fabulous hedge against rising inflation during the 1970s, proved to be a disastrous investment during the early 1980s. The price of an ounce of gold, which peaked in early 1980 at over $800 fell to $296.75 by June 1982 (Melton 1985, 66).

12.4 Laying the Foundation

The 1981-1982 recession was a very important macroeconomic event because it broke the U.S. inflationary spiral that had been going on for over fifteen years. Unfortunately, the recession also brought genuine hardship to millions of Americans in the form of unemployment, poverty, and all of the social ills associated with those problems.

Yet for the country as a whole, the hardship was worth it because the resulting disinflation helped lay the groundwork for enormous economic benefits that followed. Falling inflation reduced interest rates which helped stimulate investment spending. The disinflation also lessened the overstatement of corporate profits which lowered corporate tax liabilities and helped increase real after-tax profits. The combination of falling interest rates and increased corporate profitability (which was also brought on by the recovery that followed) led to the enormous surge in stock prices that began in 1982.

Looking back on it today, we can see how beneficial the 1981-1982 recession was for the U.S. economy. However, at the time many Americans did not see the recession as a necessary evil. Instead, they complained bitterly about closed factories, job losses, and rising poverty and focused their anger on the White House and the Federal Reserve. Ronald Reagan and Paul Volcker were the ones feeling the heat, yet both men stood firm in their efforts to break the inflationary spiral: Volcker by doing the actual dirty work, and Reagan by firmly backing his efforts. For this reason, both men deserve credit for the prosperity that followed.

Chapter 13

■ ■ ■

The 1980s Economic Expansion

"The best sign that our economic program is working is that they don't call it 'Reaganomics' anymore."
–Ronald Reagan (taken from D'Souza (1997, 122)).

After the U.S. economy bottomed out in November 1982, an expansion began that lasted nearly eight years. During the upturn, real GDP rose 30 percent, the unemployment rate fell from 10.8 percent to 5.3 percent, stock prices nearly tripled, and double-digit inflation rates became a distant memory. This economic boom ranks among the longest in U.S. history.

This chapter examines the 1980s economic expansion, and addresses two questions: (1) What were its major causes? and (2) What role did Reagan's economic program play in it? Reagan's supporters contend that his economic program was instrumental in creating the boom because the 1981 Economic Recovery Tax Act unleashed a major demand and supply stimulus that allowed the economy to grow for several years without rising inflation. In addition, they believe that it is virtually inconceivable that the United States could have experienced such rapid growth if inflation had not been conquered first. They go on to claim that Reaganomics had positive affects years later because the tax cuts played an important role in creating the huge explosion in venture capital that funded the 1990s technology revolution.

Reagan's critics claim that his economic program had little to do with causing the good times. Instead, they view 1982-1990 economic expansion as just a period of normal growth brought on by stimulative monetary and fiscal policies. Furthermore, they argue that Reaganomics was actually harmful because it created huge U.S. budget and trade deficits that eroded the growth of U.S. living standards.

13.1 Aggregate Demand

13.1.A Monetary Policy

In my judgement, the basic strategy of monetary policy in the 1980s was correct: tough medicine to reduce inflation

quickly while the public's support permitted the necessary contractionary policy, followed by enough monetary easing to achieve a moderately paced recovery that would avoid overheating demand.
— Martin Feldstein (1994, 11).

In July 1982, after "enough blood had been spilled that the credibility of the Federal Reserve's anti-inflationary policy was established" the central bank shifted to a policy of monetary ease (Mussa 1994, 114). Federal Reserve officials were worried about the deepening recession, as well as signs that the U.S. banking industry was becoming strained. Penn Square National Bank in Oklahoma City failed in July, and in August the Mexican government was on the brink of defaulting on loans issued by several major U.S. banks. Only a hastily arranged bailout package kept Mexico from defaulting. A demand stimulus was in order, and since the U.S. economy was experiencing a major disinflation, the Federal Reserve felt they could pursue a stimulative policy without setting off another bout of high inflation.

The growth rates of the monetary aggregates as the economy moved from recession to expansion are shown in table 13.1. In the fall of 1982, the Federal Reserve announced that they were suspending the operating procedures they had put in place in October 1979, and aggressively lowered the federal funds target rate and engaged in open market purchases. By 1982:IV the monetary aggregates were growing rapidly, in fact the Federal Reserve was so embarrassed by the high M1 growth

Table 13.1 Annualized growth of the Monetary Base, M1, and M2, and the Federal Funds Rate, 1982:II–1983:IV

Date	Base Growth	M1 Growth	M2 Growth	Fed Funds Rate
1982:II	6.3 %	3.7 %	8.3%	14.5 %
1982:III	7.1 %	5.2 %	7.5%	11.0 %
1982:IV	8.5 %	16.3 %	9.1%	9.3 %
1983:I	10.6 %	10.6 %	21.1%	8.6 %
1983:II	11.6 %	12.1 %	10.0 %	8.8 %
1983:III	7.8 %	9.4 %	6.3 %	9.5 %
1983:IV	7.6 %	7.1 %	7.2 %	9.4 %

Source: Data Resources, Inc.

rate that they announced that they would no longer target that measure of money (Mussa 1994, 116). The easy monetary policy continued during the first half of 1983 with all three monetary aggregates growing at double digit rates. Many economists consider this easy monetary policy to be a major factor in lifting the economy out of the recession.[1]

During the years of economic expansion, the Federal Reserve managed to pursue stop and go monetary policies while at the same time maintaining reasonably stable aggregate demand growth. They accomplished this feat because changes in monetary growth offset changes in velocity growth. This pattern is illustrated in table 13.2 which shows the annual growth rates of the M1 and M2 aggregates, their corresponding velocities, and nominal GDP from 1982-1989. After pursuing an easy policy in 1983, the Federal Reserve tightened in 1984 because they were worried that the rapid economic growth taking place would ignite another round of rising inflation (Mussa 1994, 118). The economy had, in fact, roared out of the recession-- real GDP rose 3.6 percent in 1983, and another 6.8 percent during 1984. In fact, not only was the

Table 13.2 - Annual Monetary Growth, Velocity Growth, and Aggregate Demand Growth, 1982-1989

	DM1	DV1	DM2	DV2	DPY
1982	8.5 %	- 5.0 %	8.5 %	- 5.0 %	3.5 %
1983	9.9 %	0.6 %	11.2 %	- 0.7 %	10.5 %
1984	5.4 %	3.3 %	7.8 %	0.9 %	8.7 %
1985	11.3 %	- 4.3 %	8.3 %	- 1.3 %	7.0 %
1986	14.4 %	- 9.5 %	8.7 %	- 3.8 %	4.9 %
1987	6.1 %	1.0 %	4.1 %	3.0 %	7.2 %
1988	4.1 %	3.2 %	5.5 %	1.9 %	7.4 %
1989	0.6 %	5.6 %	5.1 %	1.1 %	6.2 %

Note: DM1 = annual growth rate of M1 money supply
DV1 = annual growth rate of M1 velocity
DM2 = annual growth rate of M2 money supply
DV2 = annual growth rate of M2 velocity
DPY = annual growth of nominal GDP
DM1 + DV1 = DM2 + DV2 = DPY

Source: Data Resources Incorportated.

Federal Reserve worried about inflation, Milton Friedman was too. He presented a paper at the American Economics Association meetings in December 1983 where he interpreted the rapid monetary growth during 1981-1983 as suggesting that "inflation will be decidedly higher from 1983 to 1985 than it was from 1981 to 1983" (Friedman 1984, 400).

The Federal Reserve's tight policy during 1984 did help moderate economic growth. While the growth of economic activity averaged 6.8 percent that year, quarterly figures show that it was slowing markedly as the year progressed:

Quarter	Growth Rate
1984:I	11.4 %
1984:II	5.1 %
1984:III	2.1 %
1984:IV	0.6 %

Source: Council of Economic Advisors (1986, 255).

This growth slowdown led the Federal Reserve to reverse course and pursue a stimulative policy during 1985 and 1986 (Volcker 1994, 150). Another reason for the policy shift was that the Federal Open Market Committee was paying close attention to the velocity of money. Fearing a repeat of the 1981-1982 episode, they generated rapid monetary growth during the mid-1980s in an effort to offset the declines in velocity that were taking place. Velocity was falling because interest rates continued to decline which raised the quantity of money demanded (Hafer 1985).

The Federal Reserve reversed course in 1987 by switching to a tight policy. One reason for this move was simply that another inflation build-up surely would have resulted if the double digit monetary growth rates experienced during 1985 and 1986 had continued. The second factor was concerns that the dollar depreciation which had been taking place since 1985 would raise U.S. inflation. The tight monetary policy did not have a noticeable impact on aggregate demand growth, however, because velocity growth turned positive which kept nominal GDP growth on a fairly stable path. This was the case throughout the expansion: changes in monetary growth and velocity offset each other, so aggregate demand growth remained reasonably stable.[2]

13.1.B Fiscal Policy

It is ironic that for all the talk of supply-side economics, the expansion of the '80s was heavily driven by the stimulus of government-induced demand.
—Martin N. Baily (2000).

Expansionary fiscal policies were another important source of aggregate demand growth during the economic boom. Government purchases grew rapidly, largely because the defense build-up was taking place. Table 13.3 shows annual changes in real federal defense spending and real GDP, along with the proportion of the change in GDP accounted for by defense spending. Military spending was a major source of demand growth, especially from 1983-1987. The peak contribution occurred in 1985 when it accounted for over 14 percent of economy-wide spending growth. Consider, too, that these numbers actually understate defense spending's contribution because they do not include any multiplier effects. When the government buys goods and services, income is generated that accrues to the people who produce those goods and services. Some of this new income is spent, which results in additional income for others. When these multiplier effects are included, the defense build-up had an even greater impact on the economy than shown in table 13.3. Estimates of the near-term government spending multiplier are in the neighborhood of 1.5, which means that the numbers in the final column of table 13.3 should be multiplied by about 1.5 to

Table 13.3 - Changes in Real Federal Defense Spending and Real GDP, 1983-1989

Year	Defense Spending (ΔD)	GDP (ΔY)	(ΔD/ΔY)x100
1983	+ $18.1 B	+ $183.4 B	+ 9.9 %
1984	+ $13.5 B	+ $336.4 B	+ 4.0 %
1985	+ $26.0 B	+ $183.4 B	+ 14.2 %
1986	+ $19.3 B	+ $164.2 B	+ 12.0 %
1987	+ $15.8 B	+ $161.8 B	+ 9.8 %
1988	- $3.7 B	+ $215.7 B	- 1.7 %
1989	- $3.9 B	+ $196.8 B	- 2.0 %

Source: Council of Economic Advisors (1998, 282-283).

provide an estimate of the total short-term impact of the increases in defense spending on real GDP.[3]

The tax cuts legislated in the 1981 Economic Recovery Tax Act also contributed to aggregate demand growth. Income-tax rates fell in 1982, 1983, and 1984, with the total reduction being 23 percent. However, these tax cuts were partially offset by bracket creep caused by inflation (the indexing provision of the 1981 ERTA did not go into effect until 1985), legislated tax increases in 1982, and higher social security taxes that took effect in 1984.[4] Yet despite these offsetting tax increases, American households still enjoyed substantial net tax savings. The Council of Economic Advisors reports that in 1984 an American family earning the median income (at the time, about $22,400) owed $1,750 less in federal taxes than they would have if the tax cuts had not taken place (Council of Economic Advisors 1984, 32). Total federal tax savings during 1984 were estimated at $68 billion.

The legislated tax reductions also impacted businesses' demand for investment goods. Although the business tax cuts in the 1981 ERTA were partially offset by the tax increases legislated in 1982, economists estimate that businesses' user cost of capital did fall, although more for structures than equipment. For example, Slemrod (1986, 63-64) reports that the net effect of the 1981 and 1982 laws was to reduce the cost to businesses of general industrial equipment by 4.0 percent, while raising the cost of office and computing equipment by 2.0 percent. For business structures, he estimates a cost decline of 15 percent. The fact that investment spending was very robust during the expansion despite the high real interest rates prevailing at the time suggests that the Reagan tax cuts did, in fact, have a favorable impact on investment spending.[5]

The stimulative federal tax and spending policies can be seen through a measure called the natural employment surplus (NES).[6] The NES measures the federal government's fiscal position, given tax rates and levels of spending in place, if the economy were producing at estimated full employment. This measure is considered a better fiscal indicator than the government's actual fiscal position because the NES nets out business cycle effects.

The business cycle impacts the government's fiscal position because changes in aggregate income affect both tax revenue and outlays. For example, during a recession, tax revenue falls for two reasons: (1) there is less income to tax, and (2) this reduced level of income is taxed at lower tax rates because of the graduated income tax. Meanwhile falling output causes government outlays to rise because more people are out of work and collecting welfare and unemployment compensation. Thus, recessions cause the federal budget to move toward deficit which is exactly what we want to see happening because with the government spending more and taxing less, aggregate demand is stimulated.[7] The opposite situation occurs when the economy expands: tax revenues rise and outlays fall, so the budget moves toward surplus which helps contract aggregate demand growth. This cyclical behavior of the federal budget is called the automatic stabilizer feature of fiscal policy, and many economists believe it is a major reason why recessions became milder after World War II. Prior to the 1930s New Deal legislation, these automatic stabilizers were essentially nonexistent. Very few people paid federal income taxes, and those that did owed small amounts. In addition, federal welfare programs and unemployment compensation were not created until the 1930s.

The federal budget can be separated into NES and cyclical components which is shown in table 13.4. If the economy is producing below capacity, the cyclical component is negative, and if output is above full employment the cyclical portion is positive. In the unlikely event that production is exactly at capacity, the cyclical component is zero.

The fact that the government was running deficits (negative surpluses) throughout the 1980s indicates that fiscal policy was expansion-

Table 13.4 - Federal Surplus in Billions of 1987$, 1981-1989

Year	Actual Surplus	NES	Cyclical Component	|GDP/Actual Surplus| * 100
1981	-106.4	-59.8	-46.6	2.8 %
1982	-215.8	-123.5	-92.3	5.7 %
1983	-208.8	-126.4	-82.4	4.5 %
1984	-202.5	-174.7	-27.8	4.9 %
1985	-195.9	-208.4	+12.5	4.5 %
1986	-181.2	-171.5	-9.7	4.1 %
1987	-150.9	-181.6	+30.7	3.3 %
1988	-127.8	-162.1	+34.3	2.8 %
1989	-128.6	-157.7	+29.1	2.6 %

Source: Gordon (1993, A6). Data are fourth quarter observations.
Actual Surplus = NES + Cyclical Component.

ary, and the NES column shows why. Even if the economy had been producing at full employment, the federal government would have been running deficits due to the tax cuts, defense build-up, and continuing growth of transfer payments. In 1987, when the economy first reached, and then exceeded, full employment, the federal government was still running a deficit of $150.9 billion because the NES was -$181.6 billion. In other words, that year the cyclical budget component was in surplus of $30.7 billion because the economy was producing above full employment, but the large negative NES kept the overall fiscal position in deficit.

Note in table 13.4 that the 1986 Tax Reform Act (which took effect in 1987 and 1988) did not have a major impact on the NES measure. This is because the law was designed to be revenue neutral. The TRA reduced income tax rates for households, but at the same time raised taxable income by eliminating several deductions, as well as increasing the tax rate on capital gains for high income families. Meanwhile, the corporate income tax was lowered, but depreciation schedules were lengthened and the investment tax credit was eliminated. These changes in business taxes raised the cost of capital, especially when debt-financed because the lower income tax rate reduced the value of the interest expense deduction. In terms of the law's impact on aggregate demand, by raising the cost of capital its major effect was to cause a decline in business investment during the late 1980s.

13.1.C Additional Demand Factors

In addition to monetary and fiscal policies, there were other factors working to change aggregate demand during the boom. One was the stock market. Following its abysmal performance in the 1970s, equity values nearly tripled during the 1980s expansion. Rising equity values raised household wealth which helped stimulate consumption expenditures.

There are a number of reasons why stocks experienced such high returns. First was falling interest rates. Disinflation brought on by the 1981-1982 recession lowered expected inflation which reduced nominal interest rates. Falling interest rates raised the present value of expected dividends which drove up stock prices. Higher corporate profits also played an important role. Corporate earnings soared during the boom, from $159.2 billion in 1982 to $356.4 billion by 1989 (Council of Economic Advisors 1997, 401). Meanwhile, the fact that inflation was low meant that those corporate profits were not as badly overstated by inflation as had been the case during the 1970s. Another factor making equities attractive was the reduced capital gains tax rate legislated by the 1981 ERTA. Under the new law, the maximum tax rate on long-term capital gains was lowered from 28 percent to 20 percent. The 20 percent rate was in place until 1987 when the 1986 TRA raised the maximum to 33 percent for high income families by treating capital gains as ordinary income. All else being equal, a lower capital gains tax rate raises the attractiveness of equities relative to alternative assets such as bonds and money which are not typically subject to capital gains taxes. For this reason, a reduction in the tax rate on capital gains raises the demand for equities.

While stocks were a great investment during the economic expansion, there was one major bump in the road along the way. On Monday, October 19, 1987, the stock market crashed; every stock index took a major hit, with the Dow Jones Industrial Average dropping 23 percent. In one single day, the crash "wiped out almost $1 trillion of financial wealth in the U.S." (Brimmer 1989, 11). Since no identifiable event or piece of news occurred over the weekend preceding the crash, many analysts contend that it was just a speculative bubble popping, although some economists dispute that view.[8] Some people claimed to have seen the crash coming because stock prices and interest rates had both been rising for several months prior to the event. Interest rates and equity values often move in opposite directions, especially in the late stages of an economic expansion.

The 1987 stock market crash is an especially interesting event in macroeconomics because rarely are we presented with an event which so closely fits "ceteris paribus."[9] One day, out of the blue, $1 trillion of financial wealth disappeared! Immediately afterwards, attention was focused on the crash's potential impact on the economy, and many pointed out the leading indicator properties of stock prices. A few predicted doomsday for the U.S. economy. However, the disaster scenario never materialized, instead there was little damage to the aggregate economy beyond a decline in household spending on consumer durables during 1987:IV. One possible reason why the crash did not spread to other sectors of the economy is that immediately afterwards the Federal Reserve flooded the financial markets with liquidity, and then quietly removed it several weeks later. They were highly praised for these actions. Most stock indices were back to their pre-crash levels by the summer of 1989.

While several factors worked to raised aggregate demand during the expansion years, the behavior of net exports canceled out some of the increase. Here are the figures for real net exports (NETX) from 1981 to 1989, both in levels and as a percent of GDP:

Year	NETX (billions of 1992$)	(NETX/GDP) * 100
1981	+14.0	0.0 %
1982	-14.0	0.0 %
1983	-63.3	-1.3 %
1984	-127.3	-2.5 %
1985	-147.9	-2.8 %
1986	-163.9	-3.0 %
1987	-156.2	-2.8 %
1988	-114.4	-1.9 %
1989	-82.7	-1.4 %

Source: Council of Economic Advisors (1998, 282 & 283).

These trade deficits were a major drag on aggregate demand growth, especially during the mid 1980s.

Economists generally consider two factors to be largely responsible for these trade deficits. One was the U.S. economic boom. When a country experiences rising income, the demand for goods and services increases which includes spending on imports. For this reason, when several countries' economies are growing at the same time (which was the case during much of the 1980s), the volume of world trade expands because all countries are buying more imports and selling more exports. In this case, what is important as far as net exports are concerned is the relative growth rates of the different countries' economies. For example, if country A grows faster than country B, then all else equal, country A's purchases from country B expand faster than country B's purchases from country A. Thus, net exports fall in county A (the faster growing economy), and rise in country B (the slower growing economy). This point is relevant to the U.S. trade deficits during the 1980s because the U.S. economy was growing faster than the economies of most of its major trading partners. To illustrate, here are the compound average annual growth rates of real GDP for the G-7 countries from 1982-1989:

Country	GDP Growth
Canada	4.20 %
France	2.44 %
Germany	2.51 %
Italy	2.78 %
Japan	4.20 %
United Kingdom	3.62 %
United States	3.67 %

Source: Gordon (1993, A7-A12).

Among this group of countries, only Canada and Japan grew faster than the United States.

The second major source of the large U.S. trade deficits was the U.S. dollar appreciation that took place during the first half of the 1980s. Figure 13.1 shows the behavior of the Federal Reserve's index of the trade-weighted dollar during the decade.[10] From 1980-1985, the U.S. dollar appreciated over 40 percent against the currencies of America's major trading partners. This huge rise in the value of the dollar reduced U.S. dollar prices of goods imported into the United States, and raised foreign prices of U.S. goods sold abroad. Thus, the dollar appreciation

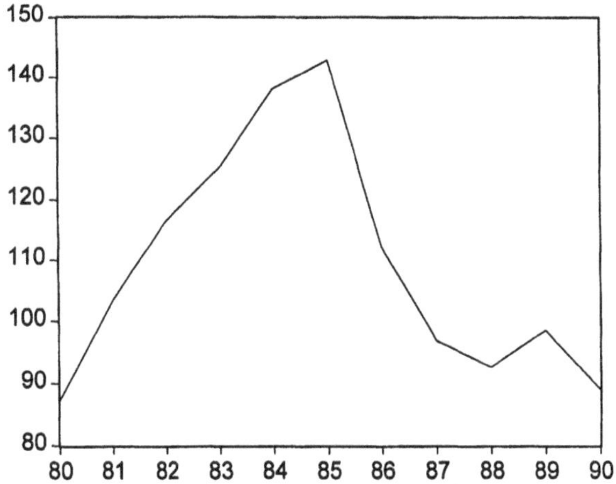

Fig. 13.1 Trade weighted value of the U.S. dollar (G-10, 1973=100)

caused the U.S. demand for imports to rise, and the foreign demand for U.S. exports to fall.[11]

Most U.S. industries producing tradeable goods were adversely impacted by the dollar appreciation, and among those particularly harmed were automobiles, steel, and agriculture. Financial losses in the U.S. auto industry were so severe that domestic automakers lobbied Congress and the Reagan administration for import protection. To their discredit, in 1981 the Washington politicians caved in and negotiated a voluntary export agreement (VER) with the Japanese. Automobile manufacturers in that country agreed to limit exports to the United States to 1.68 million units during 1981, eventually rising to 1.85 million by 1984. This agreement restricted the supply of new autos, and by doing so led to major increases in the prices of both imports and domestically-produced autos. The VER on Japanese autos is estimated to have cost U.S. consumers a total of $16.75 billion in the form of higher car prices.[12]

Why did the U.S. dollar appreciate by so much from 1980-1985? In the opinion of many economists, it was caused by a major capital inflow from abroad as foreigners were attracted by high U.S. real interest rates. According to this view, the large U.S. federal budget deficits were the root cause because they raised the borrowing needs of the U.S. Treasury which pushed up U.S. real interest rates. Real rates were, in fact, quite high, especially early in the decade. The Council of Economic Advisors (1985, 33-35) presents figures on real interest rates formed by taking the nominal rate on ten-year U.S. Treasury debt and subtracting an expected inflation series. These real rates peaked at about 8.0 percent in late 1981, and then dropped to about 4.0 percent (which is still high by historical standards) during 1983 and 1984. Short-term real rates followed a similar pattern: Barro estimates that the real return on 90-day Treasury bills averaged 5.7 percent from 1981-1985. By contrast, the same measure averaged 1.2 percent during the 1970s, and 2.5 percent in the 1960s (Barro 1997, 253-255). These high real returns were attractive to foreigners who bought U.S. dollars on foreign exchange markets in order to purchase U.S. financial assets. Thus, the demand for U.S. dollars increased which caused the dollar to appreciate on foreign currency markets.

This reasoning implies that the federal budget deficit was the major source of the U.S. trade deficit. Many called the budget and trade shortfalls the "twin deficits" and they were the subject of considerable discussion during the 1980s. Much of the debate focused on whether or not the twin deficits would result in slower growth of U.S. living standards. One group argued that the resulting high real interest rates would reduce investment spending and result in slower future economic growth. Another view contended that the twin deficits were not harmful because the foreign lending was being put to good use-- buying investment goods which raised the productive capacity of the U.S. economy.[13]

13.2 Aggregate Supply

Many economists believe that Reaganomics did generate beneficial supply-side effects during the 1980s, but that demand-side factors were more important to the economic expansion. In fact, in the eyes of some, the supply-side fruits of Reaganomics were probably greater during the 1990s than in the 1980s.

As supply-side economists predicted, the 1981 tax cuts, by raising after-tax real wages, caused increased work effort. However, the magnitude was relatively small. Several studies (many prompted by the Reagan tax cuts) investigate the responsiveness of labor supply to changes in after-tax wages.[14] Although parameter estimates vary, the results from these studies are fairly consistent in the sense that they report that the elasticity of labor supply with respect to after-tax wages is low for males (in some cases negative), but higher for females. These studies also report that the work effort of people who already have jobs varies little when after-tax wages change, but find a much greater response to higher wages by those not already employed. For example, Lindsay (1990, 69) estimates that the 1981 ERTA resulted in just a 2.5 percent increase in labor supply from 1981-1985, of which "about three-fifths...was due to the response of secondary earners in two-earner families." Along similar lines, Feldstein and Elmendorf (1989) discount the role of labor supply changes in the early stages of the 1980s economic expansion by noting that even though the unemployment rate dropped rapidly, "labor participation rates showed virtually no movement" (Feldstein and Elmendorf, 1989, p. 2). The Reagan tax cuts brought about greater work effort, but this was not a primary cause of the deluge of increased economic activity that occurred after 1982.

One thing the tax cuts did accomplish was to bring about a rise in reported (and therefore taxable) income. Most of this increase came from very high-income households. One reason why it was focused at the upper-end is because individuals such as business owners and corporate executives receive their compensation in several forms, some of which is taxable (salary, stock options), and some of which is nontaxable (health-care insurance, use of a company car, access to the company's country club membership). If the marginal tax bracket is 70 percent–the top rate before ERTA was passed–high-income workers have a fairly strong incentive to receive a given dollar of compensation in the form of nontaxable fringe benefits as opposed to taxable income. This is because at a 70 percent marginal tax rate, the choice is between receiving a dollar's worth of nontaxable fringe benefits, or 30 cents of after-tax salary income (one-dollar minus 70 cents of taxes) to spend as they choose. If the marginal tax rate is instead 50 percent (the top rate under ERTA), the choice is between one-dollar's worth of nontaxable fringe benefits or 50 cents of after-tax salary income. This is why lower marginal tax rates cause workers to desire more of their income as taxable salary, and less as nontaxable fringe benefits.

Another reason why reported income increased after ERTA took effect is because the reduction in the tax rate on capital gains inçome raised taxable capital gains income. Key features of capital gains income are (1) it can often be shifted over time, and (2) it is only subject to taxation in the year it is realized. To illustrate, suppose someone bought shares of stock several years ago, and the values of those shares rose. The appreciation in value represents a capital gain, but that gain is not taxable income until the stock is actually sold because only then is the gain realized. Capital gains can often be taken at a time that best suits the owner, and the tax rate on capital gains is a major factor in this decision. For example, if someone knew the tax rate on capital gains was going to be reduced next year, they would have an incentive to postpone realizing their gains until then so they would be taxed at the lower rate.

High-income households reported major changes in income following both the 1981 ERTA and 1986 TRA. The 1981 law dropped the top marginal rate from 70 percent to 50 percent, and the 1986 law reduced it further to 33 percent. For capital gains, ERTA lowered the tax rate from 28 percent to 20 percent, then TRA raised the maximum rate to 33 percent. Feenberg and Poterba (2000, 266-267) report that the share of taxable income reported by the top 0.5 percent of U.S. households, which was roughly the same in 1981 as it had been in the early 1960s, rose from 6.11 percent in 1981 to 11.92 percent by 1988, and they attribute this change to "high income taxpayers responding to lower marginal tax rates by reporting more of their "true" income as taxable income."[15] Lindsey (1987) calculates that after the 1981 ERTA was passed, changes in reported income resulted in tax revenues one-sixth to one-quarter higher than would have been the case if there had been no taxpayer response. Slemrod (1996, 169) describes the changes in reported income as "the stuff of legend, such as the 96.3 percent increase in capital gains realizations in 1986 compared to 1985, in anticipation of the tax increase on capital gains scheduled for 1987." Slemrod also notes (1996, 169) that from 1978-1990 the share of total income reported by the top 1 percent of U.S. income-earning households rose from 8.8 percent to 13.4 percent, and argues that the "post-1986 spurt" was caused by changes in reported income resulting from the 1986 Tax Reform Act (1996, 189).[16] Changes in reported income are a major reason why the ERTA tax cuts did not cause as large a reduction in tax revenue as critics of supply-side economics predicted would occur.

One of the major success stories of Reaganomics was its role in helping create the business investment boom of the early and mid-1980s. A burst of spending on new plant and equipment took place which benefitted the United States by having a positive impact on both aggregate demand and supply. Aggregate demand increased for the simple reason that investment is a component of spending on final goods and services. Aggregate supply expanded because investment spending influences the rate of capital accumulation which helps determine an economy's ability to produce goods and services in the future.

Table 13.5 shows real fixed business investment spending, along with its change, and the proportion of the change in real GDP accounted for by the change in investment spending.[17] The investment boom was especially powerful during the early years of the expansion because the ERTA provided inducements for firms to buy capital goods, which they did despite the exceptionally high real interest rates prevailing at the time. In addition, the strong dollar helped reduce the price of capital goods relative to prices of other goods which provided a further inducement to investment spending. The investment boom came to an abrupt halt in 1986 due to uncertainty over tax changes while the TRA was being debated, and firms' expectations that the investment tax credit would be repealed effective January 1, 1986 (Council of Economic Advisors 1987, 25). Also that year, the plunging world price of oil caused a severe cutback in domestic investment spending on oil drill-

Table 13.5 - Fixed Business Investment (FBI), Billions of 1992$, 1983-1990

Year	FBI	ΔFBI	ΔGDP	[(ΔFBI) / (ΔGDP)]*100
1983	$456.4	- $7.9	$183.4	- 4.3%
1984	$535.4	$79.0	$336.4	23.5%
1985	$568.4	$33.0	$183.4	18.0 %
1986	$548.5	- $19.9	$164.2	- 12.1 %
1987	$542.4	- $6.1	$161.8	- 3.8 %
1988	$566.0	$23.6	$215.7	10.9 %
1989	$588.8	$22.8	$196.8	11.6 %
1990	$585.2	- $3.6	$74.3	- 4.8 %

Source: Council of Economic Advisors (1998, 282).

ing equipment. Real investment spending in that industry declined $10 billion during the first half of 1986, which accounts for over half of the economy-wide decline in investment over that same period. Spending on equipment rebounded later in the decade, although spending on structures remained below its level of the early 1980s.[18]

Falling real prices of food and energy provided additional supply-side benefits. Food prices fell due to the dollar appreciation, plus the fact that world income growth was relatively slow (Council of Economic Advisors 1986, 149). Oil prices collapsed in 1986 when Saudi Arabia raised production in an effort to recapture market share. The world price of oil plummeted; a barrel of West Texas Crude fell from $30.90 to $13.75 during a span of just six-months (Council of Economic Advisors 1987, 25). This collapse in energy prices was a mixed blessing in the sense that while U.S. consumers benefitted enormously in the form of lower gasoline prices and electric and heating bills, falling oil prices also caused a regional recession in the oil-patch states. Since the United States is a high-cost producer, at $13.75 per barrel domestic oil exploration was unprofitable. There was a major decline in spending on oil drilling, and about 150,000 jobs in the oil and gas industry disappeared which spread economic pain through the South-Central United States. However, for the U.S. economy as a whole, the drop in oil prices was beneficial because it held down measured inflation, contributing to the first "significant [quarterly] decline" in the consumer price index since 1954 (Council of Economic Advisors 1987, 26). Falling inflation also raised real disposable incomes and reduced expected inflation which helped push down interest rates.

Another beneficial supply-side phenomenon during the expansion arose from the fact that labor costs grew slowly during the decade, especially when compared to what had been the case during the 1970s. Unit labor costs in the private nonfarm business sector increased by an average of 2.6 per year from 1983-1989, compared to average growth of 6.3 percent during the expansion of the late 1970s (Council of Economic Advisors 1997, 355).[19] One important reason for slower growth of labor costs was that during the first years of the expansion excess capacity existed in several sectors of the economy which resulted in a buyers' market for labor. Falling expected inflation was another factor that helped hold down wage increases. As for organized labor, the fact that some of the most heavily unionized industries such as autos, steel, Eastern coal, and farm equipment were experiencing serious problems, especially early in the decade, meant that workers in those industries were not in a position to demand large wage increases. In addition, unionized public sector workers were quiet, in part because President Reagan fired the unionized air-traffic controllers in August 1981 when they went on an illegal strike. The diminished level of union activity during the 1980s is striking when compared to what happened in the 1970s:

Years	Number of Work Stoppages	Workers Involved	Days Idle
1970-1979	2,888	14,878,000	260,098,000
1980-1989	831	5,066,000	117,571,000

Source: U.S. Department of Labor (2000, 71).

13.3 The Phillips Curve in Action

Table 13.6 shows the rates of output growth, unemployment, and inflation from 1982-1990. The economic expansion began in November 1982, and the economy followed the standard pattern during an economic recovery: rapid growth in the early stages, followed by slower growth as the expansion aged. You can see that the unemployment rate declined throughout the expansion, while inflation did through 1986. What is unusual about the 1980s expansion is the fact that it went on for as long as it did before inflation accelerated. Recalling price behavior during the prior business upturns discussed in this book, in those ear-

Table 13.6 - Output Growth, Unemployment, and Inflation, 1982-1990

Year	Real GDP Growth	Unemployment Rate	GDP Deflator Growth
1982	-2.1 %	9.7 %	6.3 %
1983	4.0 %	9.6 %	4.3 %
1984	7.0 %	7.5 %	3.8 %
1985	3.6 %	7.2 %	3.4 %
1986	3.1 %	7.0 %	2.6 %
1987	2.9 %	6.2 %	3.1 %
1988	3.8 %	5.5 %	3.7 %
1989	3.4%	5.3 %	4.2 %
1990	1.2 %	5.6 %	4.3 %

Source: Council of Economic Advisors (1998, 283, 284, & 330)

lier cases inflation accelerated soon after the economy rebounded. For example, inflation rose about two years after the 1973-1975 recession ended, and increased just a few months after the trough of the 1980 recession. This is clearly not the case here, the 1980s expansion was about five years old before inflation began to accelerate. This happened because the 1981-1982 recession was severe enough to drive output far below the full employment level. It took several years for the economy to return to full employment, in large part because major changes in economic activity take time to occur.

The Phillips curve pattern is shown in Figure 13.2 which plots the rates of unemployment and GDP deflator inflation from 1980-1989. Robert J. Gordon describes the 1980s experience as a "classic disinflation" and this figure shows why (Gordon 1998, 243). The large decline in inflation that took place from 1980 to 1982 was associated with rising unemployment which means the economy was moving along a short-run Phillips curve. Then inflation declined slowly (except in 1986 when oil prices collapsed) while unemployment fell which suggests that the Phillips curve was shifting left because of falling expected inflation. The U.S. economy first reached, and then exceeded, full employment in 1987 because that is when inflation reversed course and began to accelerate. This inflation acceleration eventually led the Federal Reserve in 1988 and 1989 to clamp on the monetary brakes which helped bring about the 1990-1991 recession. That downturn marks the end of the 1980s economic expansion.

13.4 Lasting Effects

Figure 13.2 also illustrates an important legacy left behind by Paul Volcker and Ronald Reagan. They did not panic when the economy slid into recession in 1981, nor did they panic when the recession significantly deepened in 1982. Instead, Reagan told Americans it was important to "stay the course," which meant that the United States should avoid the mistake made during the 1970s of stimulating the economy before meaningful disinflation had taken place. Instead, the recession should be allowed to run its course so inflationary pressures could be significantly reduced. Then, the recovery that followed would feature much lower inflation, expected inflation, and interest rates than had been the case in prior years.

"Staying the course" was certainly not a pleasant experience for the millions of Americans for whom recession and disinflation meant lost jobs and poverty, but the policy did lay the groundwork for the vibrant expansion that followed. And ending the era of high inflation had last-

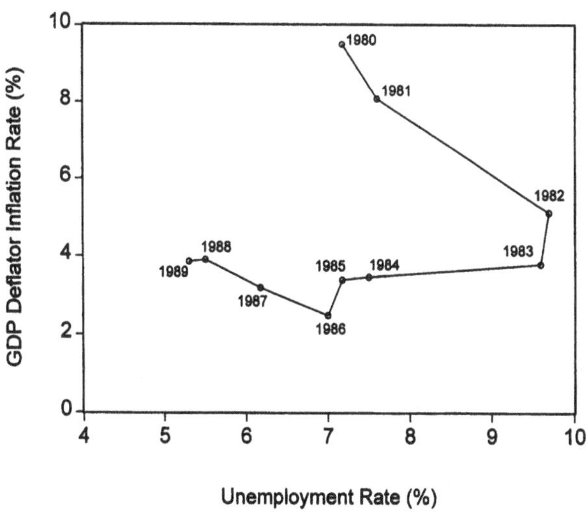

Fig. 13.2 Inflation and Unemployment, 1980–1989

ing effects well beyond the 1980s because during the 1990s interest rates remained well below their peak levels of 1979-1981.

What role did Reaganomics play in the expansion? First of all, a major sustained business upturn such as what occurred after 1982 would have been virtually impossible with double-digit inflation taking place. The U.S. tax code punishes people who hold financial assets during inflationary times by taxing nominal returns. In addition, indexing of nominal wages and prices to inflation is not widespread in the United States. As a result, the 1970s high inflation created all sorts of economic distortions that are simply not consistent with sustained economic growth. To cite just two examples, during the 1970s there was an economic incentive to store wealth in gold and real estate instead of in stocks and bonds, and firms funneled their retained earnings away from research and development spending because high interest rates made the present value of future returns low. These are patterns of behavior that do not promote economic growth.

Reagan's tax cuts and defense build-up also played large roles in the expansion. The tax cuts increased work effort some, but had a much greater impact by stimulating investment spending and raising reported income. The defense build-up was a major contributor to aggregate demand growth, especially during the mid 1980s.

The 1980s economic expansion was not all peaches and cream; there were economic problems then, just as there are economic problems today. Many workers suffered serious bouts of long-term unemployment that lasted long after the recession was over. There were concerns expressed about the increasing inequality of income and wealth. The number of homeless people appeared to be rising. The defense build-up caused some people to worry that the United States was destined to blunder into a major war. And the federal budget and trade deficits were problematic, although people still debate just how much.

Despite these problems, life for the vast majority of Americans during the 1980s was vastly preferable to the 1970s experience of high inflation, shortages, gasoline lines, and high interest rates which you could not earn unless you were wealthy. To top it all off, during the 1970s a number of politicians in Washington looked at this government-created economic mess, and told Americans that they had better lower their expectations and get used to it!

The Reagan administration made a concerted effort to reduce the federal government's presence in the economy, and allow markets to work. These policies did not bring about perfect outcomes in every case, but they were a positive change from the policies offered by previous administrations. They helped solve many of the problems that were created during the 1960s and 1970s, and for this reason there can be little doubt the American public benefitted from them.

Finally, a number of observers believe that Reagan's program had genuine long-term benefits by being partly responsible for helping fund the technology revolution that contributed to the huge economic boom of the 1990s. The major gains in labor productivity and living standards during that decade partly resulted from an increased number of computers and computer power applied to a wider set of uses. Consider what Reagan biographer Dinesh D'Sousa says (1997, p. 122):

> Reagan didn't create this [technology] revolution, but whence came the venture capital for the new industries of the 1980s?...
>
> I put this question to several Silicon Valley entrepreneurs...[and] many of them gave credit to two men: Michael Milken and Ronald Reagan. Milken created new financial reforms [the junk bond]. Ronald Reagan cut taxes and relaxed regulation, encouraging new venture investments.

Empirical evidence exists that supports the role of Reagan's tax cuts in stimulating venture capital funding. Venture capitalists fund small firms that are just starting out, or are relatively young, which they think will prosper. In exchange, the venture capitalist receives a share of the ownership of the firm. While many of these firms fall by the wayside, a few prosper in a very big way and generate enormous returns to the venture capitalists. For example, the first venture capital firm, American Research and Development (ARD) made about half its profits on one investment: a $70,000 stake in Digital Equipment Company (made in 1957), which was eventually worth $355 million (Gompers and Lerner 2001, 146).

The tax rate on capital gains influences the quantity of venture capital in two ways. First, it affects the supply of venture capital; a lower tax rate on capital gains raises the after-tax return to venture capital. Thus, a decrease in the tax rate results in a greater supply of venture capital. However, the magnitude of the impact here is probably modest because a relatively small amount of venture capital comes from sources subject to the capital gains tax. For example, in 1999, about one-fifth of new venture capital commitments were made by individuals to whom the capital gains tax would apply. The rest of the funding came from endowments and pension funds which are exempt from taxes, or from corporations and foreigners which are subject to other tax rates (Gompers and Lerner, 2001, p. 151).

A change in the capital gains tax rate also impacts the demand for venture capital. This occurs because at a lower tax rate, the return to entrepreneurship increases which raises the incentive to start new firms. According to Gompers and Lerner, this is the more important channel. Based on their statistical studies, they report that a "lower capital gains taxes seem to have a particularly strong effect on the amount of venture capital supplied by...tax-exempt investors. The empirical results suggest that the impact of the capital gains tax does not arise through its effect on those supplying venture capital, but rather by spurring corporate employees to become entrepreneurs, leading to more demand for venture capital" (Gomers and Lerner 2001, 153).[20]

Reagan's tax cuts were hardly the only policy change helping to create the surge in venture capital, because the huge increase actually began during the Carter administration when the capital gains tax rate was reduced from 35 percent to 28 percent (Poterba 1989, 49). What the 1981 ERTA did was to reduce the rate further to 20 percent, and the explosion in venture capital continued. In 1977, the last year the tax rate on capital gains was 35 percent, $68.2 million (1987$) of new commitments were made to venture capital firms. By 1986, the final year before the maximum rate was raised from 20 percent to 33 percent, $4.65 billion (1987$) was committed.

Chapter 14

■ ■ ■

A Summing Up

The Congress hereby declares that it is the continuing policy and responsibility of the Federal Government to use all practicable means consistent with its need and obligations and other essential considerations of national policy, and the assistance and cooperation of industry, agriculture, labor, and State and local governments, to coordinate and utilize all its plans, functions, and resources for the purpose of creating and maintaining, in a manner calculated to foster and promote free competitive enterprise and general welfare, conditions under which there will be afforded useful employment opportunities, including self-employment, for those able, willing, and seeking to work, and to promote maximum employment, production, and purchasing power.
—Section 2 of the Employment Act of 1946 (79th Congress, 2nd Session, February 20, 1946).

14.1 What Goes Around, Comes Around

U.S. economic policy traveled a long and arduous path from the New Deal to Reaganomics. The economic catastrophe known as the Great Depression caused an about-face in peoples' opinions on government involvement in the economy. The consensus view changed from one where a hands-off approach was the best policy toward the economy, to the notion that policymakers should actively try to manipulate the economy so as to avoid a repeat performance. That opinion changed is understandable given the depths of misery experienced during the 1930s, but the new view went far beyond advocating policies of stabilizing monetary growth, public works projects, and protecting the banking system against runs and failures. The New Deal created an enormous number of government agencies to enforce new economic controls in the form of price floors, price ceilings, and several other rules and regulations, mostly at the industry level. The federal government also began supplying goods and services such as electricity, old-age insurance, and mortgage insurance, that had previously been supplied solely by the private sector. Many of the agencies and rules established during the New

Deal still exist today.

Shortly after World War II, government involvement in the economy went a step further when Congress passed the Employment Act of 1946. This law set specific macroeconomic policy goals by stating that it was the federal government's responsibility to promote employment and purchasing power, and it created the Council of Economic Advisors to advise the president on how to achieve these goals.

To many observers, however, the economy's performance during the 1950s did not live up to the stated goals of the Employment Act. Expansions were short, which means recessions were frequent. In addition, the unemployment rates during the decade were considered high, as was inflation which reached 3.0 percent in the mid 1950s.

The economy's mediocre performance led economists to seek ways to improve it, and Bill Phillips's statistical results provided a guideline. In fact, the Phillips curve (which was based on his original results) appeared to be the perfect framework for policies to improve the economy's performance: a sustained economic expansion with reduced unemployment is possible, if society is willing to tolerate a low, steady, inflation rate.

In the early 1960s policymakers began trying to exploit the Phillips curve relationship by stimulating aggregate demand growth with expansionary monetary and fiscal policies. During the first few years, this effort was successful in the sense that unemployment fell substantially while inflation accelerated only mildly. Then problems developed: starting in 1965 the inflation rate began to accelerate by about 1.0 percentage point a year, and then in the early 1970s the situation worsened when both inflation and unemployment rose together. The inverse relationship between inflation and unemployment was revealed to be what Milton Friedman and Edmund Phelps had said it was a few years prior: just a short-run relationship.

The inability of politicians and policymakers to recognize or acknowledge the fact that a policy-induced aggregate demand expansion brought short-run benefits but long-run grief took years to sink in. The economic mess that occurred from 1965-1982 was caused in large part by policymakers' repeated attempts to exploit the short-run Phillips curve relationship, in combination with the mistaken assumption that an unemployment rate of 4.0-5.0 percent was attainable without inflation rising. Meanwhile, Arthur Burns, who headed the Federal Reserve from 1971-1978, apparently did not understand that his organization was causing the inflation which was taking place. The situation was further worsened by President Richard Nixon and his economic advisors who caved in to political pressure and imposed wage and price controls. The United States was left with a real mess on its hands in the form of severe economic instability, inflation, and shortages.

High inflation caused all sorts of problems because the U.S. economic system was not prepared to deal with it. Corporate cost accounting practices were based on the FIFO (first-in-first-out) method which assumes that historical costs are roughly equal to replacement costs. This is often the case when prices are stable, but it is certainly not true when inflation is occurring. In the high inflation environment of the 1970s, replacement costs rose above historical costs, which overstated corporate profits and, thus, corporate income tax liabilities as well. This factor helped cause the dismal performance of equity prices during the decade. In addition, the U.S. tax code, by applying tax rates to nominal income from wages, interest, and capital gains, badly distorted work and saving decisions. High inflation also wreaked havoc in the depository and construction industries because the Regulation Q deposit rate ceilings were not raised anywhere near high enough while inflation was driving up nominal market interest rates. In addition, the high U.S. monetary growth rates that caused the inflation led to the demise of the Bretton Woods system of fixed exchange rates.

During the 1950s and 1960s, free market economists fought an intellectual battle against the perverse economic policies in place, but they were largely ignored. However, during the 1970s the situation changed as it became increasingly clear that the worsening economic conditions resulted from badly designed economic policies in place at the time. It is impossible to identify a precise moment when the intellectual tide turned, but it was sometime in the mid-to-late 1970s when the industry deregulation movement gathered momentum. Paul Volcker's appointment to the chairmanship of the Federal Reserve Board of Governors in 1979, and Ronald Reagan's victory in the 1980s presidential election mark the completion of the process. Volcker and Reagan both recognized that inflation is a monetary phenomenon, and had the will to push for anti-inflation monetary policies and then stick with them when a serious recession developed. In addition, Reagan promoted tax cuts and reduced government involvement in the economy. This was a genuine intellectual revolution because these policies were essentially the opposite of what had been pursued since the New Deal.

14.2 Ongoing Controversy

> *The record of the Reagan presidency is now clear and sharp. The economic mess that Reagan inherited was cleaned up, and we are enjoying the greatest economic expansion in U.S. history–more than 90 straight months of economic growth, a dramatic lowering of personal income tax rates, inflation and interest rates down sharply, the stock market booming, almost tripling, and nineteen million brand new jobs.*
> *–Martin Anderson (1988, p. xxvii).*

> *The economic program of the Reagan years failed. It failed conservative tests, failed liberal tests, failed to achieve the goals it set for itself, and failed the American public that invested such hope and trust in it. In its failure, it left the economy with many more serious problems to solve than might have been the case if this unwarranted and deceptive program had not been adopted.*
> *–Anthony Campagna (1994, pp. 215-216).*

Years later, Reagan's economic program remains controversial. His supporters continue to argue that Reaganomics was responsible for the economic prosperity that followed the 1981-1982 recession. His critics, however, remain unwilling to give Reagan credit for the good times, instead continuing to insist that his economic program did more harm than good.

As the years have gone by, the critics' claims (arguably) appear considerably weaker. The budget deficits incurred during the 1980s may have caused U.S. economic growth to be slower than it otherwise would have been, but they did not cause economic doom for the United States. In fact, they persisted well into the 1990s, yet from 1983-1997 (the year before the federal government moved into surplus) the U.S. economy managed to create thirty million new jobs which is nothing short of phenomenal (Council of Economic Advisors, 2001, p. 318). The U.S. labor market was so strong that widespread labor shortages developed in the mid and late 1990s which led employers to advocate for increased foreign immigration to fill the vacancies. The widening gap between the have and have-nots that was blamed on Reaganomics actually began in the early 1970s–years before Reagan arrived in Washington–and continues to this day. And during the 1990s, the United States enjoyed its greatest supply-side economic expansion since the 1920s with rapid economic growth and low inflation. Many analysts attribute the magnificent U.S. economic performance during the 1990s partly to the technology revolution which Reaganomics helped create.

As far as the basic premise of Reaganomics, that tax cuts would stimulate economic activity without raising inflation, consider the comments of economist Kevin Hassett (2002, A18):

> When Ronald Reagan ascended to the presidency on a tax-cutting agenda, not many economists were willing to step forward and provide him with cover. Although Mr. Reagan was convinced that lower marginal tax rates would boost growth, there were few scholars...supporting these claims. The accusation that Reaganomics was "voodoo" was effective and memorable for a reason: There was something to it. Voters accepted Mr. Reagan's analysis largely on faith.
>
> Today the story is different. Economists of all persuasions have spent the last two decades analyzing the effects of marginal tax rate reductions on the economy and generally believe that these cuts, if properly designed, can powerfully affect our welfare. That acceptance was evident already in 1997, when economists gathered at the request of the Joint Committee on Taxation...and prepared analyses of the likely effects of fundamental tax reform. Despite disagreements about the size, all papers predicted that the positive effects would be substantial.

14.3 Be Ever Vigilant

The events described in this book suggest that a few important lessons have been learned:

1. High marginal tax rates are a restraint on economic activity.
2. Inflation is a monetary phenomenon.
3. Fixing prices does not "solve" problems, it creates them.
4. A viable policy is for the government to simply get out of the way, and allow innovation and economic growth to take place.

These are fairly simple concepts, but unfortunately some of them often conflict with the desires of vote-seeking politicians who want to be seen "doing something" for their constituents. For example, if tax rates were very low, the government would collect small amounts of revenue which would make it difficult for politicians to hand out financial favors to various interest groups. Or if the government stood aside and allowed economic growth to take place without subsidizing or otherwise protecting various industries, the public might come to think that politicians are irrelevant at best, harmful at worst.

Sometimes politicians also try to save the day by protecting their constituents from paying high prices which is why some prices end up being controlled. The market mechanism tells us that if the price of something rises, this sends a signal to suppliers to produce more, and for consumers to demand less. Unfortunately, price controls interfere with this, and we saw what trouble this caused in the 1970s when the Nixon wage and price controls were in place. Given that experience, one would think that politicians would learn to leave the price system alone. Unfortunately, a recent episode in California proves otherwise.

In the late 1990s, the state of California put into place a badly-designed regulatory system which, among other things, prevented power distributors from entering into long-term contracts to purchase electricity from suppliers at stable prices. Instead, power distributors had to buy electricity on the spot market where prices can (and do) fluctuate widely. This arrangement did not cause major problems until 2001 when a drought occurred in the Pacific Northwest which caused hydroelectric output to fall. This development was followed by rising temperatures in California which led to higher usage of air conditioners. The combination of tight supply and rising demand caused spot prices of electricity to soar, and these higher prices were promptly passed on to consumers and businesses. Electricity consumers complained, of course, and the state responded by imposing price controls on electricity at the retail level (which reduced the incentive to conserve electricity). This "solution" forced electricity distributors into the absurd position of buying electricity at unregulated high prices, and then selling it at regulated prices which were lower than the prices they were purchasing it at. As a result, the electricity companies were pushed toward bankruptcy.

With power distributors on the brink of collapse, the state decided to transfer the loss onto itself. So the state's next move was to become a middleman; California signed long-term contracts (which power distributors should have been able to do in the first place) to buy electricity from suppliers, which was then sold to the distributors. Under this scheme, the state bought electricity at prices above what they were selling it to the distributors at, meaning the state (instead of the distributors) became the loser on the transaction. This arrangement has cost California several billions of dollars which will eventually have to be covered by issuing debt or raising taxes. The entire crisis was created out of thin air thanks to bad policies that a *Wall Street Journal* editorial called "beyond stupid."[1]

A final point to raise is that despite efforts by some politicians to actually reduce income tax rates, they remain high for many Americans. The U.S. income tax system is set up so that middle-class families pay low *average* tax rates, but surprisingly high *marginal* tax rates, especially on labor income.[2] This occurs because the tax system exempts the first several thousands of dollars of income from any taxes at all (except social security taxes on labor income), but once a family's income is high enough that they are subject to federal and state income taxes, their income is taxed at high rates. Table 14.1 shows the marginal tax rates on labor income for a married couple with no children who earn $42,000 in 2001 (roughly that year's median income). The couple works in Oxford, Ohio (where the author is employed), and their earnings are subject to the social security and medicare payroll tax.[3] Using figures for the 2001 tax year, the couple is assumed to take the standard deduction of $7,600, and two personal deductions ($2,900 per person), meaning the first $13,400 of income is exempt from federal and Ohio state income taxes (but not from the social security payroll tax).[4] A couple earning $42,000 per year has a marginal tax rate of 36.51 percent.

A huge jump takes place when gross family income hits $61,300, because at that income level the federal tax rate is 27.5 percent. This is a high family income, but certainly within reach for two workers with college degrees. This couple is in a marginal tax bracket of 49.75 percent, which means that to secure one additional dollar of after-tax income, they have to earn nearly two dollars of pre-tax income. A tax rate this high creates a disincentive to earn labor income.

A large number of Americans seem unaware that they are paying such high marginal tax rates. This may be because they do not realize that their employer is matching their social security and medicare tax payments, monies which are certainly part of their compensation. Or perhaps they confuse the average tax rate with the marginal rate. Another possibility is that they have weak understanding of financial matters (which is true of a surprisingly large number of people).

Whatever the case, one point where there is very widespread agreement among economists is that the federal tax code is a complete mess. What began as a fairly simple tax system put into place just prior to World War I has evolved into thousands upon thousands of pages of law that is not only unbelievably complicated, but also works to punish some activities (earning wages) while rewarding others (owning a

Table 14.1 - Marginal Tax Rates on Labor Income, Married Couple With No Children*

Family Gross Income $42,000

Federal Income Tax Rate	15.00 %
Social Security and Medicare Payroll Tax	15.30 %
Ohio State Income Tax	4.46 %
Oxford (Ohio) City Income Tax	1.75 %
Total	**36.51 %**

Family Gross Income $61,300

Federal Income Tax Rate	27.50 %
Social Security and Medicare Payroll Tax	15.30 %
Ohio State Income Tax	5.20 %
Oxford (Ohio) City Income Tax	1.75 %
Total	**49.75 %**

* Tax rates are for year 2001. These figures are for a married couple with no children whose earnings are subject to the social security and medicare payroll taxes, and who take the standard deduction ($7,600), plus two personal deductions ($2,900 per person). Wage earners are assumed to bear the entire burden of the social security and medicare payroll tax. U.S. median family income in 2001 was approximately $42,000.

home). Many economists believe that the best thing we could do is to burn the entire U.S. tax code, and then rewrite it as a simple system with a flat (constant) marginal tax rate. This will never happen, but it is fun to consider.

Great strides were made in the area of economic policy during the past several years, and while the tide certainly turned, the battle is not over. In fact, it may never be won. The California "electricity crisis" reminds us that policymakers are prone to pursue bad economic policies, so anyone inclined to believe that we will never again see policies as poorly designed as those that caused the economic problems from 1965-1982 should think again.

ENDNOTES

■■■

Chapter 1

1. For a description of the nature and causes of the Great Depression, see Friedman and Schwartz (1963); Chandler (1970); Temin (1989); or Hall and Ferguson (1998).

2. Richard Nixon resigned over the Watergate scandal, but his resignation occurred in 1974 which is arguably the single worst year in terms of U.S. macroeconomic performance since the 1930s. Had the economy been performing better, he might have survived the scandal. Contrast Nixon's fate with that of Bill Clinton who was involved in a scandal at a time (1998-1999) when the U.S. economy was performing exceptionally well.

3. There is a general consensus that, in the absence of bank failures, the U.S. recession that started in 1929 would have been severe, but nowhere near as horrendous as what actually occurred.

4. The deposit rate ceilings are the subject of chapter 5.

5. Keynes described the cause of the recession as a lack of effective demand. Using modern terminology, we call it a low level of aggregate demand.

6. The notion that the government should be involved in promoting macroeconomic stability was embraced by Congress with the passage of the 1946 Employment Act. This law stated that it was the federal government's responsibility to promote high employment and price stability. The law also created the Council of Economic Advisors to advise the president on economic policy issues.

7. The Bretton Woods agreement is the subject of chapter 3.

8. The conference proceedings appear in Bronfenbrenner (1969). The conclusion was that business cycles were not obsolete, but that depressions of the sort experienced during the 1930s probably were.

9. The Friedman-Phelps model of the Phillips curve is discussed in chapter 2.

10. A growth recession occurs when real GDP growth falls below the long run average of 3.0 percent, but remains positive.

Chapter 2

1. The biographical details about Phillips in this section draw on the works of Blythe (1978) and Leeson (1994).

2. This is figure 2 in Samuelson and Solow (1960).

3. This statement is consistent with the Friedman-Phelps version

discussed later in this chapter.

4. This statement is consistent with the hysteresis view of unemployment.

5. In fact, there was no U.S. "missile gap" at the time because U.S. had considerably more missiles than the Soviets, but that is a whole other story.

Chapter 3

1. A grain is a measure of weight equivalent to 0.002083 ounces.

2. Both the United States and Britain were combatants in World War I, but the British were involved for three more years than the United States. Partly for this reason, the U.K. experienced considerably more inflation than the United States, so the pound depreciated against the dollar.

3. The gold flowing into the countries first experiencing recessions should have caused their money supplies to rise. However, the problem during the late 1920s and early 1930s was that the major country experiencing a recession and a gold inflow (the United States) was not allowing its domestic money supply to rise. See Hall and Ferguson (1998, 85-89) for a discussion.

4. For the details of the proposals, see Meier (1982, 21-57).

5. See Meier (1982, 57).

6. Ironically, Nixon took this same opportunity to impose wage and price ceilings upon the domestic economy. This policy was, of course, a disaster, but that is a story for chapter 6.

7. The trade-weighted dollar fell by 6.0 percent from June to December, 1971 (Council of Economic Advisors 1979, 293).

8. The 1973-1974 oil crisis is discussed in detail in chapter 7.

Chapter 4

1. Wyatt Wells (1994) wrote the definitive biography of Arthur Burns.

2. Mitchell's greatest works are *Business Cycles* (Berkeley: University of California Press, 1913), and *Business Cycles: The Problem and Its Setting* (New York: National Bureau of Economic Research, 1927).

3. Arthur F. Burns and Wesley C. Mitchell. *Measuring Business Cycles* (New York: National Bureau of Economic Research, 1946).

4. The relationship between Burns and Nixon was not all peaches and cream, however. See Wells (1994, esp. chap. 2).

5. This speech and several of his others are reprinted in Burns (1978).

6. Budget deficits cause inflation only if the central bank prints money to buy the newly issued debt.

7. Friedman and Schwartz's (1963) classic work, *A Monetary History of the United States, 1867-1960* is considered the empirical foundation of monetarism.

8. The rise in the natural rate of unemployment is discussed in more detail in chapter 6.

9. During the 1970s the M1 measure of money was considered to be the aggregate most highly correlated with spending. During the 1980s and 1990s, policymakers paid more attention to the M2 measure.

10. Since nominal GDP growth equals the sum of output growth and inflation, for a given rate of nominal GDP growth, if inflation rises, output growth must fall.

11. The 1973-1975 recession is the subject of Chapter 7. Along with reduced monetary growth, additional causes of the recession include rising oil prices and poor crop harvests.

12. Greider (1987, 342-346) presents claims that Burns was trying to influence the economy in 1972 to help get Nixon reelected, and then again in 1978 so Carter would reappoint him as chairman. However, Burns's biographer Wyatt Wells (1994) does not give much credence to these claims. The 1972 episode led to the development of the political business cycle theory which claims that politicians manipulate the economy in order to get reelected. However, the theory doesn't stand up to empirical testing particularly well, although 1972 is often held up as the best example of the cycle in action. See Chrystal (1997) for a discussion.

Chapter 5

1. The view that securities underwriting and excessive deposit rate competition were factors in the bank failures of the 1930s has been shown to be erroneous. For evidence on the role of deposit rates see Bentson (1964). See Krozner and Rajan (1994) for evidence on the role of investment banking.

2. From here on our discussion of thrifts refers to mutual savings banks and savings and loans. Credit unions accounted for a small amount of total thrift deposits during the period being discussed.

3. The 1990 Census of Housing was the most recent available when this was written.

4. In contrast, consider the case of a good such as electricity where no stocks are held because it can not be stored. If consumers' demand for electricity rose 2.0 percent, then electricity producers would produce 2.0 percent more electricity (assuming capacity exists).

5. Of course, many components of homes are commonly prefabricated such as the roof trusses. Yet the fact remains that most components of houses

could be manufactured in a more capital- intensive manner, but instead are constructed from pieces of lumber and other materials delivered to the building site.

6. Interest rates contain an inflation premium according to Fisher's equation of interest rates which states that the observed interest rate (the nominal rate) is the sum of a real rate and the expected inflation rate. Since actual and expected inflation tend to move together, actual inflation and observed interest rates do too.

7. Unless otherwise indicated, data referred to in this section are from the Federal Reserve Bank of St. Louis' online data set (FRED).

8. For a summary of the various changes, see Lash (1987, chap. 7).

9. The 1980s deregulation of banks and thrifts is discussed in chapters 10 & 11.

10. Adjusted for inflation, $1,000 in 1965 would be worth about $4,500 in today's dollars. Low denomination U.S. savings bonds were available, but they are illiquid long-term bonds.

Chapter 6

1. The New Economic Policy also included the suspension of gold conversion, some tax cuts, and the imposition of a 10 percent import surcharge tax.

2. Jawboning tactics refer to a policy of having high ranking officials make public requests for restraint. Examples include asking firms not to raise prices, or labor unions not to request large wage increases.

3. Of course, the huge negotiated wage increases in the construction industry probably contributed to the higher unemployment rate.

4. For a discussion of factors that changed the natural rate of unemployment during the 1960s and 1970s, see Ehrenberg and Smith (1991, 634-637) and Vedder and Gallaway (1993, chap. 13).

5. Rockoff (1984, 212-222) reviews several studies of the impact of the Nixon wage and price controls.

6. See, for example, "Meat Shortage: When Will it End?" *U.S. News and World Report* August 13, 1973, 15-17, and "Builders warn: No rebars, no building," *Business Week* December 8, 1973, 37.

7. The base-period profit margin was based on a firm's profit margins during the best two out of three fiscal years prior to August 15, 1971. See Kosters (1975, esp. chapter 2) for the more minute details of the wage and price controls.

8. "The Great Meat Furor," *Newsweek* April 9, 1973, 18-22.

9. In economic terminology, food is said to be a normal good because

the demand for it rises when income rises. A normal good has a positive income elasticity. In contrast, an inferior good is one where demand falls when income rises, and this type of good has a negative income elasticity.

10. Normally, not all countries boom at the same time. For example, the economic boom enjoyed by the United States during the 1990s was not experienced in most Asian and Western European countries.

11. See Federal Reserve Bank of St. Louis, *Rates of Change in Economic Data for Ten Industrial Countries*, October 1974 and September 1975.

12. "Now, Phase Three Plus," *Newsweek* May 14, 1973, 89-91.

13. "The Great Meat Furor," *Newsweek* April 9, 1973, 18-22.

14. "The Great Meat Furor," *Newsweek* April 9, 1973, 19.

15. Price controls remained on beef until September 12th.

16. The price controls on oil and natural gas are the subject of chapter 7.

Chapter 7

1. *Inter*state commerce refers to economic activity that crosses state lines. *Intra*state commerce refers to trade that takes place within a particular state. This distinction is critical because while a state can regulate its own *intra*state trade, only the U.S. federal government can regulate *inter*state commerce.

2. In contrast, trucking and railroad companies are paid to transport products between points A and B. They do not purchase the products from producers, transport them, and then sell them.

3. Browne and Syron (1976) quote prices per million cubic feet (mcf), but this is an error. The prices should be in terms of thousand cubic feet.

4. There was also quite a bit of animosity at the time between northerners and southerners, largely (but not solely) over civil rights issues.

5. Natural gas shortages are discussed further in chapter 9.

6. The modern U.S. oil industry began in 1859 when the first productive commercial oil well was drilled near Titusville, Pennsylvania by Edwin Drake.

7. See Mead (1976, 131-148) for a detailed discussion of the prorationing system.

8. A barrel contains 42 American gallons.

9. Saudi Arabian production is handled by Aramco, which is a consortium operated by Exxon, Mobil, Texaco, and Chevron. Aramco pays taxes to the Saudi government in exchange for the right to produce oil there.

10. Prices of U.S. produced oil, however, remained relatively high and stable due to the prorationing system in place.

11. The trade-weighted dollar refers to the value of the U.S. dollar against the currencies of the major U.S. trading partners, weighted by volume of trade with the United States.

12. The Arab countries formed their own association, OAPEC (Organization of Arab Petroleum Exporting Countries).

13. See Ahrari (1986) for a detailed discussion of OPEC and the political events surrounding the oil embargo.

14. There were numerous exceptions, and special programs that altered the value of an entitlement. See Kalt (1981, esp. chap. 2) for the various details of the entitlements program.

15. Griffen and Steele (1986, 288-291) compute rough estimates of the welfare loss from the combination of price controls on oil and the entitlements program, and conclude that the welfare loss was about $10.3 million per day, or $3.8 billion per year.

16. See, for example, "Why a Fuel Crisis," *U.S. News and World Report*, February 19, 1973, and "Some Steps to Stop the Oil Blackmail," *Time*, November 18, 1974.

17. The second energy crisis is the subject of chapter 9.

Chapter 8

1. The only other recessions during the century associated with rising inflation were the 1945, 1980, and 1990-1991 downturns. See Hall (1990, 15-17), and Council of Economic Advisors (1997, 305).

2. See Rasche and Tatom (1977) for a detailed analysis of the economic effects of the oil price shock.

3. Compared to the prices of other energy sources, electricity prices were relatively stable because they were determined by state regulatory agencies that were slow to approve rate increases.

4. In economic terminology, the short-run demand for food and energy is inelastic.

5. In the year 2000, the United States used approximately one-half as many BTUs to produce $1 of GDP than in the early 1970s.

6. There is also a net exports effect whereby higher spending on imported oil may cause the net export term to deteriorate. However, while this might occur in nominal terms, in real terms it may not because the physical volume of imported oil would fall because the recession and higher petroleum prices reduce consumption of oil.

7. Short term rates often rise above long term rates prior to economic recessions. See Hall (1990, 214-215) for a discussion.

8. In percent terms, spending drops much less than awarded contracts

because a large amount of construction spending reflects activity that already took place. A new building is entered in the national income accounts as investment spending when it comes on-line, which is usually not the same time-period that most of the actual spending took place.

9. Motor vehicles includes autos, trucks, and buses. Motor vehicle production data are from *World Motor Vehicle Data* (Detroit: Motor Vehicle Manufacturers Association, 1978).

10. See "Detroit Bucks a Buyer Rebellion," *Time*, December 2, 1974, pp. 35-37.

11. The higher profit margin on large cars results from the fact that Americans were willing to pay proportionately more for larger cars. In other words, a car that was 10 percent larger than another fetched a price more than 10 percent higher. See Adams and Brock (1995).

12. In October, 1973, the exchange rate-adjusted price of a gallon of gas was $0.40 in the United States, $1.06 in Germany, $0.83 in Japan, and $1.10 in France. Source: Motor Vehicle Manufacturers Association (1976, 9).

13. The descriptions of these cars come from *Wards 1975 Automotive Yearbook*, 198.

14. In 1970, the *average* auto on U.S. highways received 13.5 miles per gallon. Source: *1995 Information Please Almanac*, 79. A year 2000 model standard-size car weighs around 3,400 pounds and gets about 20 miles per gallon.

15. See Adams and Brock (1995) for an excellent discussion of the automobile industry.

Chapter 9

1. Temporary tax cuts tend to be saved as opposed to spent because they don't influence households permanent disposable income which is considered the primary determinant of consumption spending. For a discussion, see, for example, Gordon (1998, Ch. 15).

2. Another reason why Carter won the election was that many voters never forgave Ford for pardoning Richard Nixon.

3. Blinder (1979, 215) reports that most of the inflation acceleration between 1977 and 1978 can be accounted for by changes in the prices of food, home ownership (due in large part to rising interest rates), and used cars.

4. See DeMarchi (1981) for details on the political battle over energy policy during the Ford Administration, and the details of the 1975 law.

5. For a detailed discussion of the proposed National Energy Plan, see Cochrane (1981).

6. Prior to the 1976 election, Jimmy Carter sent a letter to the

of gas-producing states saying he favored decontrol of natural gas prices. See Melloan and Melloan (1978, 146-147).

7. See "President Blast Oil, Gas Industry, Urges Backing of His Energy Plan," *Wall Street Journal*, October 14, 1977, 3.

8. "Demagoguery at the White House," A paid advertisement in *The Wall Street Journal*, November 3, 1977.

9. "In Defense of the People," *The Wall Street Journal*, October 14, 1977, 24.

10. These explosives were developed by the economist J. David Ferguson, and he held a patent for this discovery.

11. An Ayatollah is a high-ranking Islamic religious leader, roughly equivalent to a Cardinal in the Catholic Church. For a discussion of the long-standing enmity between the Iranian Islamic clergy and the Shah of Iran, see Yergin (1991, chap. 33).

12. The cyclically-adjusted budget is the government fiscal position if the economy is producing at estimate full employment. A cyclically-adjusted deficit is considered expansionary, a cyclically-adjusted surplus is viewed as being contractionary. This concept is developed further in chapter 13.

Chapter 10

1. Many economists believe that inflation does not affect the poor because they are neither borrowers nor lenders. However, Easterly and Fischer (2001) present evidence that the poor are, in fact, more concerned about inflation than are higher income groups.

2. This time and energy spent altering money holdings is sometimes called the shoe leather cost, because people wear down their shoes going back and forth to the bank in an effort to minimize their money holdings.

3. "Volcker to the Rescue," *Time*, August 6, 1979, 19.

4. The FOMC has twelve members, consisting of the seven governors plus five Federal Reserve bank presidents who take turns on a rotating basis.

5. Volcker's version of events is found in Volcker and Gyohten (1992, 163-184).

6. See Melton (1985, chap. 4) for details of the Federal Reserve's change in operating procedures.

7. Lang (1980) provides a detailed discussion of the FOMC's activities during 1979.

8. See Schreft (1990) for a detailed examination of the history of credit controls in the United States.

9. These are the general components of the program. See Schreft (1990) for the details.

10. The major items in managed liabilities are time deposits of $100,000 or more, repurchase agreements, borrowings from nonmember banks or security dealers, and Eurodollar borrowings. For the precise definition of managed liabilities, see *Federal Reserve Bulletin* 66 (April, 1980), 339-340.

11. A state-charted bank can join the Federal Reserve system, but is not required to. A national bank, which is federally-chartered, must join the Federal Reserve system.

12. These are the basic provisions. See Degen (1987, 168-181) for details.

13. A situation of moral hazard arose, which happens when actions beneficial to an individual adversely impacts society.

Chapter 11

1. Energy prices were still high at the end of 1980, although the gasoline lines disappeared during the summer.

2. Reagan was also on the ballot at the 1968 Republican national convention, but he was a late entrant and it was a half-hearted attempt. See Reagan (1990, 176-178).

3. For an example of a political liberal's analysis of the Reagan presidency, see Johnson (1991).

4. A famous study by Meyer (1960) reports that the average time from decision to invest to the capital goods being economically productive assets is seven quarters.

5. See Canto, Joines, and Laffer (1981) for a formal analysis of the Laffer curve.

6. The idea that lowering tax rates can lead to higher revenue is and old one: both Smith (1776) and Keynes (1933), two giant figures in the development of economic analysis, discuss it.

7. Yet another view, called Ricardian equivalence, contends that tax cuts would have no impact aggregate demand because the public would save the entire tax cut because they know that at some time in the future they have to pay off the debt created by the tax cut.

8. Reagan himself thought the additional tax revenue would flow in quickly enough to balance the budget by 1984 (1990, 312). This turned out to be an incredibly bad forecast.

9. See, for example, Bartlett (1981, chaps. 8 & 10), and Canto, Joines, and Laffer (1981).

10. William A. Niskanen (1988, 19), who served on Reagan's Council of Economic Advisors, confirms Anderson's version of events.

11. Tax cuts of 25 percent (5+10+10) work out to a total cut of 23

percent because of reverse compounding, i.e., the tax cuts in 1983 and 1984 are percents of smaller numbers because taxes were reduced in each previous year.

12. The ERTA also allowed individuals to set up Independent Retirement Accounts (IRAs) in an effort to stimulate saving, as well as to generate a flow of funds into the ailing thrift institutions. These accounts allowed people to reduce their taxable income by $2,000 ($2,250 for a married couple with one worker) by placing that amount in an IRA. Income generated by the account is not taxed until the funds are withdrawn.

13. There were additional provisions dealing with business taxes. See Council of Economic Advisors (1982, 122-126) for details.

14. The federal gasoline tax was also raised in 1982, from four to nine cents a gallon.

15. Technically, there were just two brackets, the 15 % and 28 % rates. But high income individuals were subject to a surcharge that raised their marginal rate to 33 %.

16. For details of the 1986 Tax Reform Act, see Fullerton (1994).

17. See Feldstein (1994, 8-9) for a first-hand account of Reagan's support for the Federal Reserve's anti-inflation policy.

18. These data are taken from the Council of Economic Advisors (1996, 281 & 285).

19. See, for example, "The Great Defense War," *Time* October 27, 1980, "Defense: New Muscle for America," *U.S. News & World Report*, December 29, 1980, or several Congressional hearings held on the subject during this period.

20. These proportions are taken from Schick (1995, 190). By the early 1990s entitlements and interest on the debt accounted for 61 percent of federal outlays.

21. Entitlements here are what the U.S. Treasury calls "mandatory" spending. Source: U.S. Treasury, *The Budget for Fiscal Year 2000, Historical Tables*, Table 8.1.

22. One area where some progress was made was in the eligibility rules for welfare payments such as housing allowances and food stamps. These were changed so that only the very poor were eligible. For example, to be eligible for food stamps a person had to be 30 percent above the poverty line instead of 60 percent as specified by the old law.

23. From 1984 to 1988, nominal spending on health, medicare, income security, and social security rose 22 percent, while nominal GDP rose 26 percent (Council of Economic Advisors 1996, 280 & 369).

24. The spending data in this section are for fiscal years.

25. See Winston (1993) for a survey of industry deregulation. Petroleum and natural gas were deregulated during the Carter administration, but the rules were to be phased out over time. This is why they still existed in

1979 and 1980 when the second energy crisis occurred.

26. These studies are discussed in Yandle (1986, 115-118).

Chapter 12

1. Aggregate demand growth equals nominal GDP growth, so aggregate demand growth equals the sum of output growth and inflation.

2. For empirical evidence on inflation inertia, see Gordon (1981;1982).

3. Velocity is the number of times per year that the average dollar is used to buy final goods and services. It is calculated by dividing nominal GDP by the stock of money. If the demand for money rises, velocity falls.

4. Gordon (1983) describes the 1981-1982 recession as "the velocity recession" because he considers the behavior of velocity to be the major cause of the decline in aggregate demand growth. Others, such as Friedman (1984), hold the Federal Reserve accountable for the recession.

5. The 1980 DIDMCA was discussed in chapter 10.

6. Furlong (1983) describes how a similar change in money demand occurred in 1983 when the money market deposit accounts (MMDAs) were introduced.

7. A basis point is one one-hundredth of an interest rate. In other words, if an interest rate falls from 6.55 to 6.50, this represents a decrease of 5 basis points.

8. See Stone and Thornton (1987) for a survey of the factors that economists believe influenced velocity during the 1980s. Tatom (1983) provides evidence that the velocity decline could be predicted by the behavior of inflation, interest rates, money growth, energy prices, the change in the GNP gap, and a dummy variable for labor strikes.

9. The Federal Reserve agrees with Friedman's basic contention that heightened uncertainty helped cause the decline in velocity. See "Monetary Report to Congress," *Federal Reserve Bulletin*, March 1983, 133. Hall and Noble (1987) test Friedman's hypothesis and find empirical support, although these results have been questioned by Brocato and Smith (1989) and Mehra (1989), among others. In later work, Friedman (1988) argues that velocity is also related to stock prices and estimates an equation that closely tracks velocity behavior.

10. The goods producing sector consists of mining, construction, durable goods, and nondurable goods.

11. Klier (2000) reports that in 1982 the capacity utilization rate in automobile manufacturing bottomed out at 53.5 percent.

12. The dollar appreciation during the first half of the 1980s is

discussed in chapter 13.

13. According to Cagan and Fellner's (1983) estimates, most of the disinflation resulted from excess capacity as measured by the output gap.

14. Office of Federal Housing Enterprise Oversight, www.ofheo.gov/house/hpi_sts.txt

Chapter 13

1. See, for example, Feldstein and Elmendorf (1989).

2. At the time, many observers thought that the monetary stimulus during the mid-1980s was carried out by the Federal Reserve as part of the Plaza Accord which was an effort to reduce the large U.S. trade deficit by depreciating the dollar on foreign currency markets. Volcker, however, denies that this was a motivation (Volcker 1994, 150).

3. See Sinai (1992) for empirical estimates of the government spending multiplier.

4. See the Social Security Administration's site at www.ssa.gov/history/1983amend2.html for details on the changes that took effect in 1984.

5. This point is discussed in more detail in section 13.2.

6. See Carlson (1987) for a detailed discussion of the natural employment surplus.

7. Claiming that federal deficits are expansionary assumes that Ricardian equivalence does not hold.

8. Not surprisingly, much has been written about the 1987 stock market crash. For examples, see Santoni (1987; 1988), Baer and Strongin (1988), Pozdena (1988), Brimmer (1989), and Von Furstenberg and Jeon (1989).

9. A more recent "ceteris paribus" event was the terrorist attack on September 11, 2001.

10. The trade-weighted dollar is an index of the U.S. dollar against the currencies of remaining nine G-10 industrialized countries. Each currency's weight in the index is determined by dividing that country's world trade by total world trade of the G-10 countries.

11. The process where changes in the exchange rate cause changes in the price of imports and exports is called pass-through. See Hooper and Mann (1989) for empirical evidence on pass-through during the 1980s.

12. See Collyns and Dunaway (1990) or Adams and Brock (1995) for a discussion of the voluntary export agreement on Japanese autos.

13. Not all economist agree that the high real interest rates were primarily caused by the federal budget deficits. For example, Holland (1984) notes that the increased real rates occurred *before* the federal budget deficits

uncertainty caused by volatile monetary growth.

14. See, for example, Bosworth and Burtless (1992), Heckman (1993), Feldstein (1994), and Eissa (1996a; 1996b).

15. The numbers referred to here are taken from Feenberg and Poterba's table 1, column 3.

16. There is a large literature on taxpayer response to the changes in tax rates legislated during the 1980s. For examples, see Feldstein (1995a; 1995b), Lindsey (1987; 1988), and Slemrod (1992; 1995). Goolsbee (1999) reports that the taxpayer response to changes in tax rates was much higher during the 1980s than in earlier decades.

17. Investment spending consists of spending on new plant, new equipment, new residential structures (houses and apartment buildings), and inventory changes. Fixed business investment refers spending on new plant and equipment, and this is the component of investment that influences economic growth.

18. During the economic expansion, two major areas of equipment spending were computers and aircraft. Personal computers became increasingly common in the business world around the mid 1980s, and airline deregulation caused a boom in air travel which led the airlines to order large numbers of new aircraft.

19. Growth of unit labor costs is computed as nominal wage growth net of labor productivity growth.

20. Poterba (1989) also confirms Gompers and Lerner's contention that that capital gains tax rates have a larger impact on the demand for venture capital than on the supply.

Chapter 14

1. "Brown and Out in Beverly Hills," *The Wall Street Journal*, January 23, 2001, p. A22. See Borenstein (2002) for a detailed economic analysis of the California electricity crisis. Another recent example of politicians interfering with the price system occurred in Hawaii where the state imposed price ceilings on gasoline which are scheduled to take effect in July 2004. See Steven Chapman, "Back to the future on gasoline," *The Washington Times*, May 8, 2002, or B.J. Reyes, "Hawaii tries to cap gasoline prices," *Chicago Sun-Times*, May 5, 2002.

2. The average tax rate is the proportion of total income paid in taxes. The marginal rate is the tax rate, given a family's level of taxable income, on an additional dollar of income.

3. Half of the social security and medicare payroll tax is collected from the employee, the other half from the employer. We are assuming that the

employee bears the entire burden of the tax, as do self-employed workers. Half of the total social security and medicare payroll tax is subtracted from gross income when calculating taxable income.

4. States' income tax laws vary considerably, in fact a few states do not even have a state income tax. Ohio applies state income tax rates to federal taxable income.

Bibliography

Adams, Walter, and James W. Brock. "Automobiles." In Walter Adams and James W. Brock, editors, *The Structure of American Industry*, 9th Ed. (Englewood Cliffs: Prentice Hall, 1995), 65-92.

Ahrari, Mohammed E. *OPEC: The Failing Giant* (Lexington: University Press of Kentucky, 1986).

Anderson, Martin. *Revolution: The Reagan Legacy* (Stanford: Hoover Institution Press, 1988).

Baer, Herbert L., and Steven Strongin. "Bubble, Bubble, Toil and Trouble." *Chicago Fed Letter*, no. 15, November 1988.

Baily, Martin N. "Boom vs. Boom: '90s Beat the '80s." *The Wall Street Journal*, February 25, 2000, p. A18.

Balke, Nathan S., and Robert J. Gordon. "Appendix B: Historical Data." In Robert J. Gordon, editor, *The American Business Cycle: Continuity and Change* (Chicago: University of Chicago Press, 1986).

Barber, William J. "The Eisenhower Energy Policy: Reluctant Intervention." In Craufurd D. Goodwin, editor, *Energy Policy in Perspective: Today's Problems, Yesterday's Solutions* (Washington D.C.: The Brookings Institution, 1981), 205-286.

Barro, Robert J. *Macroeconomics*, 5th Ed. (Cambridge: MIT Press, 1997).

Bartlett, Bruce R. *Reaganomics: Supply Side Economics In Action* (Westport, CT: Arlington House Publishers, 1981).

Bentson, George. "Interest Payments on Demand Deposits and Bank Investment Behavior." *Journal of Political Economy* 57 (October 1964), 431-449.

_____. *The Separation of Commercial and Investment Banking: The Glass-Steagall Act Revisited and Reconsidered* (New York: Oxford University Press, 1990).

Biven, W. Carl. *Who Killed John Maynard Keynes?* (Homewood, IL: Dow Jones - Irwin, 1989).

Blinder, Alan S. *Economic Policy and the Great Stagflation* (New York: Academic Press, 1979).

Blythe, C.A. "Biographical Note: A.W.H. Phillips, M.B.E., 1914–1975." In A.R. Bergstrom, et. al., editors, *Stability and Inflation* (New York: John Wiley & Sons, 1978).

Board of Governors of the Federal Reserve System. *Federal Reserve Bulletin* (Washington D.C.: Board of Governors of the Federal Reserve System, various issues).

_____. "The Economy in 1974." *Federal Reserve Bulletin* 61 (January 1975), 1-10.

_____. "Record of Policy Action of the FOMC." *Federal Reserve Bulletin* 61 (February 1975), 83-88.

Borenstein, Severin. "The Trouble With Electricity Markets: Understanding California's Restructuring Disaster." *Journal of Economic Perspectives* 16 (Winter 2002), 191-211.

Boskin, Michael J. *Reagan and the Economy: The Successes, Failures, and Unfinished Agenda* (San Francisco: ICS Press, 1987).

Bosworth, Barry, and Gary Burtless. "Effects of Tax Reform on Labor Supply, Investment, and Saving." *Journal of Economic Perspectives* 6 (Winter 1992), 3-25.

Brimmer, Andrew F. "Central Banking and Systematic Risks in Capital Markets." *Journal of Economic Perspectives* 3 (Spring 1989), 3-16.

Brocato, Joe, and Kenneth L. Smith. "Velocity and the Variability of Money Growth: Evidence from Granger Causality Tests: A Comment." *Journal of Money, Credit and Banking* 21 (May 1989), 258-261.

Bronfenbrenner, Martin, editor. *Is the Business Cycle Obsolete?* (New York: Wiley-Interscience, 1969).

Brown, E. Cary. "Fiscal Policy in the 'Thirties: A Reappraisal." *The American Economic Review* 46 (December 1956), 857-879.

Browne, Lynn E. and Richard F. Syron. "The Deregulation of Natural Gas: Its Potential Impact on New England." *New England Economic Review* (September/October 1976), 45-66.

Burger, Albert E. "What Happened to the Economy in the First Half of 1980?" Federal Reserve Bank of St. Louis *Review* 62 (August/September 1980), 9-15.

Burns, Arthur F. *Reflections of an Economic Policy Maker, Speeches and Congressional Statements: 1969-1978* (Washington D.C.: American Enterprise Institute, 1978).

_____. *Our Inflation in Historical Perspective* (Washington D.C.: American Enterprise Institute, 1980).

Burns, Arthur F. and Wesley C. Mitchell. *Measuring Business Cycles* (New York: National Bureau of Economic Research, 1946).
Cagan, Phillip. *Persistent Inflation: Historical and Policy Essays* (New York: Columbia University Press, 1979).
Cagan, Phillip, and William Fellner. "Tentative Lessons from the Recent Disinflationary Effort." *Brookings Papers on Economic Activity* (1983, #2), 603-608.
Campagna, Anthony S. *U.S. National Economic Policy, 1917-1985* (New York: Praeger Publishing, 1987).
_____. *The Economy in the Reagan Years: The Economic Consequences of the Reagan Administrations* (Westport, CT: Greenwood Press, 1994).
_____. *Economic Policy in the Carter Administration* (Westport, CT: Greenwood Press, 1995).
Canto, Victor A., Douglas H. Joines, and Arthur B. Laffer. "Tax Rates, Factor Employment, and Market Production." In Laurence H. Meyer, editor, *The Supply-Side Effects of Economic Policy* (St. Louis: Federal Reserve Bank of St. Louis, 1981), 3-32.
Carlson, John B., and John N. McElravey. "Money and Velocity in the 1980s." Federal Reserve Bank of Cleveland *Economic Commentary,* January 15, 1989.
Carlson, Keith M. "Federal Fiscal Policy Since the Employment Act of 1946." Federal Reserve Bank of St. Louis *Review* 69 (December 1987), 14-29.
Carron, Andrew S. *The Plight of the Thrift Institutions* (Washington D.C.: The Brookings Institution, 1982).
Chandler, Lester V. *America's Greatest Depression 1929-1941* (New York: Harper and Row, 1970).
Christiano, Lawrence, and Christopher Gust. "The Expectations Trap Hypothesis." Federal Reserve Bank of Chicago *Economic Perspectives* 25 (Second Quarter 2000), 21-39.
Chrystal, K. Alec. "Political Business Cycle." In David Glasner, editor, *Business Cycles and Depressions: An Encyclopedia* (New York: Garland Publishing, 1997), 536-538.
Cochrane, James L. "Carter Energy Policy and the Ninety-fifth Congress." In Craufurd D. Goodwin, editor *Energy Policy in Perspective: Today's Problems, Yesterday's Solutions* (Washington

D.C.: The Brookings Institution, 1981), 547-600.

Cochrane, James L. and Gary L. Griepentrog. "U.S. Energy: A Quantitative Review of the Past Three Decades." In Craufurd D. Goodwin, editor *Energy Policy in Perspective: Today's Problems, Yesterday's Solutions* (Washington D.C.: The Brookings Institution, 1981), 685-705.

Collyns, Charles, and Steven Dunaway. "The Cost of Trade Restraints: The Case of Japanese Automobile Exports to the United States." In Philip King, editor, *International Economics and International Economic Policy: A Reader* (New York: McGraw-Hill, 1990).

Council of Economic Advisors. *Economic Report of the President* (Washington D.C.: U.S. Government Printing Office, various issues).

De Marchi, Neil. "The First Nixon Administration: Prelude to Controls." In Crauford D. Goodwin, editor, *Exhortation and Controls: The Search for a Wage-Price Policy 1945–1971* (Washington D.C.: Brookings Institution, 1975).

_____. "Energy Policy Under Nixon: Mainly Putting Out Fires." In Craufurd D. Goodwin, editor *Energy Policy in Perspective: Today's Problems, Yesterday's Solutions* (Washington D.C.: The Brookings Institution, 1981a), 395-473.

_____. "The Ford Administration: Energy as a Political Good." In Craufurd D. Goodwin, editor *Energy Policy in Perspective: Today's Problems, Yesterday's Solutions* (Washington D.C.: The Brookings Institution, 1981b), 475-545.

Dotsey, Michael, and Jed L. DeVaro. "Was the Disinflation of the Early 1980s Anticipated?" Federal Reserve Bank of Richmond *Economic Quarterly* 81 (Fall 1995), 41-59.

D'Souza, Dinesh. "How Reagan reelected Clinton." *Forbes*, November 3, 1997, 118-126.

Eastburn, David P. *The Federal Reserve on Record* (Philadelphia: Federal Reserve Bank of Philadelphia, 1965).

Easterly, William, and Stanley Fischer. "Inflation and the Poor." *Journal of Money, Credit and Banking* 33 (May 2001), 160-178.

Ehrenberg, Ronald G. and Robert S. Smith. *Modern Labor Economics: Theory and Public Policy*, 4th Ed. (New York: Harper-Collins, 1991).

Eissa, Nada. "Tax Reforms and Labor Supply." *In James M. Poterba, editor, Tax Policy and the Economy* (Cambridge, MA: MIT Press, 1996a), 119-151.

_____. "Labor Supply and the Economic Recovery Tax Act of 1981." In Martin Feldstein and James M. Poterba, editors, *Empirical Foundations of Household Taxation* (Chicago: University of Chicago Press, 1996b), 5-32.

Federal Power Commission. "National Gas Supply and Demand, 1971-1990 (1972)." Reprinted in Leslie E. Grayson, editor, *Economics of Energy: Readings on Environment, Resources, and Markets* (Princeton: Darwin Press, 1975), 319-322.

Federal Reserve Board of Governors. *Banking and Monetary Statistics, 1914-1943* (Washington D.C., 1943).

Feenberg, Daniel R., and James M. Poterba. "The Income and Tax Share of Very High-Income Households, 1960-1995." *The American Economic Review* 90 (May 2000), 264-270.

Feldstein, Martin. "American Economic Policy in the 1980s: A Personal View." In Martin Feldstein, editor, *American Economic Policy in the 1980s* (Chicago: University of Chicago Press, 1994), 1-79.

_____. "Behavioral Responses to Tax Rates: Evidence from the Tax Reform Act of 1986." *The American Economic Review* 85 (May 1995a), 170-174.

_____. "The Effect of Marginal Tax Rates on Taxable Income: A Panel Study of the 1986 TRA." *Journal of Political Economy* 103 (June 1995b), 551-572.

Feldstein, Martin, and Douglas W. Elmendorf. "Budget Deficits, Tax Incentives, and Inflation: A Surprising Lesson From the 1983-1984 Recovery." In Lawrence H. Summers, editor, *Tax Policy and The Economy* (Cambridge, MA: MIT Press, 1989), 1-23.

Freund, James L. "The Housing Market: Recent Developments and Underlying Trends." *Federal Reserve Bulletin* 69 (February 1983), 61-69.

Friedman, Milton. "The Case for Flexible Exchange Rates." In *Milton Friedman, Essays in Positive Economics* (Chicago: University of Chicago Press, 1953), 157-203.

_____. *Capitalism and Freedom* (Chicago: University of Chicago Press, 1962).

_____. "The Bank Depositor." *Newsweek,* November 7, 1966, 88.

_____. "The Role of Monetary Policy." In *The Optimum Quantity of Money and Other Essays* (Chicago: Aldine Publishing Co., 1969), pp. 95-110. (First published in American Economic Review 58 (March 1968), 1-17.)

_____. "What is the Federal Reserve Doing?" *Newsweek,* March 10, 1975, 63.

_____. "Blaming the Obstetrician." *Newsweek,* June 4, 1979, 70.

_____. "The Energy Crisis (1978)." In William R. Allen, editor, *Bright Promises and Dismal Performance: An Economist's Protest* (San Diego: Harcourt Brace Jovanovich, 1983), 141-152.

_____. "Lessons from the 1979-82 Monetary Policy Experiment." *American Economic Review* 74 (May 1984), 397-400.

_____. "Money and the Stock Market." *Journal of Political Economy* 96 (April 1988), 221-245.

Friedman, Milton, and Rose Friedman. *Free to Choose: A Personal Statement* (New York: Avon Books, 1979).

Friedman, Milton and Anna J. Schwartz. *A Monetary History of the United States, 1867-1960* (Princeton: Princeton University Press, 1963).

Fullerton, Don. "Inputs to Tax Policy-Making: The Supply-Side, the Deficit, and the Level Playing Field." In Martin Feldstein, editor, *American Economic Policy in the 1980s* (Chicago: University of Chicago Press, 1994), 165-208.

Furlong, Frederick T. "New Deposit Instruments." *Federal Reserve Bulletin* 69 (May 1983), 319-326.

Gay, Robert S., and Jeffrey D. Hedlund. "The Labor Market in Recession and Recovery." *Federal Reserve Bulletin* 69 (July 1983), 477-488.

Gompers, Paul, and John Lerner. "The Venture Capital Revolution." *Journal of Economic Perspectives* 15 (Spring 2001), 145-168.

Goolsbee, Austan. "Evidence on the High-Income Laffer Curve from Six Decades of Tax Reform." *Brookings Papers on Economic Activity* (1999, #2), 1-47.

Gordon, Robert J. "Postwar Macroeconomics: The Evolution of Events and Ideas." In Martin Feldstein, editor, *The American Economy in Transition* (Chicago: University of Chicago Press, 1980).

_____. "Output Fluctuations and Gradual Price Adjustment." *Journal of Economic Literature* 19 (June 1981), 493-530.

_____. "Price Inertia and Policy Ineffectiveness in the United States, 1890-1980." *Journal of Political Economy* 90 (December 1982), 1087-1117.

_____. "The Gordon Update." A supplemental newsletter for use with Robert J. Gordon's *Macroeconomics,* Spring 1983.

_____. *Macroeconomics,* 7th edition (Reading, MA: Addison-Wesley, 1998).

_____. *Macroeconomics,* 8th edition (New York: Harper-Collins, 2000).

Greider, William. *Secrets of the Temple: How the Federal Reserve Runs the Country* (New York: Simon and Schuster, 1987).

Griffin, James M., and Henry B. Steele. *Energy Economics and Policy,* 2nd Ed. (Orlando: Academic Press, 1986).

Hafer, R.W. "The FOMC in 1985: Reacting to Declining M1 Velocity." Federal Reserve Bank of St. Louis *Review* 68 (February 1986), 5-21.

Hall, Robert E., and John B. Taylor. *Macroeconomics,* 5th Ed. (New York: W.W. Norton Co., 1997).

Hall, Thomas E. *Business Cycles: The Nature and Causes of Economic Fluctuations* (New York: Praeger Publishing, 1990).

Hall, Thomas E., and J. David Ferguson. *The Great Depression: An International Disaster of Perverse Economic Policies* (Ann Arbor: University of Michigan Press, 1998).

Hall, Thomas E., and Nicholas R. Noble. "Velocity and the Variability of Money Growth: Evidence from Granger-Causality Tests." *Journal of Money, Credit and Banking* 19 (February 1987), 112-116.

Hansen, Alvin H. *A Guide to Keynes* (New York: McGraw-Hill, 1953).

Hassett, Kevin. "Scoring With Meg." *The Wall Street Journal,* October 9, 2002, A18.

Heckman, James J. "What Has Been Learned About Labor Supply in the Last Twenty Years?" *The American Economic Review* 83 (May 1993), 116-121.

Heller, Walter W. *New Dimensions of Political Economy* (New York: W.W. Norton, 1967).

Hendershott, Patric H., and Kevin E. Villani. *Regulation and Reform of the Housing Finance System* (Washington D.C.: American Enterprise Institute, 1977).

Hetzel, Robert L. "Arthur Burns and Inflation." Federal Reserve Bank of Richmond *Economic Quarterly* 84 (Winter 1998), 21-44.

Holland, A. Stephen. "Real Interest Rates: What Accounts for Their Recent Rise?" Federal Reserve Bank of St. Louis *Review* 66 (December 1984), 18-29.

Hooper, Peter, and Catherine L. Mann. "Exchange Rate Pass-through in the 1980s: The Case of U.S. Imports of Manufactures." *Brookings Papers on Economic Activity* (1989, #1), 297-329.

Johnson, Haynes. *Sleepwalking Through History: America in the Reagan Years* (New York: W.W. Norton, 1991).

Kalt, Joseph P. *The Economics and Politics of Oil Price Regulation: Federal Policy in the Post-Embargo Era* (Cambridge: MIT Press, 1981).

Keynes, John Maynard. *The Means to Prosperity* (New York: Harcourt, Brace and Co., 1933).

_____. *The General Theory of Employment, Interest, and Money* (London: Macmillan, 1936).

Kimmel, Jean, and Thomas J. Kniesner. "New Evidence on the Labor Supply: Employment versus Hours Elasticities by Sex and Marital Status." *Journal of Monetary Economics* 42 (October 1998), 289-301.

Kindleberger, Charles P. *The World in Depression, 1929-1939* (Berkeley: University of California Press, 1973).

Klein, Lawrence R. *The Keynesian Revolution* (New York: Macmillan, 1947).

Klier, Thomas. "Structural Change and Cyclicality of the Auto Industry." *Chicago Fed Letter* November 2000.

Kosters, Marvin H. *Controls and Inflation: The Economic Stabilization Program in Retrospect* (Washington D.C.: American Enterprise Institute for Public Policy Research, 1975).

Kroszner, Randall S., and Raghuram G. Rajan. "Is the Glass-Steagall Act Justified? A Study of the U.S. Experience with Universal Banking Before 1933." *American Economic Review* 84 (September 1994), 810-32.

Lang, Richard W. "The FOMC in 1979: Introducing Reserve Targeting." Federal Reserve Bank of St. Louis *Review* 62 (March 1980), 2-25.

Lash, Nicholas A. *Banking Laws and Regulations: An Economic Perspective* (Englewood Cliffs:Prentice-Hall, 1987).

Leeson, Robert. "A.W.H. Phillips M.B.E. (Military Division)." *The Economic Journal* 104 (May 1994), 605-618.

_____. "The Political Economy of the Inflation-Unemployment Trade-Off." *History of Political Economy* 29 (Spring 1997), 119-156.

Lindsey, Lawrence B. "Individual Taxpayer Response to Tax Cuts: 1982-1984, With Implications for the Revenue Maximizing Tax Rate." *Journal of Public Economics* 33 (July 1987), 173-206.

_____. "Did ERTA Raise the Share of Taxes Paid by Upper-Income Taxpayers? Will TRA86 Be a Repeat?" In Lawrence H. Summers, editor, *Tax Policy and the Economy* (Cambridge: MIT Press, 1988), 131-160.

_____. "The 17-Year Boom." *The Wall Street Journal,* January 27, 2000, p. A22.

Luttrell, Clifton B. "The Russian Wheat Deal-- Hindsight vs. Foresight." Federal Reserve Bank of St. Louis *Review* 55 (October 1973), 2-9.

Mayer, Thomas. "A Case Study of Federal Reserve Policymaking: Regulation Q in 1966." *Journal of Monetary Economics* 10 (September 1982), 259-271.

_____. *Monetary Policy and the Great Inflation in the United States* (Cheltenham, UK: Edward Elgar, 1999).

McNeill, Charles R., and Denise M. Rechter. "The Depository Institutions Deregulation and Monetary Control Act of 1980." *Federal Reserve Bulletin* 66 (June 1980), 444-453.

Mead, Walter J. "Petroleum: An Unregulated Industry?" In Robert J. Kalter and William A. Vogely, editors, *Energy Supply and Government Policy* (Ithaca: Cornell University Press, 1976).

Mehra, Yash P. "Velocity and the Variability of Money Growth: Evidence from Granger Causality Tests: A Comment." *Journal of Money, Credit and Banking* 21 (May 1989), 262-266.

Melloan, George, and Joan Melloan. *The Carter Economy* (New York: John Wiley & Sons, 1978).

Melton, William C. *Inside the Fed: Making Monetary Policy $*

(Homewood, IL: Dow Jones-Irwin, 1985).

Meyer, T. "Plant and Equipment Lead Times." *Journal of Business* 33 (April 1960), 127-132.

Mitchell, Wesley C. *Business Cycles* (Berkeley: University of California Press, 1913).

_____. *Business Cycles: The Problem and Its Setting* (New York: National Bureau of Economic Research, 1927).

Motor Vehicle Manufacturers Association. *Motor Vehicle Facts & Figures '76* (Detroit: Motor Vehicle Manufacturers Association, 1976).

_____. *World Motor Vehicle Data* (Detroit: Motor Vehicle Manufacturers Association, 1978).

Mussa, Michael. "U.S. Monetary Policy in the 1980s." In Martin Feldstein, editor, *American Economic Policy in the 1980s* (Chicago: University of Chicago Press, 1994), 81-145.

Neikirk, William R. *Volcker: Portrait of the Money Man* (Chicago: Congdon and Weed, 1987).

Nixon, Richard M. *The Memoirs of Richard Nixon* (New York: Touchstone, 1978).

Niskanen, William A. *Reaganomics: An Insider's Account of the Policies and the People* (New York: Oxford University Press, 1988).

_____. "Organizing the Government for Policy-Making." In Kenneth W. Thompson, editor, *Reagan and the Economy: Nine Intimate Perspectives* (Lanham, MD: University Press of America, 1994), 27-44.

Nordhaus, William D. "Oil and Economic Performance in Industrial Countries." *Brookings Papers on Economic Activity* (1980, #2), 341-399.

Okun, Arthur M. *The Political Economy of Prosperity* (New York: W.W. Norton, 1970).

_____. "A Postmortem of the 1974 Recession." *Brookings Papers on Economic Activity* (1975, #1), 207-221.

Perry, George L. "What Have We Learned About Disinflation?" *Brookings Papers on Economic Activity* (1983, #2), 587-602.

Perry, James M. "Down and Out: Idle Mills, a Dearth of Hope are Features of Ohio's Steel Towns." *The Wall Street Journal,* January

20, 1983, 1.

Phillips, A.W. "The Relation Between Unemployment and the Rate of Change of Money Wage Rates in the United Kingdom, 1861-1957." *Economica* 25 (November, 1958), 283-299.

Pierce, Richard J. Jr. "Reconstituting the Natural Gas Industry from Wellhead to Burnertip." *Energy Law Journal* 9 (1988), 1-57.

Poole, William. "Monetary Policy During the Recession." *Brookings Papers on Economic Activity* (1975, #1), 123-139.

_____. "Eulogy for Darryl Francis, 1912-2002." Federal Reserve Bank of St. Louis *Review* 84 (March/April 2002), 1-2.

Poterba, James M. "Venture Capital and Capital Gains Taxation." In Lawrence H. Summers, editor, *Tax Policy and the Economy* (Cambridge: MIT Press, 1989), 47-67.

Pozdena, Randall Johnson. "October Postmortem." Federal Reserve Bank of San Francisco *Weekly Letter,* October 29, 1988.

Pyle, David H. "The Losses on Savings Deposits from Interest Rate Regulation." *Bell Journal of Economics and Management Science* 5 (Autumn 1974), 614-622.

Rasche, Robert H., and John A. Tatom. "The Effects of the New Energy Regime on Economic Capacity, Production, and Prices." Federal Reserve Bank of St. Louis *Review* 59 (May, 1977), 2-12.

Reagan, Ronald. *Ronald Reagan: An American Life* (New York: Simon and Schuster, 1990).

Rockoff, Hugh. *Drastic Measures: A History of Wage and Price Controls in the United States* (Cambridge: Cambridge University Press, 1984).

Rolfe, Sidney E., and James L. Burtle. *The Great Wheel: The World Monetary System* (New York: McGraw-Hill, 1973).

Samuelson, Paul A. *Economics: An Introductory Analysis,* 6th ed. (New York: McGraw-Hill Book Company, 1964).

_____. "Needed Economic Policy" (1968). *In The Samuelson Sampler* (Glen Ridge, NJ: Thomas Horton and Company, 1973).

_____. *The Samuelson Sampler* (Glen Ridge, NJ: Thomas Horton and Company, 1973).

Samuelson, Paul A., and Robert M. Solow. "Analytical Aspects of Anti-Inflation Policy." *American Economic Review* 50 (May, 1960), 177-194.

Santoni, G. J. "The Great Bull Markets 1924-29 and 1982-87: Speculative Bubbles or Economic Fundamentals?" Federal Reserve Bank of St. Louis *Review* 69 (November 1987), 16-30.

_____. "The October Crash: Some Evidence on the Cascade Theory." Federal Reserve Bank of St. Louis *Review* 70 (May/June 1988), 18-33.

Schick, Allen. *The Federal Budget: Politics, Policy, Process* (Washington D.C.: The Brookings Institution, 1995).

Schinasi, Garry J. "Business Fixed Investment: Recent Developments and Outlook." *Federal Reserve Bulletin* 69 (January 1983), 1-10.

Schreft, Stacey L. "Credit Controls: 1980." Federal Reserve Bank of Richmond *Economic Review* 76 (November/December 1990), 25-55.

Shepherd, William G., and James W. Brock. "Airlines." In Walter Adams and James Brock, editors, *The Structure of American Industry, 9th ed.* (Englewood Cliffs: Prentice Hall, 1995), 247-272.

Simpson, Thomas D. *Money, Banking, and Economic Analysis, 2nd ed.* (Englewood Cliffs: Prentice-Hall, 1981).

Sinai, Allen. "Financial and Real Business Cycles." *Eastern Economic Journal* 18 (Winter 1992), 1-54.

Slemrod, Joel. "Taxation and Business Investment." In Philip Cagan, editor, *Essays in Contemporary Economic Problems, 1986: The Impact of the Reagan Program* (Washington D.C.: American Enterprise Institute, 1986), 45-72.

_____. "Do Taxes Matter? Lessons from the 1980s." *The American Economic Review* 82 (May 1992), 250-256.

_____. "Income Creation or Income Shifting? Behavioral Responses to the Tax Reform Act of 1986." *The American Economic Review* 85 (May 1995), 175-180.

_____. "High-Income Families and the Tax Changes of the 1980s: The Anatomy of Behavioral Response." In Martin Feldstein and James M. Poterba, editors, *Empirical Foundations of Household Taxation* (Chicago: University of Chicago Press, 1996), 169-189.

Smith, Adam (1776). *An Inquiry into the Nature and Causes of the Wealth of Nations* (New York: The Modern Library, 1938).

Snyder, Frank R. "Imports Come Alive, Take Record Share in 1975." *In Ward's Automotive Yearbook, 1976* (Detroit: Ward's

Communications, 1976).

Stone, Courtenay C., and Daniel L. Thornton. "Solving the 1980s' Velocity Puzzle: A Progress Report." Federal Reserve Bank of St. Louis *Review* 69 (August/September 1987), 5-23.

Sutton, Antony C. *Energy: The Created Crisis* (New York: Books in Focus, 1979).

Taggart, Robert A., and Geoffrey Woglom. "Savings Bank Reactions to Rate Ceilings and Rising Market Rates." *New England Economic Review* (September/October 1978), 17-29.

Tatom, John. "Was the 1982 Velocity Decline Unusual?" Federal Reserve Bank of St. Louis *Review* 65 (August/September, 1983), 5-15.

Temin, Peter. *Lessons From the Great Depression* (Cambridge: MIT Press, 1989).

Thornton, Mark. *The Economics of Prohibition* (Salt Lake City: University of Utah Press, 1991).

Tussing, Arlon R., and Connie C. Barlow. *The Natural Gas Industry: Evolution, Structure, and Economics* (Cambridge, MA: Ballinger Publishing, 1984).

United States Congress. Joint Economic Committee. *Hearings on the 1974 Economic Report of the President.* 93rd Congress, 2nd Session, 1974, Part 1.

_____. Joint Economic Committee. *Hearings on the Current Economic Situation and Outlook for the Housing Industry.* 94th Congress, 1st Session, 1975.

_____. Senate. Committee on Banking, Housing, and Urban Affairs. *Hearings on the Nomination of Paul Volcker.* 96th Congress, 1st Session, 1979.

_____. House. Committee on Armed Services. *Hearings on Military Posture and H.R. 2970 [H.R. 3519] Authorization for Appropriations for Fiscal Year 1982.* 97th Congress, 1st Session, 1981.

_____. Joint Economic Committee. *Employment-Unemployment Hearings Before the Joint Economic Committee.* 97th Congress, 2nd Session, 1982.

United States Department of Commerce. *Handbook of Cyclical Indicators* (Washington D.C.: U.S. Department of Commerce, 1984).

_____. *1990 Census of Housing: General Housing Characteristics United States* (Washington D.C.: U.S. Department of Commerce, 1992).

United States Department of Labor. *Handbook of Labor Statistics 1978* (Washington D.C.: U.S. Government Printing Office, 1979).

_____. *Employment, Hours, and Earnings, United States, 1909-1990, Volumes I and II* (Washington D.C.: U.S. Government Printing Office, 1991).

_____. *Compensation and Working Conditions Winter 2000* (Washington D.C.: U.S. Government Printing Office, 2000).

Vedder, Richard K., and Lowell E. Gallaway. *Out of Work: Unemployment and Government in Twentieth-Century America* (New York: Holmes and Meier, 1993).

Volcker, Paul A. *The Rediscovery of the Business Cycle: The Charles C. Moskowitz Memorial Lectures, Number XIX* (New York: The Free Press, 1978).

_____. "Statement to Congress." *Federal Reserve Bulletin.* March, 1983, 167-174.

_____. Comment on "U.S. Monetary Policy in the 1980s," by Michael Mussa. In Martin Feldstein, editor, *American Economic Policy in the 1980s* (Chicago: University of Chicago Press, 1994), 145-151.

Volcker, Paul A., and Toyoo Gyohten. *Changing Fortunes: The World's Money and the Threat to American Leadership* (New York: Times Books, 1992).

Von Furstenberg, George M., and Bang Nam Jeon. "International Stock Price Movements: Links and Messages." *Brookings Papers on Economic Activity* (1989 # 1), 125–167.

Ward's Automotive Yearbook, various issues. (Detroit: Ward's Communications).

Warren, Melinda, and Murray Weidenbaum. "The Rise of Regulation Continues: An Analysis of the Budget for the Year 2000." *Regulatory Budget Report* 22 (St. Louis: Washington University Center for the Study of American Business, August 1999).

Weicher, John C. "The Reagan Domestic Budget Cuts: Proposals, Outcomes, and Effects." In Philip Cagan, editor, *Essays in Contemporary Economic Problems, 1986: The Impact of the Reagan Program* (Washington D.C.: American Enterprise

Institute, 1986), 7–44.
Weintraub, Robert E. "Private Housing Starts and the Growth of the Money Supply." In M. Bruce Johnson, editor, *Resolving the Housing Crisis* (San Francisco: Pacific Institute for Public Policy Research, 1982).
Wells, Wyatt C. *Economist in an Uncertain World: Arthur F. Burns and the Federal Reserve, 1970-1978* (New York: Columbia University Press, 1994).
Wojnilower, Albert M. "The Central Role of Credit Crunches in Recent Financial History." *Brookings Papers on Economic Activity* (1980, #2), 401–452.
Worrall, John. "After Months Out of Work: 'I Feel Betrayed.'" *U.S. News & World Report* October 18, 1982, 73.
Winston, Clifford. "Economic Deregulation: Days of Reckoning for Microeconomists." *Journal of Economic Literature* 31 (September 1993), 1263–1289.
Yandle, Bruce. "The Evolution of Regulatory Activities in the 1970s and 1980s." In Philip Cagan, editor, *Essays in Contemporary Economic Problems, 1986: The Impact of the Reagan Program* (Washington D.C.: American Enterprise Institute, 1986), 105-145.
Yergin, Daniel. *The Prize: The Epic Quest for Oil, Money, and Power* (New York: Simon and Schuster, 1991).

About the Author

■■■

Thomas E. Hall is a Professor of Economics at Miami University in Oxford, Ohio. He received his B.A. in economics from the University of Colorado - Boulder (1976), and his M.A. (1978) and Ph.D. (1982) degrees from the University of California - Santa Barbara. His fields of specialization are macroeconomics and econometrics. He has published a number of articles in economics journals, and is author of *Business Cycles: The Nature and Causes of Economic Fluctuations*, and coauthor (with J.D. Ferguson) of *The Great Depression: An International Disaster of Perverse Economic Policies*. He has been employed by Miami University since 1982, and during academic year 1988-1989 served as a Visiting Senior Economist at the U.S. State Department in Washington D.C. where he monitored economics conditions in the United States and Western Europe. He lives in Wyoming, Ohio with his wife Chris and son Alex.

Index

www.ingramcontent.com/pod-product-compliance
Ingram Content Group UK Ltd.
Pitfield, Milton Keynes, MK11 3LW, UK
UKHW040227290926
15471UKWH00001B/40

9 780761 826811